LANGUAGE

MACHINES

ESSAYS FROM
THE ENGLISH INSTITUTE

Since 1944, the English Institute has presented
work by distinguished scholars in English and
American literatures, foreign literatures, and
related fields. A volume of papers selected for
the meeting is published annually.

Also available in the series from Routledge:

Comparative American Identities:
Race, Sex and Nationality in the Modern Text
Edited with an Introduction by
Hortense J. Spillers

English Inside and Out:
The Places of Literary Criticism
Edited with an Introduction by
Susan Gubar and Jonathan Kamholtz

Borders, Boundaries and Frames:
Essays on Cultural Criticism and
Cultural Theory
Edited with an Introduction by
Mae Henderson

Performativity and Performance
Edited with an Introduction by
Andrew Parker and
Eve Kosofsky Sedgwick

Human, All Too Human
Edited with an Introduction by
Diana Fuss

ROUTLEDGE

NEW YORK

LONDON

LANGUAGE

MACHINES

TECHNOLOGIES

OF LITERARY

AND CULTURAL

PRODUCTION

Edited by

JEFFREY MASTEN

PETER STALLYBRASS AND

NANCY VICKERS

Published in 1997 by

Routledge
29 West 35th Street
New York, NY 10001

Published in Great Britain in 1997 by

Routledge
11 New Fetter Lane
London EC4P 4EE

Library of Congress Cataloging-in-Publication Data

Language machines: technologies of literary and cultural production / edited by Jeffrey Masten, Peter Stalleybrass [i.e. Stallybrass], Nancy Vickers.
    p.   cm. —(Essays from the English Institute)
  Includes bibliographical references.
  ISBN 0-415-91863-4 (alk. paper).   ISBN 0-415-91864-2 (pbk. : alk. paper.)
  1. Language and culture. 2. Technological innovations. I. Masten, Jeffrey. II. Stallybrass, Peter. III. Vickers, Nancy. IV. Series.
P35.L334 1997   97-7321
306.44—dc21   CIP

CONTENTS

ACKNOWLEDGMENTS

Language Machines presents new work on the technologies of literary and cultural production from a variety of historical, theoretical, and disciplinary perspectives. We thank the Supervisors and Trustees of the 1995 English Institute for giving initial shape to the conference where early versions of these essays were presented and for generously assisting us in defining the contours of the subsequent volume. Many of the participants attending the Institute provided invaluable criticism and comment during the sustained and sometimes contentious discussions that followed each of these papers; we want especially to thank Elizabeth Pittenger and Franco Moretti for their contributions both to the meeting and to our thinking about this collection. Thanks also to the following individuals whose generous collaboration made *Language Machines* possible: John Brenkman, who chaired the full conference and directed the panel on "Presses"; Joseph R. Roach, who directed the panel on "Voice"; Suzanne Marcus, who flawlessly coordinated the conference; Lois Leveen, who meticulously read, criticized, and helped assemble the final manuscript; and William Germano, who encouraged us through both his patience and his timely impatience. We are particularly grateful to Harvard University and to the nationwide roster of colleges and universities whose sponsorship permits the Institute's work to continue. Among them, the University of Pennsylvania and the University of Southern California provided critical support for the completion of the volume.

JEFFREY MASTEN, PETER STALLYBRASS, AND NANCY VICKERS

INTRODUCTION

LANGUAGE

MACHINES

LANGUAGE MACHINES analyzes a range of technologies that have shaped literary and cultural production. As a whole, this collection of essays pursues two central claims: first, that material forms regulate and structure culture and those who are the agents or subjects of culture; and second, that new technologies redefine and resituate, rather than replace, earlier technologies. Underpinning both claims is the belief that language is not a disembodied essence ("in the beginning was the Word") but rather a set of productive practices. Language is now and has always been produced by a variety of *machines*. In emphasizing the notion of language as produced by machines, we want to draw upon the complexities (both conceptual and historical) of the term "machine."

In 1650, John Bulwer referred to "the curious Machine of Speech," the human machine that functions through the bodily parts of lips and tongue and vocal chords and nose.[1] The "machine" of speech is the physiological mechanism that makes speaking possible. And the machine of speech is located in what Hamlet, writing to Ophelia, refers to as the machine of the body itself (Hamlet signs his letter, "*Thine euermore most deere Lady, whilst this Machine is to him,* Hamlet" [*Hamlet*, 2.2.124]).[2] The vocal apparatus and the body, when conceptualized as machines, are resolutely untranscendental. Indeed, the term "machine," in its early uses, describes less what we now think of as technology than manual work. The "mechanique office[s]," wrote John Donne,

were those that belonged "to the hand," like writing, carving, and playing, and later writers referred to "Labouring and Mechanick men" and
to "the mechanic and farming classes."[3] These early notions of the machine
and the mechanical are illuminating because they trouble the post-
Enlightenment opposition between the manual and the technological,
just as Bulwer's notion of the machine of speech works against any simple opposition between transcendental language and materiality.

The idealist tradition has constantly attempted to separate language
from its machines. Language, if it was to be the defining human characteristic, needed to be segregated from the material forms which implicated
all forms of life. Indeed, language itself was often politically segregated
even within the human social order, so as to differentiate those with the
right to speak and interpret from those "Mechanick, Ignorant fellows,"
whom, Charles I claimed, had no right to preach or interpret Scripture.[4]
The fantasy of an immaterial language has a long history. As Elizabeth
Pittenger has shown, the mechanical arts were, in the view of Hugh of St.
Victor (1096–1141) "adulterate."[5] Hugh derived his concept of the
mechanical from the Greek *moicos* and the Latin *moechus*, meaning an
adulterer. The mechanical was in this view the perversely fleshly, which
contaminated and deformed the divine inscriptions upon the soul.
Language, then, at its purest, must be separated from the adulterations of
materiality, and consequently from writing itself, which, as the work of
the hand, is seen as a debased activity. The writing that takes place in the
monastic *scriptoria* is defined as a form of penitence *because* it is a manual and mechanical labor. In contrast to Hugh, Alanus of Lille imagines
Genius as holding in his right hand a pen and in his left "the pelt of a
dead animal, shorn of its fur of hair by the razor's bite" (i.e., the vellum
on which the pen writes).[6] Genius is thus resolutely materialized.

To Alanus's image of the materiality of writing should be added a
sense of the materiality of reading. For reading is shaped by the technologies of the scroll, the codex, the book, and the screen. Perhaps one
of the most persistent modern myths of reading is the myth of teleological narrative: the myth that "the book," as a technological form, is
organized so as to be read from page 1 to page 2, from page 2 to page 3,
and so on to the end of the book. This is of course a *possible* way of
reading a book, and one that was encouraged by the development of
narrative fiction in the eighteenth century. Indeed, the highest compli-

ment to be paid to a story within this paradigm is that it is a "page-turn-er": a language machine in which the text itself seems to perform as a perpetual motion device, turning its own successive pages. But this view can be seen as a curious, if culturally productive, deformation of the book as a technology. For if the printed book is a development of the codex, the codex, in turn, is a radical subversion of the technology of the scroll. The scroll, so central to Judaism, is a technology that depends upon a literal unwinding in which the physical proximity of one moment in the narrative to another is both materially and symbolical-ly significant. One cannot move easily back and forth between distant points on the scroll. But it is precisely such movement back and forth that the codex permits and encourages. Moreover, as Roger Chartier notes, the scroll required the use of both hands, so that reading required a very full physical participation. The codex, by contrast, when resting on a lectern, released the reader's hands for a different kind of physical participation: that of writing. As Chartier points out, the characteristic medieval depiction of "reading" shows two books: one that is read, and one in which the reader transcribes what is read.[7].

We might, indeed, consider the codex and even more the book as language machines through which Christianity came to define its rela-tion to Judaism. Christianity *cut up* the Judaic scroll by means of the codex. Typological reading, the reading which Christianity as a liturgical insti-tution demanded, required that a passage in what was now defined as the "old" testament be read not in conjunction with what came immediate-ly after it but with a passage from the "new" testament. The book, following the codex allowed one to move rapidly back and forth between the "old" and "new" testaments, to read page 1,000 a second or two (if one had marked the place) after reading page 1. Try to imagine doing that with a scroll. Christianity deliberately cut into the Judaic scroll to create a dis-continuous practice of reading. The story of the sacrifice of Isaac would thus be read less in terms of its proximate narratives in Genesis than as a prefiguration of the "Son's" crucifixion, the book's technology allowing for the rapid superimposition of the later narrative upon the earlier. Such a superimposition was encouraged both by the liturgical practice of read-ing lessons from the old and new testaments at the same service and by the later cutting up of the biblical text into numbered verses, which facil-itated the move from one specific passage to another. Marginal glosses also encouraged the reader to compare passages in, say, chapter 29 of Genesis with passages in Numbers, Exodus, Ruth, 1 Corinthians, and the gospels of John and Matthew.[8] The codex and the book were thus established as technologies of discontinuous reading. Far from emphasizing a chronological narrative, they intercut different historical and theological moments. Whatever our romantic associations with the book as a form of teleological narrative, one of the most persistent uses of the book as a machine has been as an *indexical* form. Imagine the problems of consulting a telephone scroll, *Scrolls in Print*, a dictionary scroll.

If there are general implications to the stitching together of cut pages, there are also technological distinctions among codices and books at the simple level of size. A folio volume, for instance, is not something that can easily be held in the lap or in bed, nor is it easily carried about as one walks. The folio volume is thus usually implicated in an institutional setting: a church or a library, a place to which the reader has to go. A small octavo book, on the other hand, can be carried in a pocket or in the hand; it can be picked up and put down without strain; it can even, like letters, be concealed about the person. Size has cultural implications: the Bodleian library, when it was set up in the Renaissance, explicitly excluded quartos and the theatrical "trash" published predominantly in quarto format. Bodley described such texts as "baggage books," emphasizing their disgraceful potential for vagrancy, for being carried around in hand or pocket from place to place.[9] These "baggage" books have as their extreme antitheses the chained books of medieval cathedrals and universities: books that are designed (by size, weight, and security measures) to stay in place. It was these latter books that came to define "culture" in its elite sense. To become a classic (a book that would endure because preserved in a library), Shakespeare's plays had to be produced, after his death, in folio form.

If, from the standpoint of their *consumption* as texts, the codex and the book need to be understood as particular forms of language machines, we also need to attend to the ways in which they were *produced* (in written and printed forms) and to the ways in which even the most interesting theoretical work on reading and writing often assumes a problematic distinction between the manual and the mechanical production of texts. To take one striking example: in an argument that ignores the materiality of written and printed forms, Roland Barthes argues for the "writerly" text (which requires the active work of the reader) over the "readerly" work (which is already shaped for passive consumption). Yet it might be said that at a material level the "readerly" work simply did not exist in Europe until some seven centuries after Christianity had been founded for the simple (but little-known) fact that both Latin and vernacular texts were written in *scriptio continua*. That is, in scribal texts as they were produced there were nobreaksbetweenwordsnopunctuationnocapitalletters. The "breaking up" of this stream of letters into words and logical units was the work of the reader or of the orator who would perform them. And *scriptio continua* could, of course, be broken up in a variety of ways. In the late seventh century, Irish scribes began to separate words in Latin texts, and later still such word separation was extended to the Celtic, Germanic, and finally Romance languages. Only after words had been separated did systems of punctuation and capitalization develop in various scriptoria.[10] And after the advent of printing, it was the job of the compositor (a reader who is also the producer of texts), not the author, to divide the text into paragraphs, add punctuation, add italic emphases, and so on.[11] In other words, the "work" of the reader (which some theorists take to be characteristic of modernism) was already embedded in the reading and printing practices of the codex and the early book.

The work of recent historians of the manuscript, the codex, and the book implicitly demonstrates how narrow our assumptions of the typicality of a certain kind of book and a certain kind of reading have been.[12] What is closest to us, as Wittgenstein noted, is what is often least visible. In naturalizing our own writing, reading, and printing machines, we cease to see how they have shaped, and continue to shape, our cultural practices. It is, no doubt, partly the emergence of new forms of cultural technology (film, TV, video cassettes, computers, CDs, the Web) that helps us to see the specificities and peculiarities of books and of reading techniques. We can, for instance, begin to articulate the differences between books and films as modes of storing language and images. The modern cinema has reinstalled the scroll as its technological form. A spool unwinds at a fixed speed, with no going forward or backward, without pause. We are here at the furthest remove from the reading practices that Christianity culturally privileged and technologically made possible. It takes the VCR and the video disk to "add" to the scroll technology of film and videotape the "reading" technologies of the codex: skipping, going back, pausing.

As anyone who has taught film or video knows, the *consequences* of these different language machines are all too apparent. Teaching film with the aid of a projector, the instructor resorts to the most primitive of techniques: pieces of paper, stuck at particular points in the reel or scroll of film, to which he or she laboriously fast-forwards as the class waits in increasing irritation. And there's the familiar moment at a conference when the lecturer tries to find the beginning of a particular song on tape or a particular clip on video, rewinding and fast-forwarding in ever greater desperation. The emergence of film and of music as modern academic disciplines is bedeviled by the specific problems of their developing technologies, as the history of art is bedeviled by inadequately darkened rooms and the malfunctioning of slide projectors. The "matter" of our disciplines cannot be divorced from the machines through which we study, for the "matter" only emerges within our cultural technologies.

If the first claim of *Language Machines* is that material forms regulate and shape cultural practices, the second is that new technologies do not just replace, but rather draw upon, absorb, displace, and resituate (re-place) earlier technologies. It would seem that the particular "sequence" of machines that this collection explores is necessarily implicated in a familiar scenario of Western teleological progress: the pen succeeds the voice, the press succeeds the pen, the screen succeeds the press. The contributors to this volume, though, resist any simple notion of progress, demonstrating the persistence rather than obsolescence of technologies over time and the ways in which different technologies coexist with, impinge upon, and transform each other. They explore, for instance, how the writing hand was itself shaped in the nineteenth century by printed penmanship manuals; how the "voice" was transformed by the tele*graph* and the radio; how the complexities of Indian scripts necessitated new developments in European metallurgy and the design of print; how television and computers draw upon the cultural authority of the book; how the Renaissance book has been transformed by surveillance technologies developed in World War II.

Though *Language Machines* seems to trace a familiar chronological path, from earlier to later technologies, one aim of the collection is to insist that penmanship—the use of the hand—is in no sense prior to technology. Most recent work on cultural technologies has been over-obsessed with novelty, as if the hand preceded technology. Against such a view, Jonathan Goldberg's important book *Writing Matter* has developed the work of Engels to argue that

> human evolution ... has taken place through the labor of the hand, through the extension of the hand into the world through the instrument, the tool, the machine. Engels's essay allows one to think that the origin of the human hand is one with the machine.[13]

But the "machine" of the hand is resituated by later scholarly practices within a regime of authorship and authenticity, which radically separates the imaginative writer from the mere scribe.[14] Moreover, the era of the printed book is accompanied from the first by a nostalgia for handwriting. A printer's letters included ligatures—joined letters, like "s" and "t" or "f" and "l" which, made in a single mold, simulate cursive handwriting.

"Pens," the first section of this volume, both addresses and troubles that nostalgia. As Meredith McGill argues in "The Duplicity of the Pen," Edgar Allen Poe won the literary prize of the *Baltimore Saturday Visitor* for a book that was indeed written by hand, not printed. But the book was written in Roman characters, in imitation of a printed book. More generally, handwriting was increasingly taught in the nineteenth century through *printed* texts. Handwriting, in other words, was derived from printed sources, the press in such cases being literally prior to the pen. But McGill shows how Poe's editors warded off the anxiety conjured up by Poe's derivative and mechanical hand, distancing him from the modern market by depicting him with quill in hand.

But the authorial hand has always been the site of bifurcation, as Goldberg has argued. Writers quite regularly wrote in more than one "hand." In the early modern period, for instance, a letter in secretary hand is often followed by a signature in italic hand, the hand that became associated with humanist authorship. The very notion of the "secretary" hand, though, troubles the imagined hand of authorship. For, in the Renaissance and later, secretaries were trained to simulate their master's or mistress's hand (or their *several* hands). And the word "signature" itself refers not only to the penned name of a writer but to the printed mark at the bottom of the page (A, A2, A3 and so on), a mechanically reproduced sign that has to do not with authorship but with the sequence in which pages should be folded, cut, and stitched together.

In his contribution to this volume, "The Female Pen," Goldberg interrogates the opposition between "mere" penmanship (the work of scribes and functionaries) and the hand of "authorship." He shows how the recent scholarly enterprise of detecting the "right writing" of the authorial hand inscribes a gendered and classed narrative. In the Devonshire manuscript, Goldberg examines a poem ("O Happy dames") that has been identified as being written in the hand of Mary Shelton. The poem is seemingly spoken by a woman. Yet the supposedly "bad" hand of Shelton is taken as evidence that she is a mere scribe, masking the authorial hand of Henry Howard, Earl of Surrey. Goldberg's essay questions the gender and sexual politics through which modern scholarship has assigned ownership of the pen and, through it, the hand.

The image of the quill-holding author remains crucial to the post-Enlightenment attempt to establish authorship prior to and distinct from the language machines by which texts are produced. But as Roger Stoddard puts it, "whatever they may do, authors do not write books."[15] Stoddard makes a material, rather than a theoretical, point: a book is an object, produced by a publisher, which is *printed*, not *written*. And the producers of that object are not authors but paper-makers, ink-makers, the founders of metal types, compositors, pressmen, proofreaders, binders, and so on. The second section of this collection, "Presses," pursues the implications of the book as a made object, an object that usually bears no material inscription by an author. This, as Jeffrey Masten argues in "Pressing Subjects," becomes a central problem in postwar bibliography. How are we to know what Shakespeare wrote if all we have are the printed words of potentially unreliable compositors? Bibliography becomes the attempt to get "behind" the printed book to the authorial hand, the attempt to strip away the "veil of print" so as to "see" the hypothetical authorial manuscript behind it. On the one hand, compositors figure a falling away from authorship, the interruption of a deviant materiality. On the other, as Masten shows, "authorship" (the differentiation of one hand from another) is simultaneously projected onto the compositors, distinguishing the competent from the incompetent. The collating machine that supposedly "detects" these compositorial differences was a direct outcome of surveillance techniques in the Second World War. And those techniques, now used to detect the "good" from the "bad" compositor, are, as Masten shows, implicated in the Cold War attempt to distinguish the loyal from the treacherous, the straight from the queer.

While Masten addresses the relation between seventeenth-century print culture and the twentieth-century state, Vinay Dharwadker analyzes the material hybridity of Indian print culture, a culture that cannot be seen as simply having received the imprint of the colonizer, but as having made its own substantial impression upon the material technologies (and institutions) of Europe as well as Asia. In Masten's essay, a crisis is precipitated when the author (at the imagined center of cultural production) is dislocated by the presence of the compositor (at the supposed margins). In Dharwadker's analysis, a crisis is precipitated when we are forced to recognize the extent to which not only India but also Europe are linguistically imagined not from the supposed center (say, London, Paris, Amsterdam) but from Calcutta. For it was in Calcutta that Fort William College established professorships of Arabic, Persian, Sanskrit, Bengali, and Hindi-Marathi, among other languages, nearly thirty years before any English university established a professorship in its own vernacular. And between 1800 and 1840 the Serampore Press printed 212,000 items in forty languages (thirty Indian languages, plus Arabic, Armenian, Burmese, Chinese, Javanese, Malay, Maldivian, Persian, Singapuri, and Thai). Calcutta thus became "the single most important site in the histories of Indo-European and general linguistics." As Dharwadker shows, even most critiques of the center/periphery argument operate within its terms, effacing the material and ideological labor in the making of the Calcutta print industry and the "cultural ambidexterity" of its makers, working as they did between an extraordinary range of languages and literatures.

The third section of *Language Machines*, "Screens," returns to questions about the relations among technologies: how is the technology and the authority of the book used, displaced, and transformed by cinema, television, and computer; how is television resituated by the emergence of hypertext and interactive technologies; how is film narrative problematized by its relation to the contingency of the still photograph? As Mary Ann Doane argues in "Screening Time," early silent cinema was in fact dominated not by narrative but by topical films (films about floods, executions, fires, and prize fights, for instance). This predilection for contingent events is related, both historically and formally, to the contingency of the still photograph, which was resistant to the structurings of film narrative. Within narrative cinema, the concept of the event domesticates the contingent, staging its significance within an unfolding story. But early silent films, Doane argues, are fascinated by the challenge to representation that the contingent detail represents, even as they wrestle to control the detail within the limits of documentary. The still photograph haunted the moving images of the cinema with the possibility of a contingent event not yet given a narrative place and significance. Far from being a technology made obsolete by the cinema, photography continued to trouble the emergent temporality of the cinema, with its attempts to distinguish between the event and "dead time," between the meaningful detail and the arbitrary image.

While Doane looks at the ways in which the older technology of the still photograph disturbs and disrupts the relentless forward movement of the cinematic apparatus, Marsha Kinder's essay "Screen Wars" explores the power of new cultural technologies to absorb and transform older ones. Kinder analyzes how the cinema screen was theorized by Eisenstein in relation to methods of framing in Japanese drawing, to the narrative strategies of Dickens, and to theatrical experiments. The cinema screen thus accommodates previous technologies even as it threatens them with obsolescence. Kinder then turns to the ways in which the television screen begins to simulate the multimedia hypertext in Peter Greenaway's and Tom Phillips's *A TV Dante*, a video palimpsest that draws both upon the older technologies of the codex and upon recent developments in computer technology. She concludes that, just as television resituated and attempted to incorporate a wide range of previous technologies (the codex, the theater, the cinema), so hypertext repositions the technology of television, revealing its limitations as an interactive form.

Katherine Hayles, in the concluding paper of "Screens," examines the ways in which computer technology has been problematically envisioned as technology-free. Drawing upon the construction of an information/materiality dualism in molecular biology, computer theorists have made their own distinctions between information and matter (or between message and signal), presenting information as context-free and unchanged by its instantiation within any specific medium. Hayles argues that this binarism is profoundly misleading, reproducing a fantasy of transcendence. The latest technology is imagined as going beyond technology itself. At the same time, previous technologies are both drawn upon and displaced. The book is reconfigured as an anachronism even as it becomes the site of a nostalgic desire for sensuousness and physicality. Hayles argues that it is more useful to look at the ways in which hypertext establishes both new technical procedures and new subject-positions, with the body's boundaries being extended or disrupted through the interaction of screen and user. That interaction in fact foregrounds the discontinuities which were such a striking aspect of the codex as opposed to the scroll. For although one scrolls through a text on a computer, the actual achievement of hypertext is to establish a series of interactive links between networks of discrete, discontinuous units. Thus, through a wholly different technology and different procedures, it enforces the nonlinear "reading" that we argued above was such a distinctive feature of the emergent codex. But the interaction between user and screen is no longer regulated by the margins (all too easily filled up) of the medieval codex. The virtual subject of computer technology is a different cyborg from the written subject of the codex and the book. The virtual subject emerges from the recognition that all material objects (including the book and the cinema screen) are interpenetrated by informational patterns, just as those patterns are organized by the material technologies we use.

The final section of *Language Machines* includes three essays on "Voice," which, like the essays on screens, analyze the technophobic and anti-materialist desire to detach language from the machines that produce it. All three essays also explore the dislocation of the voice—Jay Clayton in his analysis of the telegraphic voice, Peggy Phelan in her account of Artaud's performing voice, and Gregory Ulmer in his meditations on the hybrid forms of hypertext, radio, and steel guitar. In "The Voice in the Machine," Clayton looks at the struggle between aural and visual technologies in the development of the telegraph. In fact, as Clayton shows, an early *optical* telegraph was established in France in 1794, and it developed eventually a visual relay of 556 telegraph stations. Even the Morse Telegraph Company at first regulated against the use of sound systems, preferring visual ones. But as the sound telegraph developed, it was not its disembodiment that struck contemporaries but its "queer" and "odd" noise. It was, in fact, the "voice" of the telegraph that fascinated writers like Thomas Hardy and Henry James, as previously the "voice" of the letter bell that announced the arrival of the mail carrier had obsessed William Hazlitt with the permeation of everyday life by cultural technologies. Clayton notes that the voice of the telegraph was experienced in a variety of embodied ways: through the hand of the sender; through the mouths of repairmen, who placed one wire above and another below their tongues; through electric shocks as one held the wires in one's hands. There was thus nothing abstract about the voice of the telegraph, which was experienced as a dislocation of an existing aural world. It was a voice that transformed the relation between sound and distance, bringing together operators and receivers in different cities and on different continents. Clayton argues that the telegraphist, usually a woman, became a cyborg undergoing what Henry James called a "queer extension of her experience."

In "Performing Talking Cures," Peggy Phelan analyzes the crisis that Artaud felt at the queer dislocation of the voice that early sound films effected. For while Artaud's project was the radical unification of voice and body, the dubbing of the early cinema mechanically joined different voices and bodies. Artaud thus experienced the sound film as a challenge to theatrical presence, a terrifying technological introduction of "parasites" into the body's organs. Against the iterability of the sign that Derrida insists upon, Artaud dreamed of a sound that would be fully embodied, even as it shattered the bones. But Artaud's insistence on vocal presence is directed toward the production of a voice that we do not yet know, a voice that inhabits not only the orifice of the mouth and that must be heard not only through the orifices of the ear. If Artaud's desire seems technophobic, a yearning for a flesh-speech uncontaminated by parasites or even by the localized machines of speech and hearing, it is also a challenge to the hierarchical divisions of the physical body and the social body, an insistence on the curative function of the spectacular utterance of the theater.

"Kubla Honky Tonk," the essay by Gregory Ulmer that concludes this collection, is a meditation on the dislocation and hybridization of the voice through the technologies that we inhabit. If Artaud dreamed of a shattering scream, Ulmer argues that the networks in which we live are already shattered, at least from the perspective of a previous culture of literacy. The attempt to undo that shattering, to reconstitute and restore the "active voice," the grammatical voice of agency, is itself a yearning for transcendence. The "active voice" of rhetorical handbooks is praised precisely because it is transparent: the voice of the self-possessed and fully present subject. Ulmer, on the contrary, tries to track a voice that is necessarily hybrid: a voice inhabited by the conflicting voices of a local radio station and a station that plays new rock music; a voice that is situated, both literally and phantasmatically, by the conflicting locations of a house and a mobile home; a voice articulated through the imagined syncretism of country music and samba. The emphasis on the "active voice" is itself an evasion of the creolization of our voices, which is also the creolization of the technologies that we inhabit and that inhabit us.

We ourselves have produced this introduction in multiple locations, collating a poly-vocal and dispersed volume. A draft was "written" on a screen in London, printed by fax in Boston and Los Angeles. This draft was rewritten online and on screens in other locations, typed on "desktops" that have "windows," and reworked in the margins of "facsimile" pages in several hands; it was voiced on answering machines and through the cyborg technology of "voice mail." Finally, it appears as a printed book, published from a disk, although that "finally" may also be misleading since it was a contract with Routledge that initiated the collection in the first place. This introduction will inscribe, in ways we ourselves cannot know, its formation (its formatting, and ours) through the technologies deployed in its production. But *Language Machines* is not a celebration of the inevitable triumph of new technologies of information and communication. Whether this is a better or a worse book than one produced writing together at a table is a question that cannot be answered. But it is a different book, situating us as different writers and subjects as a result of the technologies that we have used (and are "used to"). The subject of scroll technology is not the same as the subject of codex technology; the subject of hypertext resituates the subject of television. We write as cyborgs, inventing the language machines that reinvent us.

NOTES

1. John Bulwer, *Anthropometamorphosis: Man Transformed, Or the Artificial Changeling* (London: 1650), p. 92.

2. See Jonathan Goldberg, "Hamlet's Hand," *Shakespeare Quarterly* 39 (1988), pp. 307–27. *The Tragedie of Hamlet*, in *Mr. William Shakespeares Comedies, Histories & Tragedies* (London: by Isaac Iaggard, and Ed. Blount, 1623), as reproduced in *The Norton Fascimile: The First Folio of Shakespeare*, prepared by Charlton Hinman (New York: Norton, 1968), TLN 1151–52.

3. John Donne, *LXXX Sermons* (London: 1640), p. 364. For an analysis of the "mechanical" to which we are deeply indebted, see Patricia Parker, "'Rude Mechanicals'" in *Subject and Object in Renaissance Culture*, ed. Margreta de Grazia, Maureen Quilligan, and Peter Stallybrass (Cambridge: Cambridge University Press, 1996), pp. 43–82.

4. Charles I, *Works*, vol. 2 (London: 1662), p. 170.

5. Elizabeth Pittenger, "Explicit Ink" in *Premodern Sexualities*, ed. Louise Fradenberg and Carla Freccero (New York and London: Routledge, 1996), pp. 223–242. This paragraph is indebted to Pittenger's fine essay.

6. Alanus of Lille, *The Plaint of Nature*, trans. James J. Sheridan (Toronto: The Pontifical Institute of Medieval Studies, 1980), pp. 165–66.

7. See Roger Chartier, *Forms and Meanings: Texts, Performances, and Audiences from Codex to Computer* (Philadelphia: University of Pennsylvania Press, 1995), pp. 18–20. Chartier also notes the close connection between the codex and Christianity: "the roll was earliest and most effectively replaced by the codex in Christian communities: from the second century, all recovered manuscripts of the Bible take the form of a codex written on papyrus, while 90 percent of the biblical texts and 70 percent of the liturgical and hagiographic texts we possess from the second through fourth centuries are also in the form of the codex" (18).

8. On biblical glossing, see Evelyn B. Tribble, *Margins and Marginality: The Printed Page in Early Modern England* (Charlottesville: University of Virginia Press, 1993), pp. 11–56.

9. See Margreta de Grazia, *Shakespeare Verbatim* (Oxford: Clarendon Press, 1991), p. 32. The *Oxford English Dictionary's* first definition of "baggage" is "[t]he collection of property in packages that one takes with him on a journey; portable property; luggage."

10. See M. B. Parkes, "The Contribution of Insular Scribes of the Seventh and Eighth Centuries to the 'Grammar of Legibility'" in his *Scribes, Scripts and Readers: Studies in the Communication, Presentation and Dissemination of Mediaeval Texts* (London: Hambledon, 1991), pp. 1–18. See also John Lennard, *But I Digress: The Exploitation of Parentheses in English Printed Verse* (Oxford: Clarendon Press, 1991), pp. 2–3.

11. On the changing relations between theatrical manuscripts and printed plays in the early seventeenth century, as compositorial practices began to be incorporated into the actual writing of plays, see Antony Hammond, "The Noisy Comma: Searching for the Signal in Renaissance Dramatic Texts," in *Crisis in Editing: Texts of the English Renaissance*, ed. Randall McLeod (New York: AMS Press, 1994), pp. 203–49.

12. See, for instance, M. B. Parkes and Roger Chartier (both cited above), and the work of D. F. McKenzie and Paul Saenger.

13. Jonathan Goldberg, *Writing Matter: From the Hands of the English Renaissance* (Stanford: Stanford University Press, 1990), p. 312.

14. On the ideological implications of the distinction between "scribe" and "author," see Scott McMillin, *The Elizabethan Theatre and The Book of Sir Thomas More* (Ithaca: Cornell University Press, 1987), pp. 156–59.

15. Roger E. Stoddard, "Morphology and the Book from an American Perspective," *Printing History* 17 (1987), pp. 2–14. On the implications of Stoddard's observation, see Roger Chartier, "Texts, Printing, Readings" in *The New Cultural History*, ed. Lynn Hunt (Berkeley: University of California Press), pp. 154–75.

PENS

JONATHAN GOLDBERG

THE

FEMALE PEN

WRITING

AS A

WOMAN

THE **DOUBLE TITLE** of this essay is meant to be doubly legible. On the one hand, the two phrases placed in apposition could simply be tautological, and, indeed, in what follows the possibility will be entertained that even at the material level of manuscript production, early modern writing practices can point to a female hand at work.[1] In seeking to identify these hands, these pages wish to affirm the gendered difference of writing in the period. However, there are massive problems in so doing, and the title of this essay registers this also. For, on the other hand, "female pen" could be read as an oxymoron, especially if one subscribes to the theory that women in this period are largely rendered silent not merely by the continually intoned prescriptions entailing female chastity, obedience, and submission, but also, and more to the point here, by the massive illiteracy of women, especially in terms of writing ability. While the pen is female in most Indo-European languages that gender their nouns, "female pen" nonetheless sounds like a virtual impossibility, and for the further reason that pen sounds so much like and is so often analogized to penis. That the pen could be viewed as an instrument of power and one gendered male would therefore imply that when a woman wields it a revaluation of the sense in which the writer remains female in any cultural sense of the word is required. So much too is suggested by "as" in the second half of my title; writing as a woman could be an act of transvestism, and indeed several recent studies, notably those of Wendy Wall and Elizabeth Harvey, have from different angles approached these questions; writing as a woman does not guarantee the gender of the author.[2]

This essay draws on materials from *Desiring Women Writers in the English Renaissance*, a forthcoming book-length study of female-authored texts, and my hope is that a problematization of questions of female authorship does not foreclose possibilities for women writers that might seem caught in a bind of simulation. For, in fact, each of the possibilities raised by this title is problematic: on the one hand there is an understanding of the woman writer that risks essentialism and dehistoricization; on the other hand, an understanding of women-as-constructed, with all its dangers of the erasure of women and of gendered difference. This is not least the case if the double situation that I have read out of this doubly-titled paper remains caught within the familiar terms of the essentialism/constructionism debate, but, even more importantly, within a binarism that genders essentialism as female; and construction, male. This double bind has, of course, often motivated the repudiation of theory in feminist criticism in the hope of clearing a space for women.[3] Yet, as I see it, what is needed is first of all to break this deadlock; to do so one must recognize how the theoretical division is maintained by the division of the sexes. Again, let me stress, the point in doing this would not be to arrive at some third term or third sex, some indeterminate middle or divine androgyne. Gendered difference is real, and real not least because of the massive work that social discourse and regulation does to maintain it, that somatic and psychological inhabitation of these categories enforces. Nonetheless it is only by questioning the divide that one can also understand its own regulatory effect and our contribution to it by insisting upon it; for by so doing the categories male and female that are thereby maintained are also impoverished.

I take my cue for this position not merely from any number of theorists I could cite—and the list would have to begin with Eve Kosofsky Sedgwick and Judith Butler—but from the instance of women's writing that is the subject of this paper. I want to look more closely here at an example that I touched on briefly in *Sodometries*.[4] In a chapter on "The Making of Courtly Makers," I argued, based in part on an anecdote from Puttenham's *Arte of English Poesie*, that a consideration of gender transitivity—of cross-gender identifications—in the sixteenth century might enlarge our sense of the range and possibilities for cultural activity in the period. Puttenham's anecdote centered on an ambiguous word, "weemen," that could as easily be read as an affirmation of the solidity of male identification (but which also thereby entailed the real possibility of male-male desire) or as an endorsement of cross-gender desire, of the desire of men for women. One consequence of this, I suggested, was that "women" could move into the position of "we men" without simply being erased in so doing, since Puttenham's term "wee men" refused the absolute closure of gender difference or, more to the point, was not bound to a syntax of heteronormativity since the opening for women represented by Puttenham followed from the presumption that male desire might as easily be satisfied by men or by women. While it must be stressed that, in Puttenham's account, "women" remained in a subservient position to men and to male desire, it need not be assumed that such would always be the situation, and I offered some examples to that effect.

One instance to make that case, which I summoned up in a cursory fashion in *Sodometries* and to which I return in this essay, had to do with a poem assigned to the authorship of Henry Howard, styled Earl of Surrey, in its first printing in the 1557 volume of *Songs and Sonnets* that has come to be called *Tottel's Miscellany*.[5] There, Tottel titled the poem "Complaint of the absence of her lover being upon the sea" (Tottel #17), and the presumption that the speaker of the poem is a woman has been repeated ever since. However, before the poem found its way into print, it circulated in manuscript; there is extant one such text of the poem entered into what is usually called the Devonshire manuscript (BL Add.17492) in all likelihood in the 1530s, perhaps early in the 1540s, but at any rate sometime before Surrey's execution in 1547, that is, at least ten years before the poem was printed. Differences between the manuscript and the printed text make it very likely that Tottel did not set the poem from the Devonshire manuscript but from another manuscript, perhaps one like the contemporary Arundel Harington manuscript, a collection of poems compiled as a self-conscious anthology, in which groups of works by the same author are gathered on sequential leaves. *Tottel's Miscellany* looks like that: its first printing includes groups of poems by Surrey, Wyatt, and Nicholas Grimald, followed by a long section of poems by uncertain authors. However, manuscript ascriptions are not always reliable; even the Arundel Harington manuscript is rather vexing around some poems supposedly by Surrey.

For the argument in *Sodometries*, what was of crucial importance to me was the fact that the poem that begins "O Happy dames, that may embrace / The frute of your delight" (Tottel #17) was written in a hand that had been identified as Mary Shelton's. I argued—or rather, held open as a possibility—that the poem seemingly spoken by a woman (as indicated by Tottel's title for it and the subsequent consensus that takes the female speaker of the poem to represent an act of male ventriloquism) might be a poem *written* by a woman, by Mary Shelton in fact.

No one has ever entertained that supposition, I assume because of the authority of Tottel's attribution of the poem to Surrey. But while her authorship of the poem has never been suggested, the ways in which Mary Shelton's hand in the Devonshire manuscript has been described has virtually precluded such a consideration. In *Sodometries*, I quoted S. P. Zitner's description of her hand as a scrawl, and noted that Zitner was simply repeating Richard Harrier's characterization in his study of *The Canon of Wyatt's Poetry*.[6] I pointed out, however, that Mary Shelton had more than one hand: her italic signature can be found on the torn page that now serves as the front leaf of the Devonshire manuscript. This signature meant, very simply, that Mary Shelton was an extremely literate person; the fact that she used italic for her formal signature aligns her with the most progressive humanistic educational programs of the period, and provides an indicative mark of the kind of high literacy that must also be related to poetic production in the Tudor period. That her ordinary hand was a "scrawl" would not distinguish her from many other writers of the period, who reserved italic for signatures or for writing in Latin. Indeed, one sign of high literacy in the period has precisely to do with the ability to manage several hands. In short, once the scrawl in which "O Happy dames" appears in the Devonshire manuscript is recognized as *one* of the several hands of Mary Shelton, it is not, as "scrawl" would seem to imply, an indication of minimal literacy.

In the Devonshire manuscript, "O Happy dames" is untitled and no authorship for it is provided. This is not unusual for manuscripts of the period, and indeed the fullest systematic study of the manuscript that has been undertaken, that of Richard Harrier mentioned above, has precisely to do with this fact. The Devonshire manuscript contains a number of poems that are attributed to Wyatt elsewhere, and Harrier sought to establish which other poems in the manuscript might safely be ascribed to him as well. This scholarly activity, which clearly has a place, accounts for most of the work that has been done on the Devonshire manuscript, indeed on most early manuscripts. There is no need for me to elaborate the conditions of modern scholarship that have dictated the assignment of authorship as the main protocol in the study of manuscripts, in part because it has been the subject of recent work by Arthur Marotti, who has frequently remarked that its effect has been to slight other social significances that such materials have.[7] While I do not believe that the desire to name Mary Shelton as the author of a poem supposedly by Surrey is identical to Harrier's efforts to sort out which poems in the manuscript deserve to be considered Wyatt's, my argument and his are sufficiently alike to raise the necessary and uncomfortable question of whether the discovery of women writers must succumb to the lure of the canonical and the mystification of the singular author. In *Sodometries* I limited my remarks on "O Happy dames" to a provocative paragraph, in part because I did not think I could convincingly argue the case for Mary Shelton's authorship, that it could only be raised as a possibility. In truth, I still think this is the case; but I think it is also the case for Wyatt. If it were obvious which poems were his, there would be no problem in establishing the canon.

This is a potentially embarrassing fact for any notion of sovereign authorship, and one upon which I want to build. When one recognizes that it is not obvious what poems Wyatt wrote; that the canon is disputed; that attributions, even in Wyatt's lifetime, are contradictory; that manuscripts that seem to group poems by authors don't do so consistently; that even the Egerton manuscript that contains poems and corrections to them by Wyatt in his own hand did not stop other hands from marking his poems, one arrives at a number of important conclusions: that there is no intrinsic evidence for authorship; that assignment of authorship is dependent upon extrinsic evidence, for example, on coincidences of attribution; but, above all, that it is dependent upon the notion that assigning authorship is what matters. And even the Egerton manuscript does not suggest that such a principle had been established in the 1530s, while *Tottel's Miscellany*, which, on its title page, advertises the name of the Earl of Surrey (although inside the book more poems are attributed to Wyatt than to Surrey) does so because Surrey's name is important to Tottel—not, however, simply as the name of an author, but as an authorizing name. It is an aristocratic title, a style that is announced and to which the poems are subsumed— a style, which, as everyone knows, is Tottel's imposition in terms of editorial changes, rewritings, the provision of titles for poems, and the like. Some of these features go back to manuscripts, and they reflect upon authorial habits in the period.[8] Wyatt's autograph manuscript testifies to numerous revisions; there is no guarantee that even he thought of producing authoritative and final texts of his poems or sought to regulate their form as they circulated from hand to hand.

These facts about manuscript production raise significant questions about the version of "O happy dames" in the Devonshire manuscript. For even if Surrey were its original author, Shelton's version might make it, in some sense, her own. The manuscript provides a way of further thinking through this point, as well as some further evidence for why Shelton's authorship has not yet been given a proper hearing. The final dozen or so entries in the Devonshire manuscript, usually said to be in Shelton's hand, are texts transcribed from Thynne's 1532 edition of Chaucer.[9] In his edition of "Unpublished Poems in the Devonshire MS," Kenneth Muir referred to these as "a group of short poems in the same handwriting, some of them apparently composed by a woman" (p. 255), as he also opined was the case with another poem in the manuscript that opens, "For thylke grownde that bearyth the wedes wycke / Beareth eke these holsome herbes as ful ofte," a set of lines, in fact, from *Troilus and Criseyde*.[10] His conclusion about the value of the poems in the manuscript was that aside from the poems by Surrey and Wyatt and a poet who might be Wyatt's imitator, "the poetical level of the verse in the manuscript is not high" (p. 258). This judgment includes the Chaucer selections, and it is not difficult to believe that seeing a woman's hand kept Muir from recognizing Chaucer; but it has also to be added that Muir's failure reminds us that decontextualized Chaucer might not be recognizable. Moreover, some of the Chaucer in the manuscript is no longer thought to be Chaucer; and some that is has been mistranscribed, or, rather, has been rewritten in ways that seem intentional. All the verses anthologized from Thynne deal with women, and some have been reworded in order to make their representations far more positive than they are in the printed text. These revisions offer the strongest suggestion that, putting a text into her own hands, Mary Shelton also made it her own.[11] That Muir couldn't recognize Chaucer, out of context, scrawled in a woman's hand, is certainly fuel for the argument I want to make here. It leads one to doubt that if "O Happy dames" had not been claimed for Surrey by Tottel, its presence in the Devonshire manuscript would have led to that authorial ascription. There is, after all, no other poem among the 180 or 190 in the manuscript that is Surrey's (and only one other poem that ever has been claimed as his—by G. F. Nott in 1815, a claim that was refuted definitively in 1871 when it was shown that the signature after a poem that Nott read as "Surrey" in fact said "Somebody").[12]

Did Mary Shelton write "O Happy dames"? The arguments I have been making to problematize Surrey's authorship of the poem and to hold open a more capacious notion of authorship that would assign value to Shelton's hand build on an assumption which, however, needs to be examined: that the version of the poem in the Devonshire manuscript is in fact in Mary Shelton's hand. Assignment of the poem to her hand was first made in a frustratingly brief account of the manuscript offered by Edward Bond in the 1871 essay referred to above; not only is it difficult to know which leaves of the manuscript Bond thought Shelton wrote and why he thought so, but he also assigns the final series of Chauceriana to the hand of Margaret Howard; indeed, he declares them to be her own compositions (as other poems in the manuscript certainly are).

Muir admits that he has "not been able to identify the numerous handwritings in which the MS. is written," although he claims that "Surrey's 'O happy dames' is scribbled by Mary Shelton" (p. 254). In his notes to the poems he prints from the manuscript he refers to a number of them as being in the "same hand" without quite saying whose hand it might be; these poems in the "same hand" include the Chaucerian stanzas, but presumably not "O happy dames." The "same hand," in other words, does not appear to be Mary Shelton's. In Raymond Southall's work on the manuscript—work distinguished by the fact that Southall did not think that establishing authorship was his prime task—indeed, he doubts that Wyatt's authorship is an ascertainable item—Southall finds three hands to predominate in the manuscript (he thinks there are at least twenty-three); he assigns "O happy dames" to Mary Shelton, along with the Chauceriana and about about twenty other leaves of the manuscript; hers is, for him, the main hand in the manuscript, followed by that of Mary Fitzroy (Surrey's sister and the wife of Henry Fitzroy, Henry VIII's illegitimate son) and Margaret Howard.[13] Southall offers no opinion about who provided much of the marginalia to the volume; it, however, is assigned to Shelton by Harrier, who also reassigns a number of the leaves of the manuscript that Southall thought were Mary Shelton's to other hands; of "O Happy dames," he is only willing to say that it is "probably by Mary Shelton's hand" (p. 51). Moreover, he does not follow Southall in assigning her the Chaucerian verses, finding the "neat hand" of those leaves quite distinct from her "scrawl." However, as Paul Remley notes in a recent essay devoted to the question of Mary Shelton's hand in the manuscript, Harrier does elsewhere identify a neat hand as Shelton's, and, as Remley argues, the writer that could produce an italic signature and who at least twice, perhaps three times, inscribed her name in the volume in a cursive script that is not identical either to the italic signature or to the "scrawl" obviously could have done "neat" writing as well. For the point is, to reiterate, Mary Shelton did not have one hand. Moreover, differences in hands arise from numerous conditions (speed of writing, cut and quality of the quill being used) which often make it difficult to know whether different hands belong to different persons (hence Southall's "conservative estimate" of twenty-three hands in the manuscript does not in fact tell us how many writers contributed to it).

Remley assigns the final Chauceriana to Shelton and makes much of her rewritings as a kind of feminine (perhaps feminist) protest literature; so too he sees the marginalia as hers and as serving the same function, as when she writes "forget this" beside a poem. (Others have assumed that such marginal remarks are meant to be directions for someone copying the manuscript, indicating which poems should or should not be copied; Bond, on the other hand, tooks these comments to be Margaret Howard's responses to poems that particularly touched or angered her.) However, because Remley knows that it is exceedingly difficult to assign hands to bodies, he accepts only as Shelton's those pieces of text that are proximate to her signatures or that seem to him consistent with the version of Shelton that the marginalia (as he reads it) and the Chauceriana suggest—Shelton as a "subversive" voice of protest. Scrupulous about the material evidence of hands, Remley falls into a much too easy notion of a real person (with an agenda obviously shared by Remley) who dictates what in the manuscript is hers. Moreover, while Remley notes that Bond assigned "O happy dames" to Mary Shelton and that "this view has persisted" (p. 48), he nowhere considers the possibility in his essay that the poem is in her hand, and thus implicitly calls that assumption into question, presumably because he does not find in that text evidence of the kind of "personal protest" he assigns to the name Mary Shelton. However, as Remley himself points out, we know scarcely anything about Mary Shelton, not even when she was born. The few traces of her name that survive, including those instances in the Devonshire manuscript, have been read in numerous ways, most of which testify to the fantasies of modern scholars, usually (not surprisingly) about Shelton's supposed love life.[14] It is this paucity of evidence, however, which also renders suspect the notion that a real Mary Shelton can be extrapolated from the hands in the Devonshire manuscript.

I would not want to give the impression in reviewing these efforts to identify Mary Shelton's hand in the Devonshire manuscript that I feel capable of doing what these scholars, far more skilled as paleographers than I am or ever will be, can do. I think it is clear that without some independent examples of Shelton's hand on documents that must have been written by her, we have little hope of being able to distinguish what exactly in the Devonshire manuscript is hers (and even such documents would not necessarily be conclusive since handwriting changes over time and is often in the early modern period different depending on the kind of text being written). In many respects, for the argument I have been making here, finding the real Mary Shelton is not the point. That the multiplicity of hands in the manuscript belong variously to three women is as useful for my purposes as the possibility of definitively ascribing texts to them; there are certainly poems in the manuscript by Margaret Howard, and just as certainly some by Mary Shelton. G. F. Nott remarked long ago that the hand of "O Happy dames" looks like that of Mary Fitzroy, and the example he provided in facsimile does bear a striking resemblance to the hand in the Devonshire manuscript (2: 591). There is a strong resemblance between the hands of these three women in this manuscript, and they are performing enormously important cultural work. A reduction of it to the question of who did what—and to the assumption that authorship is the most important category to be ascertained—limits one's understanding of the extent to which this manuscript participates in the creation of Tudor culture. This activity may not be, *pace* Remley, subversive, marginal protest; the rewriting instanced in the Chauceriana, for example, is not surprising in manuscript culture, which is is not to suggest that how Chaucer is rewritten is inconsequential. More to the point may be the importance of recognizing these women's hands as participating in and shaping the materials of cultural transmission. The failure to recognize this fact— the persistence and importance of manuscript culture in the period —is a product of print culture, theirs and ours.

I mentioned earlier that Tottel's version of "O Happy dames" is not the one offered in the Devonshire manuscript. There is, of course, no reason to suppose that he was avoiding reproducing in print a woman's hand and, indeed, the manuscript he worked from could have been another instance of the same phenomenon. However, it does have to be noted that every modern edition of Surrey reprints the poem from Tottel and not from the Devonshire manuscript; this does seem like an active suppression of the woman's hand.[15] There is no way to argue that the Devonshire manuscript offers a better text of the poem than Tottel does, if by better one means closer to Surrey's original, which is what better must mean to an editor of Surrey's work; but there is also no reason to assume in these terms that Tottel's text is any closer to the authorial holograph. We know that *Tottel's Miscellany* rarely prints its sources verbatim, and in most cases will be one step away from the manuscript(s) behind it. Ordinary editorial procedure would lead a modern editor in such instances to prefer a contemporary manuscript to the printed text, and in fact both of Padelford's 1920s editions of Surrey, as well as Emrys Jones's 1964 Oxford edition, do prefer manuscripts whenever possible. That is, in every instance but this one. That is, in the one case where a woman's scrawl has been identified as the manuscript hand.

What does the poem look like in the manuscript? Admittedly, it is a scrawl, or as Padelford writes in a note to the transcription he provided of the manuscript version in a 1906 essay on "The Ms. Poems of Henry

Howard, Earl of Surrey," "the hand is very slovenly" (p. 338).[16] However, once one admits the possibility that the hand that wrote this poem could also write neatly, the slovenly scrawl may simply indicate that it is not the neat hand of a copyist, not, that is, the neat copying hand. In the characteristic scrawl that most scholars agree is Mary Shelton's, that hand is found when she is composing, even when she is signing her name to one of her scrawled compositions. Mary Shelton's compositions in the manuscript commonly take the form of short verses, usually characterized by commentators as doggerel, a word that Shelton herself uses in one of these entries.[17] These entries often constitute *ex tempore* responses to some text in the manuscript. The first thing therefore to remark about "o happy dames" in the Devonshire manuscript is that if it is in Mary Shelton's hand it is in her composing hand. Moreover, as Padelford goes on to note, "words and even lines are scratched out to be replaced by slightly different spellings."[18] Were one dealing with a modern text, it would be easy enough to assume that these indicate a copyist recognizing and correcting a spelling mistake. However, there is no standardized spelling in the period; indeed, what makes the texts certainly by Mary Shelton in the manuscript particularly elusive and difficult to transcribe is that their spellings allow quite alternative readings. If Shelton did not have any sense of correct or singular spelling (a fact, let me hasten to add, that is no sign of impoverished literacy, since, as has often been pointed out, modern editions of Renaissance texts often lose potential meanings by modernizing spellings and thereby deciding on one meaning when the old spelling preserves multiple possibilites), these crossings out and substitutions might then indicate her rethinking whether or not the word she just wrote is the word she wants, and then deciding that it is—or, perhaps, deciding that the respelling says better what she wants.[19] At any rate, I don't think such crossings out and substitutions of the same word constitute proof that the writer of these lines is attempting to be true to some text being copied. Only once does a substitution suggest that the author may be a copyist, when "hartte" has been scratched out and "mynde" substituted—a substitution necessary to maintain the rhyme scheme. This is an "error" of the kind frequently noted in terms of memorially reconstructed texts, since "hartte" does appear two lines further down. Such accounts of mistaken transcription assume that the transcriber has memorized what is being copied and then errs by misremembering where the word properly belongs, often producing the kind of doubling that would have here had two "hart[t]e"s, one clearly in the wrong place. The trouble with this explanation is that such errors also happen when one is writing, especially when writing quickly. The hand that wrote "hartte" and then crossed it out may be recognizing that it has gotten ahead of itself. There is a similar mistake noted by Padelford in the final line of the poem when, as the absent lover is imagined return- ing, the manuscript first read, "nowe he comes wylle allas no no," and then added above the line, between "wylle" and "allas," the words "he cume." "Now he comes wylle he cume allas no no" is a proper ten- syllable line, formally congruent with the final lines of each of the stan- zas. But most of the lines in the poem have eight syllables, and the shorter version of the line is as intelligible as the longer one. Which is to say, it may not be an instance of Shelton leaving out what was in the version she was copying as of her rushing to a conclusion, still in the basic meter of the poem, and then reconsidering the end. I submit, therefore, as a real possibility, that the failure to use the Devonshire manuscript as the basis for modern texts of this poem is a refusal to grant what this account of the manuscript aims to suggest: the authority of the manuscript as (per- haps) a poem in the author's hand.[20]

But did a woman write "o happy dames"? What is the gender of the speaker? As I indicated earlier, modern editors have followed Tottel in assuming that the speaker of the poem is a woman. In his 1920s edi- tions of Surrey, Padelford provided an explanation of sorts for this by claiming that the poem was in all likelihood written by Surrey "for the Countess of Surrey, to voice her impatience at their separation during Surrey's absence on military duty in France" (an explanation that Jones repeats); alternatively, Padelford opines, perhaps, since it is in Shelton's hand in the Devonshire manuscript, Surrey wrote it for her, to express her desire for Thomas Clere, Surrey's companion in France, who died there in 1545. This explanation can be faulted on bibliographic grounds, since it assumes a somewhat later date for the Tudor entries in the Devonshire manuscript than is usual. Moreover, and much more to the point, this account assumes that women can't write for themselves. Additionally, this explanation that a poem voicing intense desire for an absent beloved male must be written in a woman's voice aims to guar- antee that there is nothing of Surrey's desire to be found in the text.

Indeed, the only reason I have to want to go on thinking that this poem is by Surrey has precisely to do with the possibility for the representation of male-male eros that it represents, a possibility that I believe the current account of the poem as written for and as a woman seeks to erase, although I think even in its own terms some sense of gender transitivity can be reclaimed from the scenario that Padelford first suggested.[21]

Elizabeth Harvey has noted how transvestite poems of the period often involve placing a female speaker in the position authoritatively prescribed by the example of the poems that comprise Ovid's *Heroides*, one of which is a source for this poem as well, the woman lamenting the absence of her beloved, usually his betrayal and abandonment of her.[22] But as Ann Rosalind Jones has observed, there are instances of female-authored texts in the period that reclaim and reappropriate this Ovidian tradition.[23] In "o happy dames," the speaker initially addresses women "that may enbrayes / the ffrwte off your delyet"; the poem does not assume abandonment as the ordinary situation of women, and accounts for happiness in erotically charged ways, as virtually every term in these lines suggests; some lines later, the speaker will once again invoke the situation of "owther lowers" who "en armes acrosse / rejoyes ther cheffe dellyet," imagining lovers embracing in the context of the speaker's description of sleepless nights and pained awakening to loss after dreaming of former delights. In that nocturnal, bedroom context, these embraces must also be sexual ones. The speaker sees women as sexual and is flooded with memories of union with the beloved, repeatedly aroused as the return of the beloved is anticipated, indeed is reexperienced. The final line of the poem, cited earlier, "nowe he comes wylle he cume allas no no," is the climactic instance in which he is almost present, and then is not. If this is a poem written by a woman, it represents female sexuality as unabashedly active and desiring, rather than contained by the familiar prescriptions, or allowed their transgressions (as in Padelford's scenario) only if one can assume that a man (preferably a husband) really wrote the poem.

It may be the forthrightness of this subject-position that has contributed to the supposition of male authorship, but, framed that way, it needs to be questioned for its reliance on a definition of gender difference plotted along the familiar axes of activity and passivity. Within the terms that the poem sets—in which the gender of the speaker is in fact never specified, and where it is only the presumption that if the desired object is male, the speaker must be female—what seems more to the point is the way in which the ordinary syntax of heteroerotic desire seems to have been reversed. If this places the speaker in the active male position, that need not mean that the poem is male authored. But it does mean that, no matter who wrote it, the presumed hetero desire in the poem also vehiculates male-male desire. This, indeed, would be the case even in Padelford's scenario, since it assumes that in writing for his wife, Surrey was writing to himself; Padelford's plot thus inscribes an imaginary heteroerotics within a narcissistic cover for homoerotics.

Not only the manipulation of subject/object positions in the poem allows for its gender transitivity. As the absent male is conjured up, he becomes an occupant of the speaker's mind, as, for instance, in the third stanza of the poem:

alas howe ofte in dremes I see
thoos yees that were my ffoode
wyche ssumetyme sso dellyted me
that yet they do me good
where with I wake with his retourne
whoosse abssente fflame dooth make me boren
but when I ffynde the lake lorde howe I mowren.

These lines display an intense incorporation and identification with the absent beloved; the seeing and the seen change positions, "thoos yees" become the speaker's I, still doing good, indeed ensuring the life of the speaker, as food and as the flame that still burns.

The phantasmatic identification and incorporation of the dream state also marks the writing of the poem in another way, guaranteeing that this is not the kind of straight autobiography that Padelford assumed. From the second stanza on, in which the absent beloved sails "en a shepe ffrawoghte wth remiemberances," to the fourth in which, projecting onto the beloved's absent state, the speaker exclaims, "loo whate amarryner lowe hays made me," the sea voyage of this poem is one that involves crossings of identity. The beloved contains the speaker and is thereby burdened by memory, and thus assumed to be in the same state of simultaneous connection and loss as is the speaker, whose transportations of the beloved, bringing him to mind, are also the exile of the speaker, at sea with the absent lover. These strong marks of identification in fact explain an otherwise puzzling feature of the poem, that it is impossible often to tell whether the speaker thinks the beloved is sailing away or sailing home. The traffic works in both directions, just as the "remiemberances" of the poem coupled with the failures and lack ("lake") suggest a trading of presence and absence, of possession and dispossession, terms that could be marked as male and female, but, if so, only to note them as moveable marks of gendered identity. If this is a poem by a woman, the positions usually gendered male and female are destabilized; indeed, insofar as it is easier to read this poem as (at the least) spoken by a woman, that position of writing seems to enable the other possibility that the poem voices—and not necessarily through a female speaker: the possibility of a male-male erotics. This poem feels transgressive of the prescribed boundaries of female desire and expression; if it latches on to or produces this through the imagined occupation of a male desiring position, it also pushes beyond usual representational limits in the male-male desire avowed in the poem. It is, of course, possible to read this poem as a male-authored one in which the presumed female speaker is simply a screen, in which there is no woman in the poem. However, other women are invoked in the poem, and the speaker seeks to occupy their positions of satisfied desire, which is one reason why it is difficult to read this poem and erase the possibility that a woman is the speaker. Even if a male author has foisted his desiring position onto the women in this poem, it cannot be read, I think, as a male-authored text that simply appropriates women, since the text articulates a position for women as desiring subjects. And, of course, if this really is a poem written by Mary Shelton or one of the other women whose hands appear in the Devonshire manuscript, this enlargement of possibility, however much it is founded in a rewriting of an Ovidian tradition and in the gender-transitive reversal of its syntax of male and female positioning, does not represent the marginal transgression and subversion that one might assume to be the only place possible for a woman writer; it is an occupation at the center.

Before concluding that a woman wrote this poem, however, there is some further evidence for Surrey's authorship that needs to be considered, for there are two other poems attributed to him that also have—and much more explicitly than is the case with "o happy dames"—speakers who are gendered female. One of these ("Good ladies, you that have your pleasure in exyle," Jones #24) seems to be another version of that poem, involving the same situation. Padelford thought it certainly written for Surrey's wife, and the poem's inclusion of a reference to her lord (as the beloved is insistently called) returning ("And playng wheare I shall hym fynd with T. his lytle sonne" [l.22]), would seem to refer to their first child, Thomas, born in 1536. The poem appears in the Surrey section of Tottel, where it is titled "Complaint of the absence of her lover upon the sea" (#19), although the line that I have just cited only appears in the version of the poem in the Arundel Harington manuscript.[24] There, in fact, the poem is not attributed to Surrey; it is signed Preston. Ruth Hughey, the editor of the manuscript, opines that Preston may be the author of the poem; in all likelihood the full name to be attached to the ascription, she argues, is Thomas Preston, who offered himself to Cromwell's services in 1533 by sending him a "specimen" of his "fashion of writing." As Hughey observes, this may allude to his compositional skills—which would lend support to his authorship of the poem —but is much more likely to refer to his script. Why would a copyist (not the copyist, it should be added, whose hand appears in the Arundel Harington manuscript) sign that transcription of the poem? Hughey explains that letters often sent by others' hands, and in their hands, would have the copyist's name on it, as was the case when Preston served as one of Princess Mary's Gentleman Waiters and carried her letters. Following Padelford's scenario, Hughey concludes that when Surrey sent the poem to his wife it was in Preston's hand. The problem with this explanation is that every example that she offers tracing Preston's activities locates him in England, not in France with Surrey. That is, if Thomas Preston did copy this poem for someone, the someone in question may have been Lady Frances de Vere, the Countess of Surrey. She did not accompany Surrey to France.

As for the other poem spoken by a woman assigned by modern editors to Surrey's authorship, which begins "Girt in my giltlesse gowne as I sit here and sow," it does appear in Tottel. It was, however, first included among the poems of uncertain authorship (#243). In its second printing, the poem was moved to the Surrey section, following one that begins "Wrapped in my careless cloke, as I walke to and fro" (Tottel #26); there it is titled, "An answer in the behalfe of a woman of an uncertain aucthor." Although modern editors print "Girt in my giltlesse gowne" as Surrey's, Tottel lends no support for this ascription. Clearly, he moved the poem to the Surrey section in recognition that it was an answer on behalf of the woman described in Surrey's poem. This poem also appears in the Arundel Harington manuscript, in a version twice as long as that in Tottel.

However, the presence of the poem in the Arundel Harington manuscript does not immediately support Surrey's authorship, since, as Hughey notes, the poem does not clearly belong in the Surrey section of the manuscript. The poem immediately following it is not his, and there is a gap of eleven missing leaves in the manuscript (lost in the eighteenth century when they served as printer's copy for the *Nugae Antiquae*). The poems that follow this lacuna are Surrey's, but there is no way of knowing whether all the leaves missing were too, and hence no way of knowing where the Surrey group began and whether it included the poem in question. The very form of the poem furthermore makes Surrey's authorship doubtful; as Mary Shelton's practice in the Devonshire manuscript shows, other hands often penned responses. "Girt in my giltlesse gowne" is likely a woman's response to Surrey's poem.

Finally, it is worth noting that "O happy dames" probably once did appear in the Arundel Harington manuscript; the poem is printed in *Nugae Antiquae* (1769), presumably from one of the lost leaves of the manuscript. There it is headed, "By JOHN HARINGTON, 1543, *for a Ladie moche in Love*." Hughey in fact prints the poem as Harington's,[25] although in her notes she indicates that she is "inclined to accredit the poem to Surrey" (p. 289). For my purposes here, it is enough simply to notice this ascription; it registers the possibility that the manuscript was correct insofar as it ascribed "O Happy dames" to a hand other than Surrey's, just as it most certainly is in another's hand in the Devonshire manuscript. John Harington in fact often served as his own copyist in the Arundel Harington manuscript, and "by JOHN HARINGTON" at the head of the poem, like the name Preston appended elsewhere, may register his function as the poem's copyist, not as its author. In which case, if he wrote it "*for a Ladie moche in Love*," "for" is not doing the work it did when Padelford said that Surrey wrote "O Happy dames" for his wife; "for" here would name Harington as the hand that made this copy of a female-authored text.

Mary Shelton's and Surrey's names appear together once in a line of a poem in the Surrey canon, an impassioned sonnet/epitaph on Sir Thomas Clere, Surrey's long-time companion after the death of Henry Fitzroy, and the supposed "sweetheart" (as the editors are fond of saying) of Shelton. In that poem the fatal trajectory of Clere's life is traced along a path in which "Shelton for love, Surrey for Lord thou chase." It was, in fact, in the context of a reading of this epitaph that S. P. Zitner, to whom I alluded at the beginning of this essay, referred to Shelton's scrawl; Zitner also noted what for him was only a muted homoeroticism in the "tac-tile immediacy" of another line in the poem, "Thine Earle halfe dead gave in thy hand his Will," assuring his readers that the line offered "no problem" since Surrey's relationship with his wife was quite "regular" while his devotion to Clere, and to Henry Fitzroy earlier, had been quite public (pp. 516, 524). Zitner's assumptions about "regularity" (or should we say straightness?) are based on the questionable belief that marriage and same-sex relations are necessarily incompatible, that open expressions of male-male love must necessarily not be erotic (same-sex erotics pre-sumably must be secret and closeted). His account tallies with those we have observed explaining how Surrey wrote poems "for" the Countess. It was left to Jonathan Crewe, following Zitner where he would not go, to read Surrey's homoerotics as explicit, and to note that in this poem, in the line "Shelton for love, Surrey for Lord thou chase," Shelton is vir-tually "one of the boys," as Crewe puts it, her gender erased, or, if there, only as a sign of "cynical inclusion/exclusion," a kind of subliminal trace of a heteroerotic sanction for a "homosexual consummation" from which, Crewe opines, "Shelton has to be temporarily absent."[26] Crewe's read-ing, noting Surrey's virtual effacement of the woman in the poem—or claiming that as what is happening—restores Shelton as female to the line, only for her, in Crewe's reading, to show up the fatality of homo-sexuality, which in this account not only kills men but also cynically abuses women. Yet, the line that names Shelton places Clere in the same position with her and with Surrey, behind each of them ("Shelton for love, Surrey for Lord thou chase"); places them, therefore, in a locus of substitution which is not the same thing as the erasure of difference. All three in the poem, as in life, are related to each other, cousins through the figure of Anne Boleyn, who appears as a kind of vanishing point in the poem—crowned in one line and displaced as "battered Bullein" a few lines later—for a kind of gendered violence which Crewe fails to note but which also structures relations in this poem. Clere is, in this poem, not merely the site of desire; he is also the site of identification for the poem's speaker, and the exchange of will is one place where this occurs. But what occurs there? "Thine Earle halfe dead gave in thy hand his Will." Clere writing; Surrey coming; Surrey half-dead; Clere dead; and yet the place from which Surrey has his life. Clere, memorialized, the site of a remembrance: the site of writing that writes Surrey beyond his own life. The hand is that of the copyist who nonetheless is also the author. The one who comes behind also comes before. That hand might be Mary Shelton's.

I mean this almost literally; so, as a final note, let me add this. This poem on Sir Thomas Clere does not appear in Tottel, nor does it survive in any sixteenth-century manuscript. It is first recorded in 1605 in William Camden's *Remaines*, an inscription copied by Camden from the tomb of Thomas Clere. It is Camden who ascribed it to Surrey—to, as it happens, "the noble *Thomas* Earle of *Surrey*."[27] This renaming of Henry Howard as Thomas Howard is not an error caused by the fact that Clere's first name was Thomas, not a confusion of identity of the sort that the poem itself encourages. It is rather, as in the case of a Holbein drawing of Surrey, also mislabelled Thomas, the register of the fact that Henry Howard was only styled Earl of Surrey; his father Thomas and his son Thomas legitimately occupied the title. The Surrey style is not Surrey's proper name. Camden giving a name to an unsigned inscription on a tomb uncannily reminds us that it is out of traces that are, properly speaking, anonymous that Surrey is made. From other hands. Anonymous, Virginia Woolf noted some time ago, was often the name of a woman.[28]

NOTES

1. On this point, see Jonathan Goldberg, *Writing Matter* (Stanford: Stanford University Press, 1990); for the identification of the gender of the writer on the basis of the hand, see also the passing comment by Arthur Marotti, "Malleable and Fixed Texts: Manuscript and Printed Miscellanies and the Transmission of Lyric Poetry in the English Renaissance" in *New Ways of Looking at Old Texts*, ed. W. Speed Hill

(Binghamton, New York: Medieval and Renaissance Texts and Studies, 1993), p.163, and the slightly extended reworking of this passage in Marotti, *Manuscript, Print, and the English Renaissance Lyric* (Ithaca: Cornell University Press, 1995), pp. 25–26. For the importance of manuscripts for female authorship in the period, see Margaret J. M. Ezell, *The Patriarch's Wife* (Chapel Hill: University of North Carolina, 1987), esp. ch. 3, and Ezell, *Writing Women's Literary History* (Baltimore: Johns Hopkins University Press, 1993), ch. 2, esp. pp. 50–65.

2. See Wendy Wall, *The Imprint of Gender* (Ithaca: Cornell University Press, 1993); Elizabeth D. Harvey, *Ventriloquized Voices* (London: Routledge, 1992). In raising these questions, I am guided by Denise Riley, *"Am I That Name?": Feminism and the Category of "Women" in History* (Minneapolis: University of Minnesota Press, 1988), while the discussion here parallels concerns raised by Peggy Kamuf, "Writing Like a Woman" in *Women and Language in Literature and Society*, eds. Sally McConnell-Ginet, Ruth Borker, and Nelly Furman (New York: Praeger, 1980), p. 298.

3. On these questions, see Diana Fuss, *Essentially Speaking* (New York.: Routledge, 1989).

4. *Sodometries* (Stanford: Stanford University Press, 1992). See p. 60 for the particular question of female authorship to which I return in this essay.

5. All citations in my text are from Hyder Edward Rollins, ed., *Tottel's Miscellany*, 2 vols. (Cambridge: Harvard University Press, 1965).

6. S. P. Zitner, "Truth and Mourning in a Sonnet by Surrey," *ELH* 50 (1983): 513; Richard Harrier, *The Canon of Sir Thomas Wyatt's Poetry* (Cambridge: Harvard University Press, 1975), pp. 24, 27.

7. See Arthur Marotti, "The Transmission of Lyric Poetry and the Institutionalizing of Literature in the English Renaissance," in *Contending Kingdoms*, eds. Marie-Rose Logan and Peter L. Rudnytsky (Detroit: Wayne State University Press, 1991), as well as "Manuscript, Print, and the English Renaissance Lyric" in *New Ways of Looking at Old Texts*, and their further elaboration in *Manuscript, Print, and the English Renaissance Lyric*.

8. On this point, see the basic and influential essay by J. W. Saunder, "From Manuscript to Print," *Proceedings of the Leeds Philosophical and Literary Society* 6 (1951), pp. 507–28. For a recent essay stressing the ways in which modern authorship does not govern Renaissance manuscripts, see Max W. Thomas, "Reading and Writing the Renaissance Commonplace Book: A Question of Authorship?" in *The Construction of Authorship*, eds. Martha Woodmansee and Peter Jaszi (Durham: Duke University Press, 1994), pp. 401–15.

9. This was first established by Ethel Seaton, "The Devonshire Manuscript and Its Medieval Fragments," *RES* 7 (1956), pp. 55–56.

10. Kenneth Muir, "Unpublished Poems in the Devonshire MS," *Proceedings of the Leeds Philosophical and Literary Society* 6 (1947), pp. 253–82.

11. This thesis is developed by Paul Remley, "Mary Shelton and Her Tudor Literary Milieu," in *Rethinking the Henrician Era*, ed. Peter C. Herman (Urbana: University of Illinois Press, 1994), pp. 55–58. Marotti includes in his brief treatment, "Women and the Manuscript System" in *Manuscript, Print, and the English Renaissance Lyric*, pp. 48–61, a consideration of the Devonshire manuscript that rehearses some of the

standard information about its female contributors, ending with citations of some of the Chauceriana as exemplary of poems in praise of women (pp. 55-57); Marotti gives no indication of the presumed authorship of these pieces, nor is he quite certain that they are to be taken straight; for one he holds open an "ironic reading," and another is said to engage in hyperbole (p. 57).

12. See G. F. Nott, ed., *The Works of Henry Howard and of Sir Thomas Wyatt*. 2 vols. (London: T. Bensley, 1815), vol. 1, pp. 162–63, and Edward A. Bond, "Wyatt's Poems," *The Athenaeum* 2274 (27 May 1871), pp. 654–55.

13. Raymond Southall, "The Devonshire Manuscript Collection of Early Tudor Poetry, 1532-41," *RES* 15 (1964), pp. 142–150, and *The Courtly Maker: An Essay on the Poetry of Wyatt and His Contemporaries* (New York: Barnes and Noble, 1964), pp. 15–25, 171–73.

14. Remley, "Mary Shelton and Her Tudor Literary Milieu," pp. 42–43, sorts out many of the confusions to be found in previous scholarship about Shelton's ancestry, including being mistaken for a sister who was possibly Henry VIII's mistress; Eric Ives, for example, names the Shelton of the Devonshire manuscript "Madge," and conflates her with Margaret Shelton, Mary's sister, in *Anne Boleyn* (Oxford: Basil Blackwell, 1986), pp. 86, 242–43. Mary Shelton's relationship with Thomas Clere is, however, the most common shorthand way scholars have to identify her; "Mary Shelton is best known as the sweetheart of Surrey's friend Thomas Clere," Harrier writes (p. 26), opening a paragraph in which he assigns her the wrong parents; "Mary Shelton, who was beloved of Sir John Clere," as A. K. Foxwell identifies her in an appendix on the history of the Devonshire manuscript in her edition of *The Poems of Sir Thomas Wiat*, 2 vols. (London: University of London Press, 1913), vol. 2, pp. 244–45, basically repeating her point in *A Study of Sir Thomas Wyatt's Poems* (New York: Russell & Russsell, 1964 [1911]) that "Mary Shelton's name appears in connection with the Howards" (p. 127); Padelford, in *The Poems of Henry Howard Earl of Surrey* (Seattle: University of Washington Press, 1920, rev. ed., 1928), is Harrier's immediate source, when he describes her as "Mary Shelton, the sweetheart of Sir Thomas Clere" (p. 186 [1920 ed.], p. 215 [1928 ed.]).

15. The editions I have in mind are those of Frederick Morgan Padelford and that by Emrys Jones, Surrey, *Poems* (Oxford: Clarendon Press, 1964).

16. *Anglia* 29 (1906): pp. 273–338. Citations of the poem from the manuscript depend on and reproduce Padelford's transcription of it on pp. 337–38.

17. The comment, "ryme dogrel how many myle to meghlemes," occurs after a poem (#40 in Muir, "Unpublished Poems in the Devonshire Manuscript," p. 277) that may be Mary Shelton's.

18. Padelford, "Manuscript Poems of Henry Howard," p. 338.

19. Among Randall McLeod's essays on this subject, see "Spellbound: Typography and the Concept of Old-Spelling Editions," *Renaissance and Reformation*, n.s. 3 (1979), pp. 50–65; "Unemending Shakespeare's Sonnet 111," *SEL* 21 (1981), pp. 75–96; "UnEditing Shak-speare," *Sub-Stance* 33/34 (1982), pp. 26–55.

20. There are, as well, the usual reasons for preferring the manuscript version to Tottel: it is less regular in meter; some of the variants, while not in any way obviously superior to the version in Tottel, are also obviously just as good as what Tottel prints. The untitled manuscript, as might be expected, gives evidence of the poem in a less smoothed-out version than that offered by Tottel.

21. The best study of gender transitivity in Surrey, and in this poem in particular, remains Anthony Scott's unpublished essay, "The Fatality of Surrey's Desire." G. F. Nott, in his 1815 edition, provides in his titles and notes to the poems some oddly interesting comments along these lines. His apparatus is entirely dominated by the notion that all of Surrey's poems are part of his romance with Geraldine; thus, while Nott believes that "O Happy dames" was written for someone else, he thinks it gave Surrey the opportunity in this poem nonetheless to voice his longing for Geraldine (see vol. 1: 12, p. 262). Nott thus reads the genders in the poem as completely reversible. Of another poem to which I turn below, "Girt in my giltlesse gowne," which Nott titles "The Fair Geraldine retorts on Surrey the charge of artifice" (vol. 1: p. 31), Nott expresses the hope that someone else wrote this poem for Geraldine, going on to say however that "she who can wound the feelings of a deserted Lover by copying what another dictates, makes the insult her own, and has little to plead in her defence" (vol. 1: p. 314). Nott, that is, takes the question of surrogacy a great deal more seriously than Padelford and recognizes the investment of the hand in writing, in this case, I assume, because of the high cultural value that Nott ascribes to Renaissance poetry.

22. The other poems in Tottel explicitly labeled as spoken by a woman (all by "uncertain authors") follow this paradigm; one (#190, "The Ladye Praieth the Returne of her Lover Abidying on the Seas"), while close in subject matter to "O Happy dames," posits an unfaithful lover and an abandoned woman; such also is the case with #222, "The Lady Forsaken of her Lover, Prayeth his Returne, or the End of her own Life," while #275, "The beginning of the Epistle of Penelope to Ulisses," translates Ovid.

23. See Jones, *The Currency of Eros* (Bloomington: University of Indiana Press, 1990), p. 43, on Isabella Whitney.

24. See Ruth Hughey, ed., *The Arundel Harington Manuscript of Tudor Poetry*, 2 vols. (Columbus: Ohio University Press, 1960), vol. 1, p. 132 for the text of the poem, vol. 1, pp. 30–31 and vol. 2, p. 112 for Hughey's comments on Preston summarized below.

25. Ruth Hughey, *Sir John Harington of Stepney* (Columbus: Ohio State University Press, 1971), pp. 131–32.

26. Jonathan Crewe, *Trials of Authorship* (Berkeley: University of California Press, 1990), p. 66.

27. Camden, *Remaines of a Greater Worke*, p. 50.

28. Virginia Woolf, *A Room of One's Own* (New York: Harcourt, Brace and Jovanovich, 1929), p. 49.

2

THE
DUPLICITY
OF THE
PEN

IN OCTOBER OF 1833, the prize committee of the Baltimore *Saturday Visiter* met in the parlor of John Latrobe's house to evaluate the poems and tales that had been anonymously submitted for an award of fifty dollars and publication in the weekly newspaper. According to Latrobe, all three of the judges were taken by a "small quarto-bound book" which stood out from the "bundles of manuscript that it had to compete with" both because of its bulk—it consisted of six tales bound together—and because of its handwriting: "Instead of the common cursive manuscript, the writing was in Roman characters—an imitation of printing."[1] Finding the tales in this volume "far, so very far, superior to anything before us," the judges struggled only to decide to which of these six tales to award the prize, finally settling on one entitled "MS. Found in a Bottle."[2]

This is one of the founding stories of Edgar Allan Poe's emergence as an author, useful for its simultaneous depiction of Poe's obscurity and his distinction. In Latrobe's multiple tellings of this tale, the anonymity imposed by the newspaper contest serves to accentuate Poe's difference from his peers. The distinctiveness of his "wonderfully graphic"[3] style produces both financial reward and long sought-after recognition as "MS. Found in a Bottle" becomes the first of Poe's stories to be published with his name attached.

One does not need to know the full story of how this anecdote became a central piece of Poe hagiography[4] to be suspicious of its allegory of the fortuitous encounter of unrecognized merit and just reward, the ideal coalescence of authorship and ownership within an emergent market for literary goods. Indeed, Poe's previous submissions to a newspaper contest had met with a fate more typical of antebellum prose fiction: failing to win the prize, they had become the property of the Philadelphia *Saturday Courier* and were published anonymously, neither profit nor credit accruing to their author.[5] Nevertheless, Latrobe's story of the discovery of the manuscript of the "MS. Found in a Bottle" offers uncommon insight into the way in which a relation between handwriting and print structured both Poe's and his critics' understanding of the literary marketplace. In this story, an anonymous, handwritten manuscript that gives the appearance of print wins the right to appear in the medium it imitates. Able to publish only one of the tales in this unpublished "Book,"[6] the judges choose a story which grounds its authority in its claim to be handwritten, a story in which the transition from handwriting to print is unnarratable and coincides with the death of the narrating subject. A disjunction between handwriting and print— the modes, respectively, of composition and reception—is foreclosed by Poe in the mode of composition, but opened up in the tale itself, represented by the utmost extremity of the polar abyss.

At the risk of leaving us all "whirling dizzily" in the "immense concentric circles" of the story's denouement,[7] I should also note that Latrobe's account of Poe's coming into authorship was first written, and later embellished, as a defense against the most famous attempt to discredit Poe—Rufus Griswold's disparaging obituary and "Memoir," a thinly veiled attack prefixed to most nineteenth-century editions of Poe's *Works*.[8] It is Griswold who first raises the question of the nature of the hand that got Poe into print. In Griswold's account, however, it is not a pre-emptive printedness but Poe's "exquisite calligraphy" that convinces a lazy and drunken prize committee to give him the award on the basis of penmanship alone.[9] These heavily invested, conflicting accounts of literary origin prompt one to ask not simply about the complex copresence of handwriting and print—the authority that a relation to printedness can carry in handwriting, and the phantom presence of handwritten forms in print—but also about the strange impropriety of the hand—how it is that the corruption of literary judgment and the manipulation of the press can be associated with ornamental penmanship.

In this essay I will take up some of the ways in which handwriting shifts its significance in a culture in which print was prior, both in terms of the teaching of literacy, which in the nineteeth century proceeded from widespread instruction in the reading of printed texts to the selective teaching of the reading and writing of handwriting,[10] and in terms of its cultural status. In the nineteenth century, print had come to take over many of the legal and administrative offices of the hand and bore a privileged relation to civic authority. As Michael Warner has argued, republican discourse regarded print as coextensive with the public sphere and relied on the generality of the printed text to represent and to legitimize popular sovereignty.[11] While by the 1820s republicanism had lost much of its force in literature and in practical politics, a republican emphasis on the publicity of print did much to determine the shape of the emergent market for books. Holding that individual rights in printed texts were eclipsed by the state's interest in their circulation, the American courts defined handwriting and print as different objects under the law. On going-into-print, an author surrendered his perpetual right to his manuscript for a limited right in a printed text; the state severed the connection between handwriting and print and inserted itself as the principle of their articulation.[12]

While linking property rights in texts to a distinction between handwriting and print did much to place copyrights in the hands of publishers, the most significant effect of the alignment of print with public property was the century-long resistance to international copyright. The legalization of international literary piracy spurred the growth of the reprint trade. Unlike the London market, which worked according to a dynamic of center and periphery, the market for books in America developed under conditions of decentralized mass-production. Not only was the national market for books distributed across multiple, loosely affiliated, regional publishing centers, each of the major cities—Philadelphia, New York, and Boston—claimed to be the center of national culture. Cutting across these internal divisions was a flourishing trade in cheap, reprinted British books, which, because unconstrained by copyright, achieved a remarkable national distribution in the form of competing, regionally produced editions. A handful of literary periodicals, which also commonly circulated without the benefit of copyright protection, were able to achieve something like national distribution through the mails. Yet not only did these magazines remain unprofitable, they were freely excerpted by other periodicals, some of which amounted to little more than a compilation of reprinted texts. Unauthorized reprinting was so widely practiced in the antebellum period that the designation of a poem, article, or tale as an "original" referred not to the quality of its contents, but to the fact that the book or periodical in which it appeared was the site of its first printing. Within the culture of reprinting, dissemination ran in advance of, and often stood in lieu of, payment. Circulation outstripped authorial and editorial control.

In this context, it is easier to understand the proprietary force of Poe's construction of a manuscript "Book," a manuscript that never made it into print despite the newspaper's attempt to underwrite its publication by subscription.[13] The decentralized literary marketplace put questions of authorship and ownership under extraordinary pressure. How was it possible to gain access to print under decentralized mass-production, and to mark a text, once published, as one's own? What were the consequences for handwriting, given the disarticulation of handwriting and print and the suspension of different forms of property across that divide?

I hope to get some purchase on these questions by looking at the ways in which mass-produced writing manuals understand their own printedness—the ways in which mechanical reproduction transforms reproduction by hand. In the first two parts of the essay, I will examine how mastery is understood and how ownership is marked once the authority of the printed text comes to replace the authority of the pemanship instructor. In the last part of the essay, I'll examine how Poe uses handwriting to claim authority in a series of anonymous printed texts—not by signing them, but by what penmanship pedagogues might identify as the conscious cultivation of a bad hand. Throughout, I want to suggest that we regard the appearance of handwriting in the context of print as a figure, not for an authenticity or self-mastery that stands over and against the impersonality of print, but for the hand's relation to printedness. I will argue that it is the duplicity of the pen—illustrated by the near ubiquitous figure of the doubled hand in mid-nineteenth-century penmanship manuals [Figure 1][14]—that marks

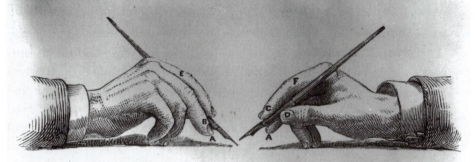

Several methods may be used with advantage to teach the scholars how to hold the pen.

1. The teacher should take a position in front of his desk, and show the correct method with a pen in his own hand.

Figure 2.1   Payson, Dunton and Scribner, *Manual of Penmanship.*

the printed text as crucially mediated. The hand in the context of print tells the story of the handedness of print itself.

I.   FROM PRINT TO SCRIPT

Changes in the physical format and in modes of address of late eighteenth-century and early nineteenth-century copybooks illustrate many of the ways in which technologies of mass-production and an emergent market for books altered the practice of penmanship and redefined its aims. In eighteenth-century America, penmanship was a specialized craft taught privately and at writing schools in urban areas, and in rural areas by itinerant writing masters who set up short courses for interested townspeople. Penmanship manuals with woodcut or copperplate engravings of a wide range of hands were printed both to secure the prestige of a particular penman and to be carried into the provinces. While many also promoted self-instruction, copybooks were generally linked with local practitioners and butressed their authority through local endorsements. Mastery of the art was still achieved by way of a conventional apprenticeship.

Nineteenth-century manuals and copybooks, however, aimed increasingly at a regional or national audience and claimed authority by virtue of public patronage or by the fact of their use in common schools and business colleges. Whereas George Fisher's *The American Instructor*, published by Ben Franklin in 1748, included a series of plates illustrating "Round Hand," "Italian Hand," a decorative "Flourishing Alphabet," a "Print Hand" for marking bales and parcels, and a modified "Secretary Hand,"[15] nineteenth-century manuals move toward a standardized, simplified curriculum of "Coarse" or "Round Hand" for beginners, followed by intensive instruction in a mercantile "Current Hand" for boys, and a short course in a diminutive "Ladies Hand" for girls. As is suggested by the model business forms that comprise nearly every copybook's final lesson, the overwhelming aim of nineteenth-century penmanship was to teach boys a business hand that would "answer the purpose of the necessary dispatch of mercantile affairs."[16] The "mending" and "painting" required for flourishes and the more elaborate scripts were discarded in favor of speed and uniformity of size and slope.[17] Along with a radical reduction in the range of hands, penmanship instruction was greatly simplified by the availability of mass-produced steel pens in the 1830s.[18] Penmanship instructors were no longer required to teach the difficult process of cutting and sharpening quills. Many of the elaborate practices that had been the mark of the master penman became reserved for ceremonial and decorative purposes.

John Jenkins' 1791 copybook *The Art of Writing: Reduced to a Plain and Easy System, On a PLAN Entirely NEW*[19] was an important catalyst for many of these changes. Jenkins pioneered what would come to be known as "analytic penmanship," a system in which the letters of the alphabet were broken down into a series of graduated and numbered "principle strokes." Jenkins's innovation takes its place in a long history of such pedagogical experiments, including the grouping of letters and grading them by difficulty, the imposition of a geometrical grid, the use of a monogram comprising all the letters of the alphabet, and an analysis of the strokes used to connect the letters.[20] What distinguishes Jenkins's system is that it takes strokes and not letters as its principal object, disassembling the alphabet into interchangeable parts that take the place of model letters at the top of the page. The penmanship systems that follow Jenkins will quibble over the proper number of "elements" and "principles" to be taught, but they share Jenkins's confidence that the breakdown of a hand into a small number of constituent parts makes both the process of writing and writing instruction significantly easier. Jenkins believed that the susceptibility of script to simplification and standardization called for a new kind of pedagogy: "as writing is in some measure a mechanical art, it should be mechanically taught."[21] Jenkins's assumption that the mechanization of the letter would lead to an automatic mastery of writing itself is perhaps his system's most enduring legacy. Jenkins not only reimagines handwriting according to the principle of moveable type, he fantasizes that analytic penmanship can democratize access to handwriting skills and standardize the nation's script, claiming that his "Plain and Easy System" is "so contrived that young gentlemen and ladies who have not been under advantages to learn to write, may immediately become not only their own instructors, but instructors of others."[22]

It is, of course, the notion that the printed writing manual can replace the writing master that is most threatening to the craft of penmanship. Jenkins's explicit pronouncements in this regard are actually rather modest: he imagines that his system will remedy "the inconvenience of living at a distance from school, . . . the want of a school" or "the unskillfulness of teachers."[23] In its ideal form, however, Jenkins's link of the mechanization of the letter to the automatic replication of the hand would eliminate not only the lengthy process of acquiring skill in writing, but also the seriality of handwriting itself, the movement of the hand across the page. Jenkins's description of competence in writing sounds more like setting or manufacturing type than the sequential formation of letters: once the principal strokes and their combination into letters have been "well impressed on the mind," they "may be instantly ready to drop from the pen when called for."[24]

The penmanship manuals that follow Jenkins elaborate a pedagogy of the writing system, demonstrating not only increasing ease with the displacement of the writing master, but also a complex relocation of the notion of mastery itself. Penmanship manuals had long theorized that writing was acquired through a two-step process of observation and execution, or, as an early eighteenth-century manual put it, obtaining "an *exact Notion, or Idea of a good Letter*" and "Command of Hand."[25] The trend in nineteenth-century penmanship, however, is toward increased emphasis on the analysis of letters, shifting attention away from the discipline of the hand.

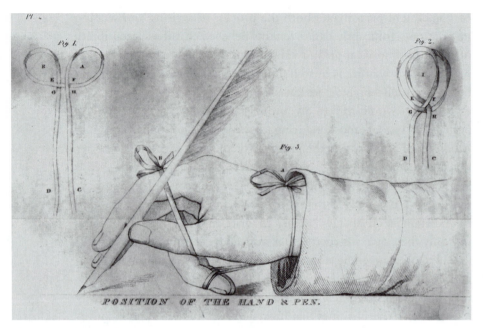

Figure 2.2 Benjamin Franklin Foster, *Practical Penmanship.*

This is not to suggest that nineteenth-century manuals ignore the hand. Mercantile penmanship's increased emphasis on speed and uniformity meant that students had to conform their bodies to a dazzling array of specifications. In order that they might be able to write for long periods without exhaustion, students were taught to distinguish whole-arm movements from forearm movements and movements of the hand and fingers. Proper writing involved the complex coordination of refractory and asymmetrical body parts so as to guarantee the uniformity of handwriting: in holding the pen the second finger was dropped below the first, so that the fingers would "act as if they were equal in length";[26] the hand and pen were required to "preserve the same elevation and the same position at the beginning, middle, and end of the same word"[27] or risk introducing flaws in proportion, slant, or spacing. Even the feet were required to maintain "a direction corresponding to the slant of the letters."[28] Benjamin Franklin Foster's 1830 copybook recommends the use of a ligature to immobilize the hand, thereby freeing the beginning student to concentrate his attention on auxiliary movements [Figure 2]. We can see here, however, the direction in which all this emphasis on uniformity and bodily correspondence is tending: the hand is tied so as to habituate the student to a set of practices that will guarantee right writing; once tied, the letter which the student would begin with is stamped upon the hand.

Foster's ligature compensates for the bodily self-discipline his system requires but has small patience for instilling. Its alphabetic configuration suggests a desire to close the gap between model letter and unhabituated hand. Concerned to short-circuit and to guarantee the process by which habits are formed—the potentially unruly business secured by the ligature—nineteenth-century copybooks begin to shift their attention away from the hand that does the writing. As the perfect replicability of the printed model letter becomes a pedagogical ideal, copybooks devote increasing amounts of time to mental discipline. They worry less about a child's ability to control his hand, and more about the fact that he might exercise faulty judgment or become the victim of a false impression. The printed copybook doesn't simply replace manual instruction: the unflinching accuracy of its impressions becomes the model for writing by hand.

Take, for example, Foster's description of a penmanship class at the Normal School in Barre, Vermont. As Foster explains, the teacher begins the class with analysis, placing ten versions of the same letter on the board, all but one of which is marked by a defect of some kind. The class is then asked to determine which letter is the most perfect and to describe in detail the particular defects of the other nine letters. If a student fails to single out the model letter, the teacher turns to the power of collective persuasion, asking "whether another member of the class is of a different opinion . . . until a unanimity of opinion is established as to the pattern or model letter."

Once consensus has been reached, the teacher turns from observation to execution, asking the students to "write a line of this letter in which all the faults specified shall be avoided, and all those beauties you have named copied." The absolutism of this request gives a good indication of the way in which a pedagogy based on emulation redistributes rather than dissipates force. Indeed, this exercise is remarkable for the way in which it shifts authority in the classroom without undoing the tyranny of the letter. As Foster explains,

> Wherever [the teacher] finds that a pupil has deviated from the model letter, he
> calls attention especially and distinctly to that point; he shows the pupil how he has
> violated his own rules, gone contrary to his own decision, copied a letter (pointing
> to it) which he had declared to be incorrect, and failed to imitate what he had pro-
> nounced a model.[29]

It is hard not to sympathize with the student who has presumably tried,
but failed to reproduce the perfect letter and has been chided for taking an
incorrect letter as his model. This drill identifies poor writing as a failure
of imitation, not of execution. It sets out to train the child's judgment,
presuming that repeated attention to differences between model and deviation will automatically take care of "command of hand." The teacher's
job is to supervise the process of emulation, making sure that the child
takes the proper object for imitation. Any failure is a failure of imprinting.

Of course, one way to insure that students are exposed to proper
models is to stop relying on the teacher's "command of hand." One
copybook suggests that the penmanship instructor purchase a "set of
Tablets made to accompany the Manual" so that "he can at all times
suspend before his class a perfect representation of whatever requires
explanation." These were especially advised for the beginning teacher
or the instructor with faulty penmanship:

> Being perfect in form and proportions, the pupils will have constantly before them
> a true model for analysis and criticism. When the Teacher has by these means shown
> the class what must be done, he has only to write upon the blackboard such errors
> and mistakes as he may discover in his examination of the scholars' writing in the
> copybooks. By continually pointing out these errors, and comparing them with the
> printed model suspended above, he will be enabled to teach as thoroughly and suc-
> cessfully as the most experienced instructor.[30]

Here the printed model letter compensates for the unreliability of the
hand, which is best confined to writing out errors. Most copybooks warn
against providing the child with "imperfect and constantly varying
forms."[31] They point out the "unwearied labor" involved in "trying to
rid the mind of a wrong idea of a letter,"[32] and decry the disadvantages
that accrue from the yearly change in instructors in the newly graded
common schools.[33] In advising the teacher on the importance of emu-

lation, they oscillate between expressing anxiety about the susceptiblity of the child to false impressions—as William Alcott warns, "through want of attention, negligent and erroneous habits are formed—perhaps fixed— often to be as lasting as life"[34]—and expressing confidence in the power of a finely tuned sense of judgment to produce right writing. Copybooks from the 1860s and 70s often devote numerous pages to a verbal drill in the analysis of written letters that is to be mastered before the child sets pen to paper. One textbook designed as a penmanship catechism includes the following exchange: "Question 72: Will you measure and analyze small w?" to which the proper answer is: "hight, one space; whole width, three spaces, distance from straight line to dot, one half space; from dot to end of horizontal curve, one-half space. Principles 2,1,2,1,2,2."[35] Drill in the analysis of letters precedes and is thought to shape writing per-formance, cutting down on the time that was to be spent in training the hand. Calling attention to "the immense importance of constant self-criticism on the part of the pupils" one manual advised, "Only let this habit be formed, and the teacher's work may be considered ended."[36]

Returning to the image with which I began [Figure 1], one can see how the doubled hand elegantly figures the penman's ambitions for the hand set within the frame of print. Opposed at pen-point, these hands represent the scene of instruction at the moment where emulation approaches the ideal of self-instruction. Offering a comprehensive view of the penhold—front and back—the illustration can represent, as its placement within the text of this copybook suggests, the hand of a teacher modelling, by facing, its double—the student's hand. And yet, these can just as easily be seen to be front and back views of the same hand. This view of the two hands pushed together suggests an idealized wholeness across the two-dimensionality of the page. Here the pens point to the place where a fold in the page would make the two hands one. The placement of the front perspective on the hand on the right side of the page—per-pendicular to the reader's axis of vision—actually places the reader in the proper position for writing, making an instructor of the book itself through the imaginary depth of the page. It is important to note, how-ever, that the individual hand—as something singular, peculiar, and proper to the person learning to write—is irrecuperable here, however you look at the image. This is a figure for the hand that is mediated by print: an image of the unreachable ideal of perfect iterability—that the student could, in doubling the model-hand, learn to perform acts of exact duplication—and of the notion of "typing" or imprinting by which mastery over the hand is thought to be accomplished.

With the drama of student emulation of the printed model taking center stage, the role of the penmanship instructor was largely reduced to regulation. It was the teacher's responsibility to assure not only that the order of the student's body would correspond with the order of his writing, but also that he conform his movements with the movements of the class. Typically, the penmanship manual recommends "Commencing and Closing the Writing Exercise" by passing out identical pens, books, and penwipers in row-order and collecting them precisely "in reverse order of their distribution."[37] Writing exercises were carried out in unison, stroke by stroke, to the sound of a bell or metronome.[38]

Penmanship systems multiply their sites of regimentation as if to compensate for the primary act of duplication over which the instructor has ceded control: the transition from model letter to student script, a transition that these systems can hardly imagine. Indeed, in describing the writing process, some of these manuals come remarkably close to disengaging writing altogether from the action of the hand. One recommends that students begin by writing over perfect copies with dry pens so that "their own attention to the instruction received is undisturbed by any dark record of their transgressions."[39] Not only the student's liability to error, but also the process of learning to write must be kept from leaving a trace. The manual goes on to advise regular alternation between observation of the model letter and execution of the copy, and yet its account of the final goal in penmanship is not much different than the dry-pen exercises with which it began: "It should be borne in mind that the great point is to make the pupil really see the copy, to transfer the forms there to mental vision, so that he can actually see them on the paper to write over."[40] The throwaway imperative is precisely to the point: the model letter is "borne in mind" and projected on the page for a passive hand to superscribe.

2. COPYING THE COPYBOOK

Drill and counting is in many ways the logical pedagogical extension of analytic penmanship: the act of writing as the simultaneous performance of discrete motions; a collective, stroke-by-stroke reconstitution of the model hand. It was hardly conducive to the development of individual style in writing, but that was its virtue. Mercantile writing carried authority because of its predictability, its regularity. Uniformity of appearance was at a premium in the promissory notes, bills of exchange, and ledger entries that these students were training to write. When penmanship manuals take up the question of individuality in writing, it is most often treated as a "bias"[41] that prevents the acquisition of right writing, or as a "deviation"[42] that occurs when classroom instruction is through. In contrast, excellence in writing is marked by a momentary uncertainty about the ownership of one's hand:

> By proper teaching and sufficient training, pupils may arrive at such exactness and uniformity of execution that when specimens of the whole class are collected in the same book, it will be almost impossible for them to identify each his own writing. To other persons examining the book, the writing will all seem to have been done by the same scholar.[43]

This exercise, in which identity in handwriting is corporate and is suddenly made legible when set within the frame of a book, is taken from *The Spencerian Key to Practical Penmanship* (1866), an instructor's manual and tribute to the "Late Platt Rogers Spencer" whose penmanship system dominated the market from the 1860s through the 1890s. Spencer's system is unusual insofar as it acknowledges the student's desire to distinguish his hand from that of the collective and creates a space for such desire within the system. Not surprisingly, the space in which uniformity opens up to variety is the capital letter, which in the Spencerian system was capable of carrying an assortment of different "proportions, terminations, combinations, and shadings." The range of difference, however, was as carefully policed as its confinement to the site of the capital letter might suggest. As the textbook puts it, "We desire . . . to encourage individuality of style, so far as it may be consistent with propriety."[44]

This shuttle between "propriety" and "individuality of style" signifies on a more important level than the Spencerians' desire to encourage the development of schoolboy expressiveness. The "Variety of Spencerian Capitals" is not so much a marker of individual style in writing as it is a marker of the individuality of this particular system.

29

Figure 2.3   *Spencerian Key to Practical Penmanship.*

The permissability of flourishes at the site of the capital distinguished the Spencerian system from its main rival, Payson, Dunton, and Scribner, whose system prided itself on its geometrical regularity and comparative plainness of style. The Spencerians' cultivation of difference across a grid in which variability was itself regular speaks to the central problem of the redefinition of mastery in the penmanship systems I have been describing: How does one assert ownership of a system which claims authority by virtue of its propriety? How is it possible to rep-

Figure 2.4   *Spencerian Key to Practical Penmanship.*

resent a claim to originality consistent with the principles of a system
dedicated to the elimination of individual differences?

Early on in his career, Platt Rogers Spencer relies on a notion of
literary originality to convey a sense of ownership: the primitive copy-
slip system with which he begins devotes an unusual amount of space to
original poems, which Spencer signs "Your Friend, The Author."[45] These
clunky couplets set outside the frame of the handwriting lesson clearly
do the job of distinguishing Spencer from his competitors, who specif-

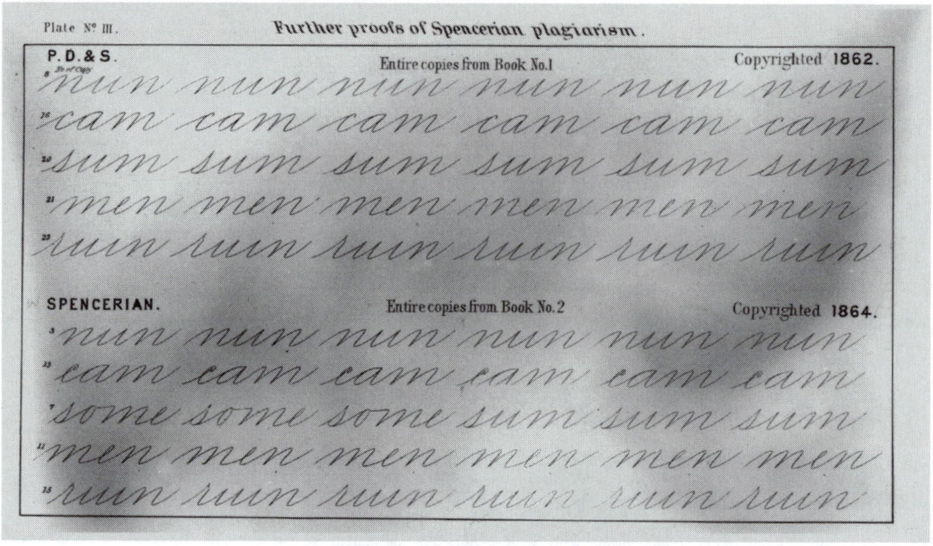

Figure 2.5   *Reply of Payson, Dunton & Scribner to the Absurd Claims of the Spencerian Authors to Originality.*

ically deride his "flights of fancy" when defining their own as a "commonsense system."[46] Spencer's literariness, however, is not enough to secure the system after his death. His five sons and a nephew—the so-called "Spencerian Authors" who inherit it—continue to claim property in the system by saturating it with marks of ownership that succeed by virtue of their detachment from Spencer. Take, for example, an illustration that conventionally accompanies comments on writing posture—a set of instructions that are common to all of these systems because they have been agreed on as proper. In the Spencerian text, if a boy follows these instructions he will find that he writes only "Spencer" [Figure 3].[47] This illustration demonstrates the hope that proper writing could come to take a proper name. And yet it also points to the difficulty of owning a hand that is authoritative by virtue of its standardization. Not only does it betray a residual anxiety about the ability of a particular system to be registered in the script—would the handwriting be recognizably Spencerian without recourse to the proper name?—it also suggests that a standard hand can no longer be claimed by its author. As the frontispiece of the volume indicates, though a mercantile script may be distinguished as Spencerian, Spencer himself cannot legitimate this script

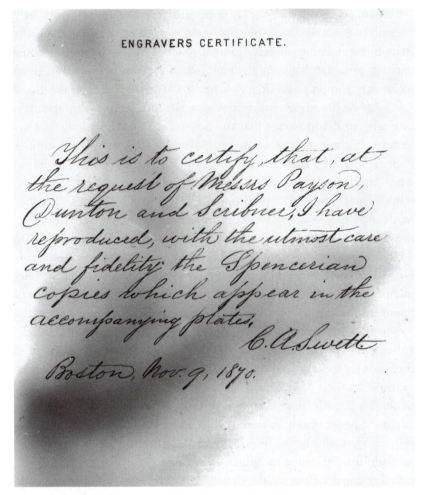

ENGRAVERS CERTIFICATE.

This is to certify, that, at the request of Messrs Payson, Dunton and Scribner; I have reproduced, with the utmost care and fidelity; the Spencerian copies which appear in the accompanying plates.

C. A. Swett

Boston, Nov. 9, 1870.

Figure 2.6   *Reply of Payson, Dunton & Scribner to the Absurd Claims of the Spencerian Authors to Originality.*

by writing in his own hand [Figure 4]. Just as the child succeeds by writing in a hand that is not proper to himself, so the writing master authorizes his writing system through recourse to an alien script—the elaborate, quill-pen flourishes of the art of penmanship that the mercantile hand has effectively displaced. The anachronism that identifies the master through recourse to a notion of mastery that the system itself denies is only intensified by the traces of the act of mechanical production—"Photo by Platt"—that has produced the authorizing image.

Spencer's rivals, Payson, Dunton, and Scribner, found it similarly difficult to mark the hand they marketed as proper to themselves. Their strategy for claiming property in their system rests on the minute comparisons of script that were the hallmark of analytic penmanship. In an incendiary pamphlet, the *Reply of Payson, Dunton & Scribner to the Absurd Claims of the Spencerian Authors to Originality*, this penmanship triumvirate tries to demonstrate that the Spencerians have stolen not only features of their style, but, more importantly, the systematic nature of their penmanship itself. Their claim is that the Spencerian copybooks were "ungraded, unsystematic and unsuited to the wants of common schools" until they lifted such organizing principles from the "mathematically exact" Payson, Dunton, and Scribner style.[48] What interests me, however, is not the legitimacy of their case, but the precise way in which their property claims do and don't find substantiation in the handwritten letter. At the back of the pamphlet, Payson, Dunton, and Scribner include a series of engraved plates in which they chart the course of Spencerian infringement. What becomes immediately apparent is that handwriting designed in the image of print cannot serve to mark individual differences. In each case, the copying that should be the mark of theft comes to look like the copying prescribed by each system. For example, in their comparison of business and social forms, the charge of theft is considerably weakened by the formulaic nature of the exercise itself. More starkly, in their comparison of "small-letter" excercises [Figure 5], it is only the homonym sum-some that secures the sameness-within-difference on which the charge of plagiarism rests. Even *with* this signal difference, the distinctive marks by which a hand could be known and ownership maintained threaten to collapse into the regularity enforced by both systems.

It is only on the last page of the pamphlet, when Payson, Dunton, and Scribner try to guarantee their own veracity, that we can see how handwriting can serve to mark ownership within the frame of print [Figure 6]. Here, the engraver of the plates testifies that he has faithfully copied the "Spencerian copies" that Payson, Dunton, and Scribner allege have been stolen from them. What interests me, however, is the way in which the "Engraver's Certificate" deflects attention from the question of theft to the act of copying that is necessary to make handwriting mass-produceable. Over and against the image produced by the copybooks—that handwriting could and should be as iterable as print—this certificate reminds us that copying by hand is done singlehandedly and serially, as opposed to the apparently agentless production of multiple copies on which the objectivity of print conventionally rests. In trying to minimize the possiblity of distortion or misrepresentation that is introduced by the presence of an additional hand, the engraver's certificate calls attention to the power of the hand to make *unfaithful* copies. It is, finally, not the handwriting itself that proves "fidelity" or theft, but the disjunction between media—the extra step by which handwriting is made amenable to print—that gives evidence of invention, design, and manufacture. The Engraver's Certificate suggests that ownership can be located not in the handwriting itself but in the hand that manipulates the press—a hand that is made suddenly visible by the differential iterability of handwriting and print.[49]

I want to return briefly to the image of the doubled hand to note the way in which it encodes not only the impossible ideal of perfect iterability prescribed by the printed copybook, but also the difference *between* the media that enables printed handwriting to suggest the manipulability of the press. The same setup that allows for complex patterns of identification with the printed hand preserves its oppositional structure despite repeated printings; the hands face each other along a transverse axis—not a mirror-structure that would recapitulate the way in which the image was imprinted on the page. As with the engraver's certificate, this image is infinitely reproduceable, and yet the form of iteration it portrays is always at odds, somehow, with the plane of the page.

3. AUTHENTIC FACSIMILES

There are many ways to take the literary measure of key features of the cultural construction of handwriting in America—the disarticulation of print and handwriting literacy, and the differential iterability of handwriting and print. Frederick Douglass's famous depiction of coming into literacy gives some sense of the cultural significance that can get attached to each medium. Taught to read by a mistress unaccustomed to slavery, Douglass discerns a connection between reading, rationality, and the right to liberty both from his master's "bitter opposition" to the practice, and from a schooltext-dialogue in which a slave wins "voluntary emancipation" through the exercise of reason alone.[50] If reading literacy can deliver the idea of individual liberty but not the fact of it, writing literacy promises a form of self-ownership that proceeds by self-effacement. Hoping someday to write his own pass to freedom, Douglass tricks local schoolboys into teaching him writing by pretending he knows more than they. Left alone in the house at night, Douglass writes in the spaces of his young master's copybooks, copying his copies until he could write "a hand very similar to that of Master Thomas."[51] Self-mastery comes through mastering a hand that is indistinguishable from his or any master's hand. Reading the printed text raises the false promise of the extension of individual rights by rationality alone; learning to write teaches self-ownership by sleight of hand.

Melville's Bartleby finds himself similarly stranded in the interstices of handwriting and print—or, more precisely, handwriting that has come to take on the characteristics of print. Bartleby first utters his signature phrase "I would prefer not to" when the manuscripts he has copied serially are to be checked against one another—the moment at which manual reproduction is authorized to appear as if mechanically reproduced. Both of these texts depict subjects who are oddly disowned and empowered in the gap that is formed—by force or by choice—between media. In what follows, however, I want to examine a couple of texts in which a claim to authority is made through the overlap of handwriting and print. In his early tale, "The Visionary" and in a spoof on celebrity called "Autography," Poe uses handwriting of a doubtful authenticity to negotiate a position between British original and American copy, and between the twin risks of antebellum publishing: the subjection of authors to a propertyless dissemination and the invisibility of editorial ownership. In both cases, the duplicity of the pen suggests an ability to manipulate the press. By keeping a nearly perfect, but identifiably flawed, facsimile in circulation, Poe claims a privileged relation to decentralized mass-production—importantly, not one of mastery but one of disruption.

Poe's Bryonic tale, "The Visionary," was first published in *Godey's Lady's Book* alongside other anonymous sketches such as "The Catholic," "The Fatalist," "The Missionary," and "The Short Gentleman." In this tale, an anonymous Poe imagines he could exert a kind of undercover authority by blurring the difference between himself and Byron—by making it impossible to tell British original from American copy. "The Visionary" is remarkable for its canny awareness of the inappropriateness of literary

gentility to mass-cultural forms. Indeed, Poe sets out to exploit this dis-
crepancy. In "The Visionary," Poe imagines exerting control over the
mass-phenomenon of Ladies' Magazine Byronism through recourse to a
conspicuous anachronism—the indeterminacy of an aristocratic script.

Pitched as an elaborate, fictional defense of Byron, who is everywhere invoked but never named, "The Visionary" sets out to dissociate
idleness and speculation from its association with "squandering" and
waste.[52] In many ways, the complex plotting of the tale is designed simply to endorse its hero's final pronouncement: "to dream has been the
business of my life" (165). While this narrative aim has obvious bear-
ing on Poe's own attempts to justify his career, the mismatch between
Byron's and Poe's predicaments is clear from the lengths to which the
story goes to establish grounds for comparison. The story opens with
an elaborate—and seemingly unnecessary—justification for withholding Byron's name from the reader. It soon becomes clear that the
purpose of this device is to bring Poe's anonymity as an author into
relation with Byron's quite different, generic namelessness. Whereas
Byron's namelessness is the product of his extraordinary fame—no one
need say his name because everybody knows it—Poe's namelessness is
a product of reprint-culture—no one *can* say his name because it is
withheld from readers. Should Poe's Byronic tale succeed, he might,
like the Byron in his tale, be everywhere known, but never named; yet
namelessness for Poe indicates anonymity and poverty, not fame and
opulence, nor the other kind of withholding that this tale is obsessed
with—the aristocrat's delight in concealing his wealth from public view.

Set in Venice by the Bridge of Sighs, "The Visionary" reaches its
denouement in a secluded space of aristocratic excess. Invited to a mysterious nobleman's private lodgings after he has witnessed an heroic rescue
of a drowning child, Poe's narrator engages the nameless "stranger" in a
discussion of his magnificent art collection. As this aristocrat explains,
his eclectic assortment of paintings and sculpture has been preserved
from the public to guard against imitation. Only the narrator and the
nobleman's valet have been admitted to these rooms, because their unusual
arrangement "has but to be seen to become the rage—that is, with those
who could afford it at the cost of their entire patrimony" (159).

After a long disquisition on originality, the aristocrat lapses into a
reverie, at which time Poe's narrator makes a singular discovery. Written

in the margin of an Italian tragedy is a poem that exposes the noble-man's true identity. At the level of plot, these "English lines" (162) confirm the stranger's liaison with the Marchesa Aphrodite, clinching Poe's tale as romantic rewriting of Byron's affair with the Contessa Guiccioli. And yet, as the narrator explains, these lines were "written in a hand so very different from the peculiar characters of my acquain-tance, that I had some difficulty in recognizing it as his own" (162). The text that follows helps to explain the narrator's difficulty. This homage to Byron has become the vehicle for the anonymous reprint-ing of Poe's Byronic poem "To One in Paradise." Poe's later title for the tale, "The Assignation," explicitly links the problem of assigning authorship to this doubly-authored poem to the illicit romantic liai-son that is the framework for the plot and the hallmark of the Byronic.

In "The Visionary," the indeterminacy of the aristocratic script stands both as an acknowledgment of indebtedness and as an attempt at tran-sumption. Poe's insertion of his own poem as the key to unlocking his Byronic hero's identity both declares his poetic dependence—despite Poe's authorship of this poem, these are indeed "English lines"—and underscores how the Byronic as a cultural phenomenon depends on such acts of imitation. In its necessary doubleness, the poetic assignation at the heart of this tale undermines the emphasis on originality that is pro-duced by the nobleman's extravagant connoisseurship.

As in "The Fall of the House of Usher," the denouement of "The Visionary" is delayed by a lengthy interlude devoted to aesthetic play—in this case, an explication of the aristocrat's aesthetic preferences more or less lifted out of Moore's *Letters and Journals of Lord Byron*. What becomes clear from this episode, however, is that Poe is not simply interested in aristo-cratic discrimination, but in the way in which such taste is vulnerable to exploitation. Poe's tale is itself an instance of such abuse. "The Visionary" takes its place in the eighth volume of *The Lady's Book* alongside a wealth of Byroniana—including a biographical memoir, a reprinted poem, engrav-ings of Byron's residences, a historical essay on Byron's Venice, and a poet-ical address to Byron written in Spenserian stanzas. Poe's consciousness of the fraudulence of his Byronic posturing can also be traced in the tale itself. The hallmark of the aristocrat in this tale is his ability to tell original from copy and his self-mocking relation to his property, an attitude that serves to double and to expose Poe's self-mocking relation to his medium. Poe's

Byron's aesthetic judgments are wickedly self-referential. Commenting on one of his statues, this aristocrat remarks: "Part of the left arm ... and all the right, are restorations; and in the coquetry of that right arm lies, I think, the quintessence of all affectation" (160).

And yet, Poe's narrator's exclusive access to his Byron's "cabinet" (159) and the tale's central scene of poetic misrecognition project an attitude more complex than simple adulation or ironic dismissal. Poe's tale banks on literary aristocracy as a popular phenomenon, yet it also seeks to distinguish itself from the Byronism that has "become the rage" with a claim of authenticity. Poe hasn't come to praise or to bury Byron, but to regulate access to the Byronic. "The Visionary" projects the author's fantasy that, by a single act of doubling that calls attention to its fraudulence or duplicity, Poe's Byron could be protected against mass-duplication.

In thinking through Poe's emphasis on the aristocrat's need to keep his art collection hidden from view, we should recall that Poe's imitation of Byron had indeed cost him his patrimony. In one of his final letters to his stepfather, John Allan, Poe asked for financial assistance in publishing a volume of poems, claiming "I have long given up *Byron* as a model—for which, I think, I deserve some credit."[53] Poe's earliest surviving poetic lines also testify to the fundamentally oppositional relation between Byronic extravagance and a credit economy. Written on the obverse of a page of calculations that represent John Allan's emergency money—an estimation of the liquidity of debts that were owed him—a youthful Poe had written the following lines:

—Poetry. by. Edgar A. Poe—
Last night with many cares & toils oppress'd
Weary, I laid me on a couch to rest—[54]

Poe's marginal identification with a generic Byron figure in "The Visionary"—one whose characteristic posture is to recline on an ottoman—represents an experiment in the possible liquidity of the Byronic persona. I would argue that it is, finally, by giving up modelling Byron *exactly* that Poe is able to generate credit. Poe's Byronic poem and the tale in which it is set hold value because they approximate without exactly reproducing the original. In "The Visionary," and in a whole host of other works that play off the difference between an aristocratic hand and the popular press, Poe's authorial strategy is to place the double or facsimile in a context where the reader is forced to question its veracity.

Poe uses handwriting of doubtful authenticity to establish his authority in a whole series of texts, including the "Marginalia," a series of fictional book annotations; the "Autography" series, which, while it began as a hoax, became the basis for two more serious attempts at criticism; and tales such as "MS. Found in a Bottle" and *The Narrative of Arthur Gordon Pym*. One might also recognize the strategy of keeping a nearly perfect but identifiably flawed facsimile in circulation as Dupin's signature move at the end of "The Purloined Letter." I want to look briefly however, at Poe's first venture into "Autography" to reinforce the point that it is through disruption of the conditions of reprint culture and not through what we'd generally call mastery of them that Poe imagines he can emerge as an author.

Poe's first "Autography" series juxtaposes printed letters, which purport to be the correspondence of statesmen and literati, with facsimile signatures and a brief editorial comment on the handwriting of each letter's author. Much of the humor of this piece lies in the burlesques of individual authors' styles. For example, Poe makes fun of Washington Irving's fastidiousness through his delicate refusal to read the manuscript "Treatise on Pigs."[55] And yet Poe's "Autography" also sets in motion a more sophisticated play on the way in which the authentic or original derives its authority only in relation to the facsimile or copy. One can see how this works by simply glancing at the format of the piece. While in a print context, the MS-signature is set off as "authentic," these are, of course, only *copies* of authors' signatures, facsimiles taken from the business letters that had accumulated on Poe's editorial desk. Similarly, while the parody correspondence is clearly inauthentic, it serves as a reminder that an author can only be said to have established his identity when his style can be imitated and recognized. Poe's witty treatment of this thematic is most evident from the way in which he designs his correspondence to produce the mark of authenticity—the sought-after signature—despite the vehement refusal of the letter writer in question. The concluding letter of the initial series nicely illustrates this triumph of circulation over the subject:

Sir.—Yours of the—came duly to hand. The fact is, I have been so pestered with applications for my autograph that I have made a resolution to grant one in no case whatsoever.

Yours, &c, [56]

What is perhaps most intriguing about this series, however, is the way in which Poe's insertion of fake signatures in a mass-produced magazine generates profits by disrupting the process of reprinting. Due to the popularity of the piece and the expense of commissioning new woodcuts of the signatures, editors who sought to reprint Poe's extravaganza found it economical to apply to the magazine in which Poe's "Autography" first appeared in order to rent the "originals."

It is also likely that Poe's "Autography" produced profits based on other magazines' *failure* to reprint it. One editor praised the series, lamenting "We wish we had the cuts, so that we might transfer it."[57] Calling attention to the magazine while neglecting to reprint its contents could only increase the value of the original. Indeed, the disruption Poe introduces into the system of reprinting actually *produces* this mass-produced magazine as an original. It is not simply the incorporation of handwriting into print that generates this value, but Poe's setting the facsimile signature within a context that raises the question of its availability, alternately asserting and denying its susceptibility to reproduction.

Even late in his career, Poe's image of the ideal coalescence of authorship and ownership involves a complex superscription of handwriting and print. Editing an elite literary magazine was a lifelong, unrealized dream for Poe. He had announced and abandoned an earlier project, *The Penn Magazine*, twice due to lack of funds. When Poe revived the project in 1843, he changed the magazine's title from a pun that was "somewhat too local in its suggestions"[58] to *The Stylus*, the name of a more ancient writing instrument that reflected the seriousness of his national ambitions.

Poe's epigraph to his *Prospectus of The Stylus* reflects the assumption that the image of inscription would counter what he saw as the unreliable publicity of the press. Poe's prospectus begins,

—unbending that all men
Of thy firm TRUTH may say—"Lo! this is writ
With the antique *iron pen.* (1033)

The hyper-rigidity of this appeal to readers is intended as an index of the periodical's promised objectivity. As opposed to ordinary magazines in which anonymous reviewers adjusted their critical commentary to suit a variety of publishing interests, Poe's magazine swore to "[hold] itself aloof from all personal bias" and to deliver "an absolutely independent criticism" (1035). The phallic inflexibility of this goal sets Poe's journal apart from the partisan monthlies and ladies' magazines that would be its close competitors. Poe's "antique iron pen" hearkens back to a mythical time before anonymity intervened to separate criticism from truth, the hand writing from what is written.

Poe's explanation of his motivations for launching his journal clarify what's at stake in this technological regression. Speaking in the third person of his dissatisfaction with previous editorial positions, Poe writes,

Having no proprietary right ... in either of these journals; his objects, too, being in many respects, at variance with those of their very worthy owners; he found it not only impossible to effect anything, on the score of taste, for the mechanical appearance of the works, but exceedingly difficult, also, to stamp, upon their internal character, that *individuality* which he believes essential to the full success of all similar publications. (1034)

Here Poe links a periodical's identity to its proprietor's control over the action of stamping. The magazine's ability to leave a strong impression on an individual reader depends on its direction by "a single mind" (1034), a relationship that is jeopardized by diversified production. Poe's "iron pen," then, takes up the individuality that he sees as potentially inscribed by the press under the ideal conditions of undivided ownership.

Poe's proposed title page for this magazine, however, undermines the association of the "iron pen" with identity, continuity, and unwavering judgment. Rather than securing the *Prospectus*'s promise of objectivity, Poe's title-page reinstitutes handwriting as the site of duplicity, asserting control of, not submission to, "TRUTH." At the center of the page [Figure 7] is a hand holding a stylus, inscribing *Aletheia*,

Figure 2.7   Fascimile Reprint, *Some Letters of Edgar Allan Poe to E. H. N. Patterson of Oquawka, Illinois.*

the Greek word for truth. Below this illustration is a Latin epigraph, which, in the source from which Poe is likely to have taken it, is rendered "sometimes a pen of gold and sometimes a pen of iron."[59] Poe's willingness to offer two modes of address—one bent to flatter and one to tell the truth—seems an astonishing reversal of his claims in the *Prospectus*. Indeed, the hand caught in the act of inscription seems to have stopped for direction, waiting on the dictates of its audience to manipulate truth.

Poe's title page and magazine proposal perform a number of complex relocations: authorial ambitions become editorial, individuality is found at the press, but control over the press is represented as the maintenance of a double relation to the reading public, a relation best represented by a duplicitous pen. We are on the whole, made uncomfortable by the fact of an author's subjection to market forces; more unnerving still is an author who is engaged in manipulating that market to advantage. Among many who have attempted to restore Poe to a version of authorship less threatening than *The Stylus* would suggest is Sara Sigourney Rice, who, for the frontispiece to her *Memorial Volume*, altered a daguerrotype of Poe so that a quill pen was placed in his outstretched hand.[60] In using different versions of Poe's signature on their covers—the mark both of originality and standardization—Burton Pollin's *Collected Writings of Edgar Allan Poe* and Floyd Stovall's edition of Poe's *Poems* have compensated for Poe's subjection to circulation and have provided a corpus for his hand.[61] What we should be aware of, however, is not simply the appropriation of the hand—that these books suggest a relation to print and to authorship that Poe did not and could not have possessed—but our own investment in disguising that appropriation, passing off our own interventions in the reprint market as if they were written in another hand.

NOTES

I am grateful to the American Antiquarian Society and to the Monroe C. Gutman Library, Harvard University Graduate School of Education, for access to their penmanship collections. My research benefited enormously from an early reading of Tamara Plakins Thornton's *Handwriting in America: A Cultural History*, forthcoming from Yale University Press in 1996. I wish to thank Jonah Siegel for patiently taking and retaking rolls of slides for the essay's initial presentation, and Jay Grossman, Jeffrey Masten, and Andrew Parker for their helpful comments on various drafts.

1. "Reminiscences of Poe by John H. B. Latrobe" in *Edgar Allan Poe: A Memorial Volume*, by Sara Sigourney Rice (Baltimore: Turnbull Brothers, 1877), p. 58.

2. Quoted in Jay B. Hubbell, "Charles Chauncey Burr: Friend of Poe," *PMLA* 69 (September 1954), p. 838.

3. Rice, 59.

4. As Hubbell explains, Latrobe's testimonial was first printed by Charles Chauncey Burr in the proslavery, secessionist New York monthly, *The Old Guard*, as part of the post–Civil War struggle to reclaim Poe for the South. See "Poe and His Biographer, Griswold," *The Old Guard* (June 1866) pp. 353-58. Latrobe greatly elaborated his

account of the meeting when he spoke at the dedication of the Poe monument in Baltimore, November 17, 1875. See Rice, pp. 57–62.

5. The *Saturday Visiter* warned authors that relinquishing their property rights was a condition of entering the contest: "We wish those who may write for either of the premiums to understand that all manuscripts submitted will become the property of the Publishers." Dwight Thomas and David K. Jackson, *The Poe Log: A Documentary Life of Edgar Allan Poe 1809–1849* (Boston: G. K. Hall & Co., 1987), p. 130.

6. Hubbell, p. 838.

7. Thomas Ollive Mabbott, *Collected Works of Edgar Allan Poe*, vol. 2, (Cambridge: Harvard University Press, 1978), p. 146.

8. "Memoir of the Author," in *The Works of Edgar Allan Poe*, vol. 3 (New York: J. S. Redfield, 1850), pp. vii–xxxix. Griswold's "Memoir" was initially placed as a preface to the third volume but was moved to the first volume in subsequent printings.

9. Griswold, p. xii.

10. See David D. Hall, "Introduction: The Uses of Literacy in New England, 1600–1850," *Printing and Society in Early America*, eds. William L. Joyce et al. (Worcester: American Antiquarian Society, 1983), pp. 1–47 and E. Jennifer Monaghan, "Literacy Instruction and Gender in Colonial New England" in *Reading in America: Literature and Social History*, ed. Cathy N. Davidson. (Baltimore: Johns Hopkins University Press, 1983), pp. 53–80.

11. *The Letters of the Republic: Publication and the Public Sphere in Eighteenth-Century America* (Cambridge: Harvard University Press, 1990).

12. For an account of the Supreme Court's definition of print as public property, see my "The Matter of the Text: Commerce, Print Culture, and the Authority of the State in American Copyright Law," forthcoming in *American Literary History*.

13. *The Poe Log*, p. 134.

14. Illustrations of the penhold that make use of the image of the doubled hand are found in all of the Spencerian and Payson, Dunton, and Scribner copybooks and manuals I cite in this essay. The image of the doubled hand is increasingly common in penmanship books published after 1840 and can be found in Chauncey Bascom, *Guide to Chirography* (Connecticut, 1832), Thomas Towndrow, *Towndrow's Guide to Calligraphy* (Salem, 1844), Levi S. Fulton and George W. Eastman, *Key to Fulton and Eastman's Chirographic Charts* (New York, 1849), and, doubtless, many other manuals I have not had the opportunity to consult. George Becker's *The American System of Penmanship* (Philadelphia, 1842), Marcus Root's *Philosophical Theory and Practice of Penmanship* (Philadelphia, 1842), and J. Nelson's *Introduction to Penmanship* (New York, 1850) work important changes on this image—Becker and Root by depicting a man and woman attached to these otherwise detached hands, and Nelson by picturing a monstrous teacher's hand on the right side of the illustration, providing a model for a boy at his desk, drawn to signficantly smaller scale. For reproductions of these images, see Ray Nash, *American Penmanship 1800–1850* (Worcester: American Antiquarian Society, 1969) pp. 215, 226, 256. It is striking that Jonathan Goldberg's

study of Renaissance handwriting manuals, *Writing Matter: From the Hands of the English Renaissance* (Stanford: Stanford University Press, 1990), turns up none of these images. The common Renaissance image of the penhold, which illustrates in parallel both good and bad ways of holding the pen—often for two scripts, secretarial and italic (Goldberg, pp. 93–94, 102–4)—suggests a wholly different relation to the process of emulation. As I will argue below, the image of the doubled hand illustrates both the pressure toward a uniform script and a typically nineteenth-century anxiety about the emulation of bad models.

15. Ray Nash, *American Writing Masters and Copybooks: History and Bibliography through Colonial Times* (Boston: The Colonial Society of Massachusetts, 1959), p. 23.

16. Allison Wrifford, *Wrifford's Mercantle Chirography* (New York, 1824), p. 14.

17. For a critique of the Italian hand and the Reversed Hand along these lines, see Benjamin Rand, *A New and Complete System of Mercantile Penmanship and New Invention of Running Hand* (Philadelphia, 1814), pp. 14–15.

18. Henry Bore credits James Perry with the popularization of steel pens. His "Perry Pens," patented in 1830, introduced flexibility into the otherwise too rigid pens through differently shaped apertures punched into the nib. See *The Story of the Invention of Steel Pens* (New York: Ivison, Blakeman & Co., 1890), p. 28 ff.

19. John Jenkins, *The Art of Writing: Reduced to a Plain and Easy System, on a PLAN Entirely NEW* (Cambridge, 1791). Jenkins substantially revised and extended this small pamphlet in 1813, in part to lay claim to his system, which had been eagerly taken up by Henry Dean, Allison Wrifford, and others. For an account of the publication history of Jenkins's system, see Nash, *American Writing Masters*, pp. 26–34.

20. I depend here on Ray Nash's assembly of comparable exercises. See his *American Writing Masters*, pp. 28–29.

21. John Jenkins, *The Art of Writing: Reduced to a Plain and Easy System, on a PLAN Entirely NEW*, Revised, Enlarged and Improved (Cambridge, 1813), p. x.

22. ibid., p. 10.

23. ibid., p. 7.

24. Jenkins 1791, p. 10.

25. John Clark, *Writing Improv'd* (London, 1714), quoted in Nash, *American Writing Masters*, p. 29.

26. Platt Rogers Spencer, *The Spencerian Key to Practical Penmanship* (New York, 1866), p. 31.

27. Benjamin Franklin Foster, *Practical Penmanship* (Albany, 1832), p. 49.

28. Spencer, p. 24.

29. Benjamin Franklin Foster, *Penmanship, Theoretical and Practical, Illustrated and Explained* (Boston, 1843), pp. 39–40.

30. Payson, Dunton, and Scribner, *Theory and Art of Penmanship: A Manual for Teachers* (Boston, 1864), p. 24.

31. ibid., p. 26.

32. Jenkins 1791, p. 11.

33. *Theory and Art of Penmanship*, p. 26; Jenkins, too, warns against "a succession of masters who write a diversity of hands" (1791, p. 10). For further discussion of the danger of emulating bad models, see Foster, who cautions that an unsupervised student "will go on heaping error upon error till his faults become habitual, perhaps beyond remedy" (1843, p. 48), and Spencer, who explicitly critiques copybooks that display "imperfect forms . . . designed to warn the pupil against the faults portrayed" (p. 91). However, even in Spencer, who goes on at length about "the susceptibility of children to impressions and permanency of these impressions" (p. 107), it is never clear why a bad model should be so much more easily impressed than a good one.

34. *On Teaching Penmanship* (Boston, 1833), p. 6.

35. *Theory of Spencerian Penmanship, For Schools and Private Learners, Developed by Questions and Answers, with Practical Illustrations* (New York, 1874), p. 24.

36. *Theory and Art of Penmanship*, p. ii.

37. *Theory of Spencerian Penmanship*, p. 5.

38. In their *Manual of Penmanship* (New York, 1873), Payson, Dunton, and Scribner explain how drill and counting can translate fractious individuality into a more tractable and efficient corporate identity: "the objections urged against the use of counting are the strongest arguments in its favor. We hold that it is precisely this restraint that the nervously irritable need, this urgency that the lymphatic require. The very fact that it tempers the impatience of the one, and stimulates the inertness of the other, proves its excellence. . . . The irritability aroused by personal restraint is unfelt in the concerted action. It is not as if his pen must be kept to a slow pace; it keeps that pace almost naturally, from the very sympathy of united movement. He loses, so to speak, the individuality of himself and pen. He is part of an acting body. He is not directing an independent pen, but one out of a number" (p. 98). Michel Foucault uses a penmanship lesson to illustrate the instantiation of disciplinary power through "the correlation of the body and the gesture" in *Discipline and Punish* (New York: Vintage Books, 1979), p. 152.

39. *Theory and Art of Penmanship*, p. 22.

40. ibid., p. 24.

41. Foster, 1832, p. 45.

42. Spencer, p. 134.

43. ibid., p. 135.

44. ibid., pp. 96–99.

45. See P. R. Spencer and V. M. Rice, *Young Misses' First Lessons in Ladies' Penmanship: A Facsimile System* (Jefferson, OH: Younglove and Co.) 1848, back page. See also Spencer & Rice's System of Business Penmanship (Geneva OH: P. R. Spencer) 1848.

46. *Theory and Art of Penmanship*, p. xiii.

47. See also the illustration of the proper writing posture while standing, which features a man at a counting house writing "Spencer" into his ledger (Spencer, p. 34).

48. *Reply of Payson, Dunton & Scribner to the Absurd Claims of the Spencerian Authors to Originality* (Boston, 1871), pp. 16, 22.

49. If it were the handwriting itself that authorized the guarantee, we would have to be able to determine whether the "Engraver's Certificate" was written in a Payson, Dunton and Scribner or a Spencerian hand. While it is entirely possible that the engraver was playing with this distinction—compare, for example, the capital "S" that begins the word "Scribner" with the extra flourish that marks the "Spencerian"— it is not the script itself to which we turn for adjudication, but the publisher to whom C. A. Swit is conscripted. Swit's "Certificate," which, in trying to minimize the engraver's agency, calls attention to the presence of an additional hand, can be seen as the disruptive return of an earlier copybook convention—the title-page distinction between "Scripsit" and "Sculpsit" that allowed for the signature of both writer and engraver.

50. Frederick Douglass, *Autobiographies* (NY: Library of America, 1994), pp. 37, 42.

51. Douglass, p. 45.

52. Mabbott, p. 151. Further references to this edition will be noted in the text.

53. *The Letters of Edgar Allan Poe*, vol. 1, ed. John Ward Ostrom (New York: Gordian Press, 1966), p. 20.

54. *The Poe Log*, pp. 62–63.

55. *Southern Literary Messenger* (February, 1836), p. 209. Mabbott also reprints the spoof, pp. 259–90. For an astute analysis of Poe's "Autography" as a meditation on the way in which "personality was seen to emerge from a generic publicity" (p. 40), see Jonathan Elmer, *Reading at the Social Limit: Affect, Mass-Culture, and Edgar Allan Poe* (Stanford: Stanford University Press, 1995), pp. 37–43.

56. *Southern Literary Messenger*, p. 212.

57. *The Poe Log*, p. 346.

58. Poe published three slightly different versions of the *Prospectus of The Penn Magazine* in June and August 1840, and January 1841. Facsimile reprints of these texts can be found in Jacob N. Blanck, *Bibliography of American Literature*, vol. 7 (New Haven: Yale University Press, 1983), pp. 116–19. Poe published his *Prospectus of The Stylus* in March 1843. It has been reprinted in G.R. Thompson, *Edgar Allan Poe: Essays and Reviews* (New York: Literary Classics of the United States, 1984), pp. 1033–35. Further references to this edition will be noted in the text.

59. For the source and translation of Poe's epigraph, see Mabbot, p. 329, and Burton Pollin, *Discoveries in Poe* (Notre Dame: University of Notre Dame Press, 1970), pp. 206–295.

60. To compare this daguerrotype to the original, see Michael J. Deas, *The Portraits and*

Daguerrotypes of Edgar Allan Poe (Charlottesville: University Press of Virginia, 1989), pp. 59 and 80. Rice's altered daguerrotype was also used by James A. Harrison as the frontispiece to Volume 4 of his *Complete Works of Edgar Allan Poe*, 17 vols. (New York: George D. Sproul, 1902). I am indebted to Bill Pannapacker for this reference.

61. See Burton Pollin, ed. *The Imaginary Voyages* (Boston: Twayne, 1981), *The Brevities: Pinakidia, Marginalia, Fifty Suggestions and Other Works* (New York: Gordian Press, 1985), *Writing in the Broadway Journal*, 2 vols. (New York: Gordian Press, 1986), and Floyd Stovall's *The Poems of Edgar Allan Poe* (Charlottesville: University Press of Virginia, 1965).

PRESSES

JEFFREY MASTEN

3

PRESSING SUBJECTS
OR, THE SECRET LIVES OF SHAKESPEARE'S COMPOSITORS

PUTTING ASIDE MY TITLE for a moment, I'll begin instead with a more modern secret life. When a twentieth-century American student—let's call him Student A—was in about the sixth grade, a teacher corrected his repeated spelling of the word *occasion* in a composition. Student A was in the habit of spelling this word *o-c-c-a-i-s-i-o-n*, because he knew that a correct spelling of this word would need to register (as his spelling did) a long "a" vowel in the second syllable. O–c–c–a–i–s–i–o–n. Student A no longer recalls the composition or most of the sixth grade, but the moment of correction—or more accurately, the memory of his confident, repeated, peculiar spelling—sometimes recurs, when he writes or types the word. How all *occasions* do inform against him, now.

As I hope to show in more detail, such a narrative would be largely impossible to have lived or told in the early modern period—say, around 1600—because, as is widely known, there was no one standard of correct English spelling with which to discipline the young student, although, as we'll see, within certain contexts there was beginning to be the idea of a standard.

... it is even more important that we should discover, if we can, through the identification of compositors on the basis of their spellings, *what kind of minds* may have affected the readings of substantive editions of Shakespeare's plays, since *this question is* fundamental to the editing of any text ...

—Alice Walker,
Textual Problems of the First Folio[1]

A [computer] password is more than just a flaky kind of fingerprint. We still want passwords to be romantic, not just utilitarian. We reveal ourselves in our passwords.... Choosing *xerxes* or *donjuan* is a grown-up equivalent of wearing Power Ranger underwear.

—James Gleick,
in *The New York Times Magazine*[2]

Second, the anecdote might be taken to suggest that there are, in a way to which I'll return, naturally occurring spelling preferences—as suggested by Student A's apparent individualized preference, when questioned in his untutored state, for the spelling *occaision* over *occasion*, and the fact that he continues sometimes to hesitate over the "i" of the keyboard when typing this word, even after years of advanced literary training. But the anecdote also obviously suggests that Student A wasn't untutored, and was attempting to conform to a notion of standardized, phonetic spelling.

The problematic of compositor study—the study of the workmen who set by hand the type of early printed books, the subjects that will occupy me for much of this paper—resides in this anecdote in another way. For if we were to apply Student A's story to the seventeenth century without attention to some important epistemic differences, we would reproduce, I think, the way in which twentieth-century bibliography has applied, without enough examination, its own assumptions about spelling, regularity, and, as we'll see, individuality, to conditions of language and subjectivity before the modern era. The words of Charlton Hinman are exemplary in this regard; writing in a 1940–41 essay that precedes and provides a rationale for his immense labor collating and dividing up the compositorial shares of the first folio collection of Shakespeare's plays, Hinman says that

> . . . *it is to be expected* that any compositor of the sixteenth or seventeenth century would develop certain individual spelling habits, and that these habits may serve to distinguish his work from that of other compositors. (79, my emphasis)[3]

Hinman here tells us what he expects, or rather what "is to be expected" of early modern spellers, but there is no evidence supplied for these twentieth-century expectations.

I'm aware—and now I return to my title—that probably most of you will find the study of early modern typesetters something less than a "pressing subject" for literary and cultural studies today. But what I hope to suggest in the course of this paper is that, first, compositor study has instrumentally affected the early modern texts we read and study, especially those texts associated with Shakespeare; second, that the paradigm within which compositor spelling analysis operates is demonstrably related to other deforming narratives about the production of early modern texts; third, that these narratives came to life within a particular mid-twentieth-century epistemology that has had, in other spheres, demonstrably toxic effects on actual persons living and dead; and finally, that there are other ways in which we might think, historically and theoretically, about the subjects that pressed the texts we read and study—ways that might be more useful for the study of the history of the book, and for the history of the subject.

I. SPELL-CHECK

If there were no spelling bees in early modern England, this is not because that culture had not perfected other modes through which the spectacle of a particular subject's submission to (or divergence from) a larger cultural value could be exhibited, but because spelling was only in the process of becoming such a value and, relatedly, only in the process of becoming an action, a transitive activity—and not yet predicated on the absorption and reproduction of particular "correct" spellings. In fact, one of the earliest meanings of the word *spell* (as a verb) in English was "To read (a book, etc.) letter by letter; to peruse, or make out, slowly or with difficulty" (ca. 1300–1850).[4] To spell in English, from about 1300 well into the nineteenth century, meant to read something, to consume a supplied text—to puzzle out a particular exemplar. A set of what the *Oxford English Dictionary* calls "figurative" meanings continued to spin out from this spelling-as-reading meaning in the sixteenth and seventeenth centuries: "To discover or find out, to guess or suspect, by close study or observation" (ca. 1587–1879); "To make out, understand, decipher, or comprehend, by study" (ca. 1635–1886). "[T]he vast discourses of wisest and most learned men," writes Kenelm Digby in 1644,

> are beyond the spellinges of infantes: and yet those discourses spring from the same roote, as the others spellinges doe, and are but a raysing of them to a greater height . . . .[5]

Digby's context (an extended metaphor within a scientific discussion) suggests that *spellinge* for him signifies reading or comprehension—the belabored understanding of children. The acting company's famous preface to the first folio collection of Shakespeare's plays can be reread, respelled, in this context: "*To the great Variety of Readers*," it begins, "FRom the most able, to him that can but spell . . . ."[6] What knowledge of spelling is required to spell Shakespeare?

That's 1623, and, as we've seen, Digby's 1644 text also invokes spelling-as-reading (he also uses the phrase "spellingly reade"), suggesting that this meaning continues to circulate even after the tentative beginnings of what we think of as spelling. According to the *OED* at least, the recognizably modern meaning of spelling—"To name or set down in order the letters of (a word or syllable)"—appears first around 1588 (ostensibly in Shakespeare), though I am not at all sure that the early examples of this usage I know of are (upon rereading) about the production of "correct spellings" in our terms. Spelling in the fully modern sense does not clearly emerge in the *OED*'s examples until much later in the next century, around 1661.

If spelling in early modern English is about reading, the ability to make sense of particular graphic shapes and forms on the page, we should also note that these shapes might be different, within a certain range, while at the same time not necessarily registering as "different words" in our understanding. As Margreta de Grazia has argued in an important essay on English prior to lexical standardization, in a culture in which there was constant, multiple graphic and phonic overlap among (what we would refer to as) discrete words, there was more polysemic possibility/activity built into this system—if early modern English can even be called a "system."[7] "Linguistic field" is a better term,[8] taken alongside Juliet Fleming's reminder that English was "not unruled, but ruled differently—perhaps in accordance with a rhetorical rather than grammatical, lexical, and orthographic order."[9]

The variability of pronunciations, the intersection of dialects, the ongoing shift from an inflected to a largely uninflected grammatical practice (and the corresponding migration of words among "parts of speech"),[10] the nonexistence of dictionaries regulating the usage/spelling of everyday words, etymological thinking that linked rather than dissevered similar words[11]—all of these factors made for a more fluid and unfixed linguistic field. What we call "single words" were spelled in multiple ways—often by the same person, and the *OED*'s focus on discrete words, sorted into particular (so-called) parts of speech, attached to particular (also discrete) meanings associated with a variety of (past) forms obscures and imposes a modern order upon the fluidity of early modern practice(s), in which *ay* sounded like both *I* and *eye/eie*, and could be spelled *I*, *aye*, *ay*, etc. Or, to take some other examples I've been thinking about, the pairs of words *conversation* and *conversion*, *precedent* and *president*, *discreet* and *discrete*, even *foundation* and *fundament*, were interchangeable. In this context, *spelling* was conceptualized as the process of *processing* these forms, not *producing* them. Production is called not *spelling*, but *writing*.

Those familiar with the decades around 1600 might say that I'm simplifying the issue: that there were in fact those in English culture who saw this linguistic situation as an issue, a problem, and attempted to fix it. In the 1560s to 1580s, with Thomas Smith's *De recta & emendata Lingvae Anglicae Scriptione*, John Hart's *An Orthographie*, and William Bullokar's *Booke at large, for the Amendment of Orthographie*, there were recurrent attempts to standardize English spelling—that is, to focus on the production of uniform spellings.[12] Such attempts continued in the early seventeenth century. As Jonathan Goldberg has importantly observed in his discussion of some of the texts of this movement, sixteenth-century spelling reform is not devoid of ideological aspirations and effects,[13] and the etymological resonance of Smith's, Hart's, and Bullokar's titles can begin to emphasize for us the cultural values with which uniform spelling is associated for its reformers. Spelling reform is about *orthography*, literally right-writing; *orthos* is straight, upright, standing, the opposite of crooked.[14] Alexander Hume's unpublished treatise *Of the Orthographie of the Britan Tongue* (ca. 1617) makes the connection explicitly:

> . . . the printeres and wryteres of this age, caring for noe more arte then may win the pennie, wil not paen them selfes to knau whither it be orthographie or skaiographie that doeth the turne . . . .[15]

Hume both dedicates his text to the King and coins a perverse opposite to rectitude in delineating his system of right-writing; *skaiographie* comes from *skaios*, "left, left-handed, awkward, crooked,"[16] related to the Latin *scaeuitas*, "[i]nstinctive choosing of the wrong; perversity."[17]

Whether orthography or skaiography doeth the turn, orthography seems always, nevertheless, to have the potential to turn against, to turn *back* on its advocates, who frequently don't fare well in the popular culture that registers their efforts. In the 1594–97? play *Loues Labour's Lost*, to take a familiar example, the spelling reformer (in this case, the advocate of more Latinate spellings in English) is often referred to in the folio's stage directions and speech headings as simply "the Pedant," rather than as Holofernes, and is associated with both sodomy and cuckoldry.[18] Bullokar's name is misunderstood as "ballocks" (testicles) and "bullocks" (castrated bulls) in the Massinger/Middleton/Rowley play *The Old Law* (1618?).[19] Or consider Benedick's description of the love-sick Claudio in *Much Adoe about Nothing*: "he was wont to speake plaine, & to the purpose (like an honest man & a souldier) and now is he turn'd ortho-graphy, his words are a very fantasticall banquet, iust so many strange dishes: may I be so conuerted, & see with these eyes?"[20] Right-writing is made to take a turn here; the right (ortho-graphy) becomes strange and fantasticall, the sign of a perverse conversion to what we would call "heterosexuality."[21] As Elizabeth Pittenger and Juliet Fleming have shown, language-learning in this period often registers complicated structures and anxieties of sex/gender.[22]

Spelling reform is thus contested;[23] neither can it be read as a positivist history, for, again as Goldberg notes, the reformers aren't successful, and when English spelling eventually becomes (more) standardized, it does not become so along the lines advocated by those who have "turn'd orthography."[24]

For the purposes of this paper, this is the crucial point about spelling as articulated in the late sixteenth and early seventeenth centuries: the spelling reform of Hart, Bullokar, Hume, and others does not have as a shared value the erasure of variable spellings of English words; the existence of multiple possibilities for the spelling of any given word does not register as a concern in these reform texts—or in *antireform* texts. Mulcaster, for example, writes against the reform of what he calls "our customarie writing"[25] without registering the spelling variances that are for us an apparent feature of period writing. Instead, spelling reform (as Goldberg's analysis demonstrates and deconstructs in detail) seeks to produce an ostensibly mimetic relation between the sounds of words and their orthography—a system in which each letter or combination of letters will be matched with a single spoken sound.[26] The development of this aspiringly mimetic system might in fact seem to eventuate in the reduction of variability, but the difference in emphasis is a central one for understanding the early modern English linguistic field. What is at stake in the early modern debate is not the reduction of variability but the cohesion of sound and graphic depiction; "in true Ortography," Bullokar writes (with a redoubled excess), "*both* the eye, the voyce, and the eare consent most perfectly, without any let, doubt, or maze."[27] The consent is among bodily members, not among spellings.

Further, the relation of spelling to allegedly "individual" members of the body politic (and here I'm building on Peter Stallybrass's important critique of the notion of the *individual*, as opposed to the *subject*, in this period)[28] is not what we have come to expect. When Thomas Whythorne goes to write what is now often said to be one of the first "autobiographies" in English, he writes his extraordinarily self-scrutinizing narrative not in conventional (i.e. *variable*) spelling, or in an idiosyncratic system of his own devising, but in a version of Hart's orthography; the individual life spells itself out by aspiring not to individuation but to standardization, uniformity. Yet even here, as the modern editor of Whythorne's manuscript notes, the autobiographical subject practices no fully auto-orthographical consistency: "'use' may be spelt 'yowze' or 'iuwz' or in ten variant ways. . . ." (lvii), and "on the same page he will write 'laf' and 'lawf' for 'laugh'" (lxvi).[29]

Thus far I've said little about my ostensible subject, the printing press, and I want to note the fact that a number of orthographers (and anti-orthographers) register the possible importance of print in their projects. Bullokar, for example, laments that "for lacke of true ortography our writing in Inglish hath altered in euery age, yea since printing began," but he argues that "printing be the best helpe to stay the same, in one order."[30] As we've seen, Hume's citation of English "skaiographie" indicts both writers *and* printers. But, contra Bullokar and the more recent print historian Elizabeth Eisenstein, we should note that the spelling of early modern English compositors may actually have *resisted* the progressive stabilization of spelling that print is said to have enacted.[31] As D. G. Scragg notes, "justification [in this period] was achieved by varying the spelling of words in a line, and words which had a variable length extending from *pity* to *pyttye* became very valuable to printers."[32] Examining the 1611 King James Bible, A. W. Pollard writes, "In my innocence I was prepared to find [the spelling] both scholarly and consistent." But he finds that the "only consistency is that the form is always preferred *which suits the spacing*."[33] This undernoticed point can from our perspective hardly be *over*emphasized, since it is utterly foreign to modern practice: where our newspapers and computers use spacing to justify a line of printed text, early modern printers used *both* spaces *and* variable spellings to fill out their lines.[34] Whatever its eventual effect in solidifying a common spelling practice, early print may have seized upon the variance of spellings that *already* existed in early modern English and may have encouraged, promoted, expanded, circulated, inculcated that variance by continuing to reproduce variant spellings that might then have been seen as even more widely available[35]—even more available to compositors themselves, who might reproduce them in contexts that required no justification.

2. SPELLING AND THE INDIVIDUAL TALENT

> *Barnardo.* WHo's there?
> *Fran.* Nay answer me: Stand & vnfold
> your selfe.
>
> —*Hamlet* (1623)[36]

The fundamental assumption of twentieth-century compositor analysis is that, even if the language as a whole did not operate according to principles of standardized spelling, each individual writer, and therefore typesetter, operated according to a personal, largely self-standardized glossary. The central study in this field, Charlton Hinman's division of compositor labor in the Shakespeare folio, is based largely on his analysis of variations in the words *do, go* and *here*; "quire tt [*Othello*]," he says, ". . . was set by a man with a marked preference for *do, go* and *heere*. And such a man was Compositor B, as he is now generally called" (*PPFFS* 1:183).[37] In contrast, some pages in gathering o, which includes parts of *2* and *3 Henry VI*,

> were quite as certainly set by someone else—by a man who, unlike B, strongly preferred *doe, goe,* and *here* to *do, go,* and *heere*. . . . This man was Compositor A; and . . . he was almost as constant to his habit of spelling these words in the manner indicated as B was to his habit of spelling the same words in a different way.
> (I: 184–85)

Hinman eventually analyzes some other spellings that aren't as seemingly common and arbitrary as these, but I want to notice here, first, the way in which letters on the page are made to produce a compositor with strong preferences and constant habits, and second, the way in which that subject is made to seem immediately to have an identity in Real Life, a name—even though that name is almost comically an obvious bibliographical construction: "Such a man was Compositor B . . . . This man was Compositor A."[38]

I'm not sure it's possible to prove to current satisfaction that compositors *didn't* have self-standardized spelling glossaries that they habitually employed and that can therefore be used to identify them. Perhaps the only way to demonstrate this empirically would be to compare known printers' records connecting particular compositors to particular pages, with the actual printed pages, and then to show how the spellings on those pages do, or do not, disclose compositors with individualized, consistent practices. We don't have such records for the Shakespeare folio or for most early seventeenth-century printed books, but in his brilliant critique of the use of spacing to distinguish compositors, D. F. McKenzie has shown that, in cases where we *do* have such records, the compositors don't line up in the way the individuating methodology of compositor study predicts.[39]

The first section of this paper has, I hope, begun to suggest the problematic of the assumption of individualized spelling practices, at a cultural level—the way in which it would require an individual speller resistant to the unstandardized linguistic context surrounding him. Hinman, in the 1940–41 essay I quoted earlier, writes that

> The standardization of spelling was of course in progress, particularly in printing houses; yet there was still, even among printers, such a variety of acceptable alternative spellings that *it would be remarkable indeed* if individual compositors did not form individual habits. ("Principles," 79)

As before, Hinman notes what he would find remarkable, if lacking, but without substantiation. Indeed, Hinman's own logic is itself remarkable: there was no larger cultural system of standardization, *so that* there must have been, compensatorily, standardization at the level of the individual. The sheer lack of a standardized linguistic field seems to *necessitate* standardization at the more local level; no individual, Hinman suggests, could countenance the variety of available spellings.

If I can only at this point cast doubt on the notion of individuated orthography, I think I *can* show that the study of compositors as individuals—as we've already begun to see—partakes of peculiarly modern notions of agency and subjectivity, and that our study of this method has something to say about our approach to Shakespeare.

Hinman says that

> The habits of Compositor D with respect to other words than "do," "go," and "here"— both his preferences and his *tolerances*—are yet to be thoroughly studied. So too are such non-spelling peculiarities as may be discovered in his work. (*PPFFS*, 1: 199).

The work of compositor analysis is to convert characters into characters—spellings into an individual constituted as a range of (ortho)graphic behaviors, habits, preferences, and even tolerances (by which term Hinman means that a compositor "tolerates" some spellings he prefers not to use himself, if they're present in the copy from which he's setting type). But the rhetoric, as we've seen it so far, is not particularly careful to distinguish apparently unconscious habits from tolerances and strong preferences; if the compositor is a creature of his habits, he's also a "man" who prefers and tolerates. Hinman's comment at the end of this passage—on Compositor D's "non-spelling peculiarities"—figures the trajectory of compositor analysis itself, for the larger point, as Walker puts it, is to know "*what kind of minds* may have affected" Shakespeare's text—to discover the peculiarities that go beyond the bounds of mere spelling.

Indeed, though most of the compositor analyses published since the 1940s have been taken up with identifying compositors in various texts, the larger editorial *use* of this analysis is said to reside in the next step: to know what kind of errors particular compositors were ostensibly prone to making and thereby to determine when a supposed error in Shakespeare's text is likely an error made by a compositor (and therefore to be eliminated through emendation)—and when it is Shakespeare.[40] The result has been a kind of composite-compositor-sketch, the delineation of characters that proliferate out from the surface of these texts: Compositor A, we learn, "was by habit conservative."[41]

Or: "The important thing to remember, in connection with A's habits, is that he was systematic" (Walker, "Compositor Determination," 15n8). So secure is A's personality that his behavior can be predicted even in hypothetical situations: "He could normally maintain a system, and I have no doubt that if A had decided to turn every tenth 'e' he could have held his head to the business" ("Compositor Determination," 15n8). Gary Taylor has attempted to reverse this characterization: "A's reputation as a uniquely reliable and trustworthy compositor, whose work editors should be loath to emend, is almost wholly unfounded."[42] In contrast, consider the "notorious"[43] Compositor B's "more erratic ways" ("Compositor Determination," 15n8), which are

> marked by a combination of misdirected ingenuity, deliberate tampering, and plain carelessness that makes him an interesting example of how far a compositor could go in the intentional and unintentional alteration of copy while setting it into type—although it should be understood that B appears to have gone a good deal further than most.[44]

Hinman's index entries for the compositors themselves read like character composites:

> Compositor E, . . . spelling peculiarities of . . . ; his spelling "mixed," much influenced by copy, his true preferences therefore hidden . . . ; no strong preferences evident at first . . . ; non-spelling peculiarities . . . ; set [type] only in absence of one or both "regulars" and used their cases . . . ; why he began with quire dd, not cc . . . ; . . . was very inaccurate, was expected to make errors, and much of his work proofed . . . ; set only for the six Tragedies which F reprints from quartos . . . ; his essential function . . . ; his dual role . . . ; set most of *Titus* and *Romeo*, all of pre-cancellation *Troilus*, had a share in *Ham.*, *Lear*, *Oth.* . . . ; was slower than B . . . ; final disappearance . . . ; although heretofore confused with B, his work now relatively easy to identify . . . ; his share in F summarized . . . . (*PPFFS*, 2: 536)

I'll return to E's characteristics, but notice here that a chronological log of E's activities in the progress of folio printing oscillates with, and becomes, a rehearsal of personality traits, with a fully bounded subjectivity—a subjectivity so complex that even some of E's "true preferences" (preferences culled from the printed page) remain somehow hidden from view. The spelling evidence may be composed of temporary aberrations, but the compositor is now a species.[45]

The kind of individuation of printing-house labor delineated here is both essential to the method of compositor analysis and, apparently, that which can thwart its success, as Fredson Bowers (Hinman's teacher and the dean of postwar American textual studies) suggests, writing in 1959:

> the uniqueness of each compositor, and of his mental and physical habits and reactions, lends to the detailed study of his work an unpredictable basis in which the human equation is often of the first importance. . . . each compositor is a law to himself, subject to all the irrationality associated with human operations under individual responsibility.[46]

Individuation, as Bowers makes clear, is at the center of this method, doubly so, for even as the passage seems edgily to approach an admission of the method's impossibility, it suggests that the ideal compositor for analysis is one who is outrageously, clinically idiosyncratic (and therefore identifiable), but at the same time absolutely consistent in his idiosyncrasy.

This methodological paradox brings us back to Hinman's Compositor E, who is, as we've seen, hardly the ideal compositor; indeed, he further suggests some of the internal inconsistencies of the methodology. For Compositor E is an impressionable individual of astonishing malleability. Hinman notes that the habits and preferences of E actually *change* over the course of the pages of the folio he works on: he begins as "a novice who had not at first had any really strong spelling preferences"; early on in the job he "follows copy" closely but quickly develops "strong spelling preferences" of his own—what Hinman calls "a *do-go* habit" (*PPFFS*, 1: 213n2). This habit also characterizes Compositor B, and Hinman in fact finds E working closely with B. Commenting on Hinman's work, T. H. Hill emphasizes "the closeness of E's working relationship with compositor B . . .[;] throughout the Tragedies, we can observe E's gradual acquisition of typographical expertise. . . . He was, as the Nurse in *Romeo* puts it, 'a man of wax.'"[47] Another bibliographer notices Compositor E's "strong imitative tendency, which has so effectively concealed his presence and caused such confusion. . . ."[48]

Once we start to notice variability, imitative tendencies, and the acquisition of others' habits—where before there had only been solid identity and consistency—these more flexible characteristics begin to appear everywhere: Hinman admits that "both [compositors] A and B now and again used non-characteristic spellings, and sometimes without ascertainable reason" (*PPFFS*, 1: 185). As we've seen, B's work is sometimes difficult to distinguish from that of Compositor E (*PPFFS*, 2: 512, 1: 226); and what characterizes E, as he's initially delineated by Hinman, is his lack of character, or lack of his own characters: he has "B-like spelling preferences but also a strong tendency to follow copy" (*PPFFS*, 1: 212). If this evidence undermines the separability of B and E, and the separation of E's work from that of the other compositors who composed Shakespeare,[49] the very flexibility and malleability of E's spellings make it possible, by Hinman's own logic, to find the impressionable E almost *anywhere* (*PPFFS*, 1: 213n2).[50]

3. HABITS AND INTOLERANCES

Spelling-habit is the way in which any person spelt; it is usage, mostly unconscious, sometimes grotesquely self-conscious. Spelling-pattern, however, is the investigator's concept of individual tendency . . .

—T. H. Hill, "Spelling and the Bibliographer"[51]

Both A and B made mistakes, but B made more than A and was especially given to particular kinds of aberration. Unlike A, Compositor B took frequent and various liberties with his copy.

—Charlton Hinman (*PPFFS*, 1: 10)

. . . for every obvious homosexual, there are probably nine nearly impossible to detect.

—*Life* magazine (1964)[52]

The analysis of compositors' spelling begins in a 1920 letter to *The Times Literary Supplement* about spellings in Macbeth, appears as an occasionally useful inferential method in R. B. McKerrow's widely taught 1927 *Introduction to Bibliography for Literary Students*, and is first employed in earnest as a textual method in Edwin Willoughby's 1932 book on the first folio.[53] Hinman publishes on spelling identification in 1940–41, but it is only after the hiatus of the Second World War that compositor study becomes central to the conduct of Shakespearean bibliography. Take down from the shelf the row of early issues of *Studies in Bibliography*, the annual volume of papers Bowers began in 1948, and you find at least one article each year on compositor identification in the period directly after the war—and then an explosion of interest in the mid-50s: five articles in 1955, four in 1956, three in 1957, three more in 1958.

But "hiatus," to backtrack for a moment, is not the best word for what happened to American bibliographic study during the Second World War, for, as I want to suggest, compositor analysis wasn't so much suspended as *produced* by the war, in some important ways. Before the United States entered the war, Bowers "had been given secret instruction as a cryptanalyst in a naval communications group being formed at the university [of Virginia]"; during the war he moved to Washington "to supervise an intelligence unit working on deciphering enemy codes."[54] Among a number of prominent literary and bibliographic scholars, the unit included Charlton Hinman (33).[55] Hinman in fact got the idea for the collating machine he later invented to compare first folio pages from "the method followed in the intelligence unit for comparing successive photographs of enemy fortifications, to see whether changes had been made" (Tanselle, 34).

Were compositors to become the code-producing enemies of postwar bibliographic scholarship? The connections between postwar bibliography and cryptanalytic work didn't escape another bibliographer, G. Thomas Tanselle, reviewing Bowers's life and work. "The goal of both activities," he writes, "is to find meaningful patterns in what at first seems to be chaotic data" (34). But surely there are other questions to ask: what are the differences between intentionally produced codes disclosing the locations of Japanese warships, and the codes, or inscriptions, of seventeenth-century spellings? What if chaotic data, as I've suggested, is instead data that lies outside our standards for the behavior of the chaotic and the ordered? But these are not the only questions to be asked of the methods of compositor analysis, and I want briefly to think more broadly about the discourses that surrounded compositor study in the late 40s and early 50s.

If the enemies of the United States and its bibliographers from 1941–1945 were fascists abroad, some of the most extravagant battles of the postwar Cold War, as a number of political and social historians have argued, were fought against (real and ostensible) homosexuals and communists within. If the publication of the Kinsey report on *Sexual Behavior in the Human Male* in 1948 taught and then sought to reassure Americans that homosexuals were potentially everywhere, the 1950 Senate inquiry into the *Employment of Homosexuals and Other Sex Perverts in Government*[56] also marshaled Kinsey's evidence to argue that homosexuals were everywhere *in the government* and necessary to detect. And like the pre-World-War One chief of Austrian intelligence (a homosexual) that the Senate committee produced as its lone example—a man who gave secrets to (not incidentally in 1950) the Russians and even altered the texts of Austrian intelligence reports—these infiltrating homosexuals were black-mailable and unstable. As the report gratuitously (which is to say, from its perspective, approvingly) added, the Austrian homosexual, upon discovery of his "traitorous acts," committed suicide (*Employment of Homosexuals*, 5).

Detection, as historian John D'Emilio summarizes the Senate report "was not an easy task . . . , because too many [homosexuals] lacked the 'outward characteristics or physical traits that are positive as identifying marks of sex perversion.'"[57] Detection was nevertheless important because "[t]hese perverts will frequently attempt to entice normal individuals to engage in perverted practices. This is particularly true in the case of young and impressionable people who might come under the influence of a pervert" (*Employment of Homosexuals*, 4).

Beginning in the early 50s, then, and extending into the sixties, as Lee Edelman has brilliantly shown,[58] the United States experienced an explosion of discourse related to the visible signs and detection of homosexuality.[59] Throughout this period the discourses of detection remain similarly constituted: surveillance is concerned with detecting homosexuality through its visible signs on the body, with the "habits," "practices," "tendencies," and "aberrations" of the homosexual, and his/her "perversion" of the larger body politic, or of the fighting corps during and after the Second World War, as Alan Bérubé has documented. During this period, in the armed forces and in postwar civilian life, more and more citizens were subject to these forms of detection, which ranged from individual interrogations of recruits and troops in the armed forces, to the homosexual gag-reflex test developed by the Army, to Rorshach testing, to the other psychiatric tests for detection advocated by the Senate committee.[60] As D'Emilio has shown, the attempt to detect homosexuals (and, almost interchangeably, communists) "extended far beyond a search for those in the military and the federal bureacracy," to states, municipalities, private industries (46), and universities.[61]

You'll have detected already the tendency of my argument, so let me provide a caveat before I proceed. I don't mean to suggest that Hinman and other Shakespearean bibliographers believe(d) that sexual preferences or behaviors can be ascertained on the basis of spelling habits, or that Hinman and others intentionally applied this rhetoric, in their work, with the virulence intended by the Senate committee or by Hinman and Bowers's colleagues in the armed forces. On the other hand, I *do* mean to suggest that the language of mid-twentieth-century compositorial study, in its search for essences/identities that can be read out from spelling habits, behaviors, and practices, bears resemblance to and is startlingly contemporaneous with other twentieth-century attempts to detect identities—*sexual* identities—on the basis of visible physical signs and behaviors.

That this rhetoric would have been available to Hinman and Bowers and the other scholars, mostly Americans, working on compositor study in the 50s—through their experience in the wartime Navy, but also simply by reading the newspaper in the early 50s—I've already tried to suggest. Hinman, who was in Washington at the Folger Shakespeare Library working on folios at his collating machine (at least in 1952–53) lived in the midst of it. President Eisenhower strengthened Truman's "loyalty" program in April 1953 and for the first time explicitly prohibited the hiring and retention of federal employees engaged in "sexual perversion" (D'Emilio, 44). At the time of the Senate report in 1950, fifteen gay employees of the Library of Congress (across the street from the Folger) were under investigation for sex perversion—nine had resigned, one was dismissed, and five cases were "pending" (*Employment of Homosexuals*, Appendix III, 25).

Nor would a certain rhetoric of homosexuality have been foreign to the University of Virginia in the 50s, where Bowers was editing the volumes of *Studies in Bibliography* and their articles on compositor identification, but also working on an edition of a new cache of Whitman manuscripts—manuscripts of the poems that had become the "Calamus" section of *Leaves of Grass*. Bowers, for his part, displays a certain avoidance of the word "homosexual" throughout his first published essay on the manuscripts (in the 1954 volume of *Studies*),[62] almost as if he had searched-and-replaced the term *homosexual* with *calamus*, which appears throughout the essay in lower case without quotation marks:

> ...another spurt of poetic activity produced additional poems, many of these of a calamus nature .... (258)
> ...one of these [poems] is perhaps the most specifically calamus poem he wrote ...(259)
> ...even this frankly calamus poem ...(259)

When Bowers does finally use the much more frankly calamus term, the syntactic discomfort is striking: "In th[e]se manuscripts . . . , there is a small amount of homosexual references but no serious emphasis on it" (258). The troubled agreement of this sentence—what is the "it" that lacks serious emphasis but the apparently unmentionable entity *homosexuality*?—can suggest for us a larger problematic we have witnessed in the rhetoric of compositor study. For, like Hinman's index entry for Compositor E, Bowers's sentence seems lodged between a series of acts or behaviors in the text ("homosexual references") and an undefined entity or identity ("it") that, however unemphasized in the texts under analysis, seems to govern the rhetoric of his reading. The trajectory of Bowers's discussion of Whitman's "homosexual references," however confused, resembles that of the compositor's aberrations and perversions lying on the surface of Shakespeare's text.

For I do think, to return to Shakespeare, that nothing less than the security of the state of Shakespeare's text, or corpus, is at stake in the rhetorics of compositor analysis. Hinman stresses again and again that Shakespeare's text is only as reliable as the trustworthiness of the compositors who set it in type. In the same volume of *Studies* that included Bowers on Whitman, Walker writes,

> we are faced with the possibility that there may be at least two hundred errors in the Folio *Lear* and *Othello* for which compositor B was solely responsible. Must we assume that these two texts are pitted with holes and corrupted by interpolations and perversions of the wording?[63]

For Hinman, at least, the security of the Shakespearean text and national security during the Cold War years might have been even more firmly linked. Hinman had been a fellow at the Folger, beginning work on Shakespeare compositors, in 1941–42 (Tanselle, 33); after Pearl Harbor and for the duration of the war, the library (which sits two blocks from the U.S. Capitol) had moved 30,000 of its most valuable books to a secret location on the more remote Amherst College campus.[64] In the midst of collating the folios, Hinman himself writes in 1953 that the Shakespeare folios had been moved again, and the Cold War resonates in his language: "As a precaution against possible disaster, only about half of the irreplaceable Folger copies are being kept in the Library in Washington; but the other copies will be brought back for collation as soon as work has been completed on the copies now available."[65]

But let another bibliographer—for reasons that will become clear, I'll refer to him as Bibliographer B—speak about the more textual disasters threatening Shakespeare:

> type-setters played a role the importance of which can hardly be overemphasized .... Thus in a given text we may find what a printing house employee *thought* Shakespeare wrote, or what he thought Shakespeare *might* have written, or—more disastrous still—what a printing house employee thought Shakespeare *should* have written, rather than what he actually wrote.[66]

Like Hinman, Bibliographer B was a dissertation student of Bowers's, and he came back to the University of Virginia after a few years elsewhere to be Bowers's colleague. He published in *Studies* on compositor analysis in a number of Shakespeare plays, and, early one morning in March of 1955—and now I'm quoting from the local newspapers— Bibliographer B, "who was 37 and unmarried, shot himself in the right side of the head with a .22 calibre pistol."[67]

I don't know much else about Bibliographer B, but it's hard not to read the signs, bodily and other, proffered by the newspaper accounts of his death as anything but, say, "a small amount of homosexual references but no serious emphasis on it." There is the gratuitous linking of his age, his (un)marital status, and the shot, which, in the logic of the sentence seems almost consequential. There is the statement that

Bibliographer B "was known to be suffering from 'extreme worry and strain' . . . according to reliable sources."

What were B's habits and preferences, I find myself wondering. There's not much to go on. He habitually appears on time for his 9 o'clock class, or else an alarmed colleague wouldn't have come looking for him. His grooming habits are likewise impeccable: "At the time he was found [Bibliographer B] was cleanly shaven and dressed." (The suggestion that one might have expected to find him in another state seems only a further sign, an offering up of the worried and strained body to further view.)

I find myself examining the habits of his prose, in the lecture on compositor study I've already quoted. Does it matter, I wonder, that he explicitly avoids discussing compositor *identification* in this talk on compositor study? "I shall not discuss the methods by which compositors can be identified, but assuming that identification is possible, I should like to examine some of the implications . . . ."[68] Does it signify that, speaking as he is to the assembled members of the 1954 English Institute, on a panel with Bowers and Walker, with Hinman in the chair[69]—speaking, a few months before his death, of the potential disasters to be uncovered by compositor study—he avoids the rhetoric of detection, perversion, aberration, and irrationality, though he is attuned to "habits"?

I don't think it matters whether Bibliographer B was gay or not—although of course he lived in a context where it mattered immensely. Either way, there seem to be no more signs, but, when I go back to Hinman and find him looking at the infiltrated, compromised fortifications of the folios through his collating machine, counting aberrant spellings not of *xerxes* or *donjuan*, but of *traitor, young*, and *grief*—the spellings that, along with *do, go*, and *here*, he tracks to detect compositors throughout the book—it's hard not to see, through that apparatus, an identity for Bibliographer B.

4. THE RETURN OF THE RE-PRESSED

. . . it is of greatest concernment . . . to have a vigilant eye how Bookes demeane themselves as well as men; and thereafter to confine, imprison, and do sharpest justice on them as malefactors: For Books are not absolutely dead things, but doe contain a potencie of life in them to be as active as that soule was whose progeny they are; nay they do preserve as in a violl the purest efficacie and extraction of that living intellect that bred them.

—John Milton, *Areopagitica*[70]

Joseph Moxon's (1683) *Mechanick Exercises: Or, The Doctrine of handy-works. Applied to Printing* is the repository of much of what we think we know about seventeenth-century English printing, outside of printed books themselves. As the first extant guide to English printing-house practice, Moxon is the basis for some of Hinman's assumptions about the conduct of printing, press-speed, and the importance of nonstop work and efficient production—assumptions that themselves lead to the narratives we've seen on the alternation of different compositors. Moxon is also in part the basis for McKenzie's important critique of Hinman's postindustrial assumptions about efficiency and standardized production. Much of the discussion of Moxon[71] centers on how reliable he is as a factual guide to English printing-house practice, and to what degree a late-seventeenth-century account is a reliable guide to early seventeenth-century practice.

But the *Mechanick Exercises* for printing—part of a series of exercises that includes smithing, joining, carpentry—is more instrumental in its intentions and effects than this discussion allows for. Moxon's publications function as do-it-yourself guides to these various "arts"— in this case as a kind of self-interpellating manual for the production of printers. To set up a press, you learn these terms for the parts of the press; you set up the parts in this fashion; you move the parts in this way to produce print. This process in itself is highly self-reflective and -reflexive; as de Grazia has shown, the parts of the press in Moxon's description are anthropomorphic and reproductive: tongues, heads, bodies, cheeks, matrices, screws, etc.[72] Moxon's title, *Mechanick Exercises* is in this context ambiguous, for *mechanick* in this period can mean "manual" *or* "mechanical"[73]; and likewise, *exercises* might signify: exercises, in the pedagogical sense, for the reader to go through, to rehearse; practices; "habitual occupation or employment"; or even a "disciplinary suffering, 'trial'" (*OED*). Are *Mechanick Exercises* the exercises of the press, or of the person training him/herself to operate the press? Who or which is (the) mechanick? Who or what is being trained, disciplined in this applied art?

There is not space in this essay to produce a larger reading of Moxon as a cultural document, but I do want at least to suggest how we might use Moxon to move toward a more historically attuned notion of the compositor—as a pressing subject, rather than as the erratic, obstructionist individual of New Bibliographic accounts.

Moxon writes of the compositor's duties as a kind of negotiation, with the compositor not as an intruding perverter in the ideally unmediated transmission of the text, but as a kind of useful double agent negotiating among others:

A good *Compositer* . . . reads his *Copy* with consideration; . . . and consequently considers how to order his Work the better . . . As how to make his *Indenting, Pointing, Breaking, Italicking, &c.* the better sympathize with the *Authors* Genius, and also with the capacity of the Reader. (2: 220)[74]

The good compositor orients himself in two directions, toward the author and toward the reader, and lest we too quickly assume, as in modernity, that only authors have genius, we should note that "*a good natural Genius*" is one of the attributes Moxon desires too in his compositor (2: 197).

But if the compositor is a negotiating agent, there are also ways in which the printing house and the press train, discipline, *produce* the compositor, as in Moxon's description of the disciplining of a printing-house employee who fails to pay fines levied for in-house infractions:

The Workmen take him by force, and lay him on his Belly athwart the *Correcting-stone*, and held him there while another of the Work-men, with a Paper-board, gave him 10 *l. and a Purse,* viz. Eleven blows on his Buttocks; which he laid on according to his own mercy. For Tradition tells us, that about 50 years ago one was *Solaced* [the term used for this punishment] with so much violence, that he presently Pissed Blood, and shortly after dyed of it. (2: 357–58)

Lain athwart the "Correcting stone" like a page to be proof-read, or a forme filled with type, disciplined too with the textuality of a "Paperboard"—the composer of text has become text, produced by, subject to, the press. It may be in this context that the impressionable Compositor E becomes, for us, if not for the New Bibliographers, the most likely model of the early modern compositor: impressionable, a man of wax, he has imitative tendencies, he follows copy closely.

You'll perhaps not be surprised that *beating* itself is a term in printing—it refers to the inking of the press. The press-man, in Moxon's words,

> keeps a constant and methodical posture and gesture in every action of *Pulling* and *Beating*, which in a train of Work becomes habitual to him, and eases his Body, by not running into unnecessary divertions of Postures or Gestures in his Labour. . . . And a *Pull* of the same strength upon the same *Form*, with the same *Beating*, and with the same *Blankets, &c.* will give the same Colour and Impression. (2: 334)

These are the mechanick exercises of the press-man. But is there any way to emerge—theoretically—from this constant shuttle of pressing subject and machine, mechanick and mechanical? I've spoken of interpellation, but the better term here—for Moxon's reader, the compositor, and the press-man alike—might be Bourdieu's concept of the *habitus*. Bourdieu defines *habitus* as

> systems of durable, transposable dispositions, structured structures predisposed as structuring structures, that is, as principles which generate and organize practices and representations that can be objectively adapted to their outcomes without predisposing a conscious aiming at ends. . . . [75]

Thinking more particularly about the compositor and his spellings, we might speak not of spelling habits but of spelling *habitus*:

> Because the *habitus* is an infinite capacity for generating products—thoughts, perceptions, expressions and actions—whose limits are set by the historically and socially situated conditions of its production, the conditioned and conditional freedom it provides is as remote from creation of unpredictable novelty as it is from simple mechanical reproduction of the original conditioning. (55)

Neither unpredictable novelty nor simple mechanical reproduction, the compositor's spelling, in these terms, becomes not a conduit of identity, but, again quoting Bourdieu, "a product of history, produc[ing] individual and collective practices—more history—in accordance with the schemes generated by history" (54). More particularly, we might define the spelling *habitus* as the collision of a number of dispositions (seen historically): public tastes and traditional practices; the availabilty of different traditions of spelling in different classes, regions, and dialects within and on the borders of English; the attempts at orthographical reform; and the exigencies of printing, spacing, and justification—the press training the compositor to spell, limiting the spellings possible.

Here's how Moxon describes the secret/inner life of the compositor:

> first [he] reads so much of his *Copy* as he thinks he can retain in his memory till he have *Composed* it. . . . And having read, he falls a Spelling in his mind; yet so, that his Thoughts run no faster than his Fingers: For as he spells A, he takes up A out of the A *Box*, as he names n in his thoughts, he takes up n out of the n *Box*, as he names d in his thoughts he takes up d out of the d *Box*; which three *Letters* set together make a Word, viz. And; so that after the d he sets a *Space*: Then he goes on to the next word, and so *Composes* on . . . . (2: 212–13)[76]

If Moxon in 1683 is some distance from the unfixed linguistic field of the earlier seventeenth century—he says the compositor should know "*the present traditional* Spelling *of all English Words*" (2: 197)—if, that is, spelling has become a process of "naming [letters] in his thoughts," of producing spellings, we should nevertheless notice that Moxon is at the same time not merely describing, but also working to *produce* such a system, to compose compositors for/in whom the production of spellings on this model will occur. Once you've gone through your Mechanick Exercises, is the "A *Box*" in the upper case, or in your mind?

Spelling, in 1683, may still be reading, and writing, from reading; the compositor "falls a Spelling in his mind": he writes, reading his mind, reading what's written in his mind, in the space(s) provided.

5. RECOMPOSING

I want, in concluding, to spell out some of what I think are the larger ramifications of a critique of compositor analysis.

If compositor analysis seems like an arcane subfield to those outside its discipline, I think it's important to note that it is part of a larger movement in twentieth-century treatments of Shakespearean and other early modern texts that insists upon a precise individuation of agents at every stage of textual production, in ways that are often strikingly anachronistic. In this way, compositor analysis closely parallels the work of scholars like Cyrus Hoy (and more recently Jonathan Hope) who have sought to discern and separate out of collaborative texts the individuated shares of particular playwrights—to separate, say, Shakespeare and Fletcher's words in *The Two Noble Kinsmen*—on the basis of "linguistic habits" or "preferences," the ostensible difference in usage of words like *'em* and *them*, *ye* and *you*.[77] (Like Hinman's work, Hoy's was also done under Bowers's supervision at the University of Virginia; Hoy's attention to "habits" and "preferences" is also a legacy of the 1950s, published between 1956–1962.) The most extreme version of this is the bibliographic treatment of a play like *Pericles*, where various related New Bibliographic methods have located two (or more) playwrights, two memorial reporters of the text, and *three* compositors (named x, y, and z, two of whom are said, in the still standard account, to be "immoral").[78] All of this individuated activity is isolated in order to explain the ostensible "badness" of a text that, as Barbara A. Mowat has recently shown, was in the early seventeenth century acted on tour from the text of the *same* printed book now so universally maligned in twentieth-century bibliography and criticism.[79]

Though space constraints have kept me from demonstrating in any particular Shakespearean instance how compositor study might affect, reform, or deform the folio text, I do at least want to suggest that the individuating energies of compositor analysis, as I have recently argued in the treatment of a supposed crux in *As You Like It*, are often marshalled to explain away, or edit out, an "error" or "easy misreading" that might, if undiagnosed, lead one to see, for example, two men holding hands in the last act of a Shakespearean comedy. If Compositor B, notorious and erratic, known for his perversions, can be said to have misread a pronoun in his manuscript, the text can be adjusted accordingly, and Shakespeare's hand—which is to say, in this case, a pair of "heterosexual" hands—can be restored. The compositor's skaiography ("his") can be replaced by Shakespeare's orthography ("hir"), and interpretation may proceed.[80]

Let me make it clear that, by offering a critique of compositor analysis, I do not seek to foreclose discussion of the labor of those engaged in producing books in early modern England. Notice though, how a historically inappropriate notion of solitary authorial genius can completely occlude what Moxon observes—as late as the end of the seventeenth century—about the function of compositors in (re)writing, (re)ordering, (re)emphasizing the text initiated by other hands. Why not produce a history of composition that is attuned to the labors of compositors in this way?—not as obstructing the ideally unmediated transmission of the authorial text, but as colaborers in the working(s), mediations, and transformations of textual production and reproduction. Mediation, after all, is what we have—all that we have.

"[T]hat some demonstrable features of Shakespeare's holographs may eventually be recovered from the prints is not entirely a dream," Bowers writes, examining Compositor E in the folio *Othello*,[81] and Walker articulates the extraordinary fantasy, even if under negation, of stripping away compositors' spellings and translating the folio texts of Shakespeare back into Shakespeare's own spellings ("Compositor Determination," 8). These authorial fantasies remain current, and current with literary and cultural critics as well; a recent book on the rise of an English national culture in the late sixteenth century, for example, modernizes spellings "[e]xcept when quoting from Spenser's verse, where archaism has authorial warrant."[82] But which archaisms, we can ask, even in Spenser, carry the warrant of authority, and which are the collective habits, or *habitus*, of the sixteenth century? What interpretive arrest is produced by this warrant? And when we recompose Shakespeare's spellings, will we have Shakespeare's spellings, or the spellings that spell Shakespeare?[83] As I hope I've begun to suggest, these are questions of more than merely philological interest.

NOTES

I am grateful to Andrew Parker and Jay Grossman, who contributed to early drafts, and to Thomas Berger, Christopher Cannon, John Guillory, Shannon Jackson, Meredith McGill, Barbara Mowat, Jeanne Addison Roberts, Marc Schachter, Susan Snyder, Susan Staves, and Peter Stallybrass for conversations and comments that contributed substantially to this paper and my understanding of issues involved in its writing.

1. Alice Walker, *Textual Problems of the First Folio: Richard III, King Lear, Troilus & Cressida, 2 Henry IV, Hamlet, Othello* (Cambridge: Cambridge University Press, 1953), p. 164, my emphasis.

2. James Gleick, "Crasswords" in *The New York Times Magazine* (April 16, 1995), p. 20, emphasis original.

3. Charlton Hinman, "Principles Governing the Use of Variant Spellings as Evidence of Alternate Setting by Two Compositors" in *The Library*, 4th ser., 21 (1940–41), pp. 78–94. References will appear parenthetically in the text.

4. As a verb, *spell* entered English in a highly generalized way, meaning "To discourse or preach; to talk, converse, or speak" (current to about 1450),and (transitively) "To utter, declare, relate, tell" (current to about 1509). The *Oxford English Dictionary* (2nd edition) is the source for cited definitions and examples unless otherwise noted.

5. Kenelm Digby, *Two Treatises in the one of which, The Natvre of Bodies; in the other, the Natvre of Mans Sovle . . .*, (Paris: by Gilles Blaizot, 1644), p. 172.

6. *Mr. William Shakespeares Comedies, Histories & Tragedies* (London: by Isaac Iaggard, and Ed. Blount, 1623), as reproduced in *The Norton Facsimile: The First Folio of Shakespeare*, prepared by Charlton Hinman (New York: Norton, 1968), sig. A3.

7. De Grazia, "Homonyms Before and After Lexical Standardization" in *Shakespeare Jahrbuch* (1990), pp. 143–56. See also Peter Stallybrass, "Shakespeare, the Individual, and the Text" in *Cultural Studies*, eds. Lawrence Grossberg, Cary Nelson, and Paula Treichler, with Linda Baughman, and with assistance from John Macgregor Wise (New York: Routledge, 1992), pp. 593–610.

8. I borrow the term from Pierre Bourdieu, while noting that his usage refers to a post-standardization linguistic situation; see, for example, "The Production and Reproduction of Legitimate Language" in his *Language and Symbolic Power*, ed. John B. Thompson, trans. Gino Raymond and Matthew Adamson (Cambridge: Harvard University Press, 1994), pp. 43–65. French has/had an earlier, more prescriptive, and more centrally institutionalized relation to its lexical standardization, with for example the formation of the *Academie Française* in 1634–35.

9. Juliet Fleming, "Dictionary English and the Female Tongue" in *Enclosure Acts: Sexuality, Property, and Culture in Early Modern England*, eds. Richard Burt and John Michael Archer (Ithaca: Cornell University Press, 1994), pp. 301–2.

10. The idea of an English grammar on the classical model is also (only) emergent in this period; see for example Jonson's attempt at an English grammar, in which orthography is extragrammatical: "*Prosodie*, and *Orthography*, are not parts of *Grammar*, but diffus'd, like the blood, and spirits through the whole"; *The English Grammar*, in *The Workes of Benjamin Jonson. The Second Volume* (London: for Richard Meighen, 1640), p. 35.

11. This list summarizes de Grazia, pp. 152–53; on dictionaries, see Fleming, "Dictionary English."

12. Thomas Smith, *De recta & emendata Lingvæ Anglicæ Scriptione, Dialogus . . .* (Paris: Robert Stevens, printer to the King, 1568), as reproduced in Latin facsimile, with an English translation, in *Sir Thomas Smith: Literary and Linguistic Works*, 3 parts, ed. Bror Danielsson, Part III (Stockholm: Almqvist & Wiksell, 1983); John Hart, *An orthographie, conteyning the due order howe to write thimage of mannes voice* (London: by William Seres, 1569); *Bullokars Booke at large, for the Amendment of Orthographie for English speech . . .* (London: by Henrie Denham, 1580).

13. Jonathan Goldberg, *Writing Matter: From the Hands of the English Renaissance* (Stanford: Stanford University Press, 1989), pp. 192–93, 196–97, and 205–6.

14. Henry George Liddell and Robert Scott, et al., compilers, *A Greek-English Lexicon*, 9th ed., (Oxford: Clarendon, 1968), pp. 1248–49.

15. Alexander Hume, "*To the maest ecellent in all princelie wisdom, learning, and heroical artes, JAMES . . . ,*" the dedication to his *Of the Orthographie of the Britan Tongue; A Treates, Noe Shorter Then Necessarie, for the Schooles*, ed. Henry B. Wheatley (London: Truebner & Co, for The Early English Text Society, 1865), p. 2.

16. Hume, editor's errata sheet inserted after 3.

17. *Oxford Latin Dictionary*, ed. P. G. W. Glase (Oxford: Clarendon, 1982), p. 1698.

18. "Yes yes," the Page (Moth) says about him, "he teaches boyes the Horne-booke: / What is A b speld backward with the horn on his head?" (*Loues Labour's lost*, TLN 1785–86, as reproduced in *The Norton Facsimile* [cited above]). My reading of this passage as sodomitical and cuckholding follows Patricia Parker's "Preposterous Reversals: *Love's Labor's Lost*," *Modern Language Quarterly* 54.5 (1993), pp. 461–465.

19. Phil. Massinger, Tho. Middleton, and William Rowley, *The Excellent Comedy, called The Old Law: Or A new way to please you* (London: for Edward Archer, 1656), p. 29. The play may also be referring to the *English Expositor* (1616), a hard-word list by Bullokar's son John.

20. *Much Adoe about Nothing*, TLN 851–55, as reproduced in *The Norton Facsimile*. Actually, the folio text reads "turu'd ortho-graphy," and I have myself "righted" the writing here, effacing what is possibly a compositor error (the turning of the letter "n") or a compositor's joke (to turn a letter in *turn*, especially when it is followed immediately by *orthography* seems particularly overdetermined). As I hint above, the word *turn* turns up with some regularity in discussions of orthography; Benedick's "conuerted" is itself an etymological relative of *turn*.

21. Cf. *Much Adoe*: "I neuer yet saw man, / How wise, how noble, yong, how rarely featur'd. / But she would *spell him backward* . . . / *So turnes* she euery man the wrong side out . . ." (TLN 1149–58, my emphasis).

22. On French lessons, see Juliet Fleming, "The French Garden: An Introduction to Women's French" in *ELH* 56 (1989), pp. 19–51. On sex/gender and scenes of early modern (Latin) pedagogy, see Elizabeth Pittenger, "Dispatch Quickly: The Mechanical Reproduction of Pages" in *Shakespeare Quarterly* 42 (1991), pp. 389–408, and "'To Serve the Queere': Nicholas Udall, Master of Revels" in *Queering the Renaissance*, ed. Jonathan Goldberg (Durham: Duke University Press, 1994), pp. 163–189.

23. Goldberg notes that a number of pedagogical writers resist sixteenth-century spelling reform, e.g. Richard Mulcaster (*Writing Matter*, pp. 195–97). Shakespeare is perhaps among the resistant—though, by citing plays mentioned above as early examples of *spell* in the modern sense, the *OED* implies that he invents or is at least coincident with the emergence of modern spelling.

24. Read a few lines of Bullokar's orthography and you may well find it strange and fantasticall; the "foreigness" effect might have been redoubled for an early modern reader,

since not only the peculiar forms of words, but the fact that the words *have* set forms, might have signalled its foreignness, its likeness to Latin and Greek.

25. Richard Mvlcaster, *The First Part of the Elementarie VVhich Entreateth Chefelie of the right writing of our English tung* (London: by Thomas Vautroullier, 1582), p. 100.

26. Goldberg, *Writing Matter*, chapter 4, passim.

27. *Bullokars Booke at large*, sig. B1, my emphasis.

28. Stallybrass, "Shakespeare, the Individual, and the Text."

29. *The Autobiography of Thomas Whythorne*, ed. James M. Osborn, old-spelling edition (Oxford: Clarendon, 1961), pp. lvii, lxvi. For Bullokar and others, the production of orthographical consent/consensus is linked to forms of political organization; his is a nationalist project (as his prefatory address "Bullokar to his Countrie" suggests), and he says his reform of consenting sound and writing is for the benefit of rich and poor within a nation containing "In one houshold (of diuers sorts) ech one in his degrée" (C2). Likewise, Spenser, in a question quoted repeatedly and with apparent approval in Richard Helgerson's recent book on the rise of a national culture in late sixteenth-century England, asks: "Why a God's name may not we, as else the Greeks, have the kingdom of our own language?" (quoted in *Forms of Nationhood: The Elizabethan Writing of England* [Chicago: University of Chicago Press, 1992], p. 1). The rhetoric of nationalism and right-ness that inheres in the debate between a phonetic spelling practice and "our customarie writing" is not incidental to the larger concerns of this paper over individual spelling practice. This debate may suggest that spelling practice itself (on whichever side of the debate) adheres with a model of period subjectivity articulated by Francis Barker as the location of the early modern subject within the larger spectacle of royal power (*The Tremulous Private Body: Essays on Subjection* [London: Methuen, 1984], pp. 14–41). Or, adjusting the model here, within the larger system of either a phonetic orthography or "our customarie writing"—the kingdom, either way, of "our own language." Within the larger frame of subjection to either model of linguistic practice, there is no attention to the questions that loom large for a modern spelling investigator like Hinman: individualized spelling practices, spelling choice, and preference.

30. *Bullokars Booke at large*, sig. D1.

31. Elizabeth Eisenstein, *The Printing Press as an Agent of Change: Communications and Cultural Transformations in Early-Modern Europe*, 2 vols. (Cambridge: Cambridge University Press, 1979), vol. 1, p. 117.

32. D. G. Scragg, *A History of English Spelling* (Manchester: Manchester University Press; New York: Barnes and Noble, 1974), p. 71.

33. Alfred W. Pollard, "Elizabethan Spelling as a Literary and Bibliographical Clue" in *The Library*, 4th ser., 4.1 (1923), p. 6, my emphasis.

34. Randall McLeod has also shown that spellings are made to vary to avoid the breakage of certain kinds of types; see "Spell-bound" in *Play-Texts in Old Spelling: Papers*

from the Glendon Conference, ed. G. B. Shand, with Raymond C. Shady (New York: AMS, 1984), pp. 81–96.

35. The relatively unstructured linguisitic field I have been describing had changed significantly by the time Richard Hodges published, in 1643, his book *A Special Help to Orthographie: Or, The True-writing of English. Consisting of such Words as are alike in sound, and unlike both in their signification and Writing: As also, of such Words which are so neer alike in sound, that they are sometimes taken one for another* (London: for Richard Cotes, 1643). This is the advent of spelling standardization, and something different from spelling reform, for Hodges assumes that there are now already correct spellings (not mimetically related to sound) that need to be inculcated. For Hodges, unlike for many of his fellow literate English subjects of the preceding century, *assent* cannot be *ascent* or "A *sent* or savour" (1). At the same time, this book registers the possibility that, as late as 1643, there are (else what market for this book?) those who could still (as we would say) "confuse" these (as we would say) "discrete" "words."

36. *The Tragedie of Hamlet* (1623 folio version, as reproduced in *The Norton Facsimile,* TLN, 4–7).

37. Charlton Hinman, *The Printing and Proofreading of the First Folio of Shakespeare,* 2 vols. (Oxford: Clarendon, 1963); citations will appear parenthetically as *PPFFS* in the text.

38. At the end of his project, Hinman tries to assign actual persons' names to compositors; see final note below.

39. D. F. McKenzie, "Stretching a Point: Or, The Case of the Spaced-out Comps" in *Studies in Bibliography* 37 (1984), pp. 106–21. There have been several important critiques of compositor analysis. McKenzie's earlier work has shown with devastating logic that Hinman's work is based on erroneous assumptions about attitudes toward labor and efficiency in the printing house ("Printers of the Mind: Some Notes on Bibliographical Theories and Printing-House Practices" in *Studies in Bibliography* 22 [1969], pp. 1–75). Peter W. M. Blayney has demonstrated that the analysis of the production of any one book requires the analysis not only of other books produced contemporaneously in the printer's shop but also of *all* books produced by other shops with which the particular printer may have shared work (*The Texts of King Lear and Their Origins, Vol. 1: Nicholas Okes and the First Quarto* [Cambridge: Cambridge University Press, 1982]). These are important critiques of bibliographic assumptions and the logic of bibliographic methods; their importance lies in revising our notions of printing house "efficiency," the fallacy of systematic/normal procedures and, as de Grazia has recently shown, our notion of jobs, labor, and wages in the preindustrial workshop ("Soliloquies and Wages in the Age of Emergent Consciousness" in *Textual Practice* 9.1 [1995], pp. 67–92.). Though enabled by and largely congruent with this work, this essay attempts a different kind of critique.

40. Or to be more faithful to the metaphors of the field: "to recover from behind the veil of compositor's spellings . . . a clearer impression of the manuscript, or other [printer's] copy, with a view to elucidating textual problems." Alice Walker,

"Compositor Determination and other Problems in Shakesperian Texts" in *Studies in Bibliography* 7 (1955), p. 9; references will appear parenthetically in the text.

41. Alice Walker, "The Folio Text of *1 Henry IV*" in *Studies in Bibliography* 6 (1954), p. 53.

42. Gary Taylor, "The Shrinking Compositor A of the Shakespeare First Folio" in *Studies in Bibliography* 34 (1981), p. 112.

43. See for example Harold Jenkins's Arden edition of *Hamlet* (London: Methuen, 1982), p. 54.

44. Philip Gaskell, *A New Introduction to Bibliography* (Oxford: Clarendon, 1972), p. 348.

45. In a way to which I'll return, I'm alluding to a well-known sentence of Foucault's; see *The History of Sexuality, Volume I: An Introduction*, trans. Robert Hurley (New York: Vintage, 1978), p. 43.

46. Fredson Bowers, *Bibliography and Textual Criticism* (Oxford: Oxford University Press, 1959), p. 34.

47. Hill, "New Light on Compositor E of the Shakespeare First Folio" in *The Library*, 6th ser., 2.2 (1980), p. 178.

48. Andrew S. Cairncross, "Compositors E and F of the Shakespeare First Folio" in *Papers of the Bibliographical Society of America* 66 (1972), pp. 395–96.

49. In a reconsideration of Hinman's and Walker's work on Compositor B, Paul Werstine confronts this problem: "perhaps an editor must conclude that compositor variability is so high, as Compositor B's is between the comedies and *1H4*, that compositor identification is a useless tool"; "Compositor B of the Shakespeare First Folio" in *Analytical and Enumerative Bibliography* 2.4 (1978), p. 260.

50. If variability can produce E's potential ubiquity, it may also produce, within this paradigm of individuation, the multiplication of discrete individuals. As Taylor puts it, "if C changed this habit between *King John* and *1 Henry IV*, then the later C might as well be another man" ("Shrinking," 110). This is a larger problematic for the methodology, for, if habits disclose individuals, what if the habit is only a phase? In the fifty years since Hinman set to work, the history of compositor study (with the possible exception of the treatment of Compositor E) has often favored reading the discovery of changed habits as evidence of new individuals, rather than variable old ones: where in the beginning, there were only A and B, Hinman found C, D, and E. Howard Hill discovered F, and Taylor more recently located H, I, and J. On this, see Blayney, who notes that Hinman's method was originally introduced to differentiate only two (*not* "more than one") compositors (*Texts of King Lear*, p. 152). See also McKenzie's comments on the dangers of "division as a function of analysis" ("Stretching," pp. 116–17). In the 1940–41 essay, Hinman emphasizes that spelling study must rely upon variations, discard evidence of continuities among parts of texts (he labels this evidence "non-significant spellings"), and continue to search for more evidence that will support the discovery of difference.

51. T.H. Hill, "Spelling and the Bibliographer" in *The Library*, 5th ser., 18.1 (1963), pp. 1–28. The quotation appears on p. 3.

52. Quoted at p. 151 in Lee Edelman, "Tearooms and Sympathy; or, The Epistemology of the Water Closet," in *Homographesis: Essays in Gay Literary and Cultural Theory* (New York: Routledge, 1994), pp. 148–70.

53. Thomas Satchell, "The Spelling of the First Folio," letter in *Times Literary Supplement*, (June 3, 1920), p. 352; Ronald B. McKerrow, *An Introduction to Bibliography for Literary Students* (Oxford: Clarendon, 1927); Edwin Eliott Willoughby, *The Printing of the First Folio of Shakespeare* (Oxford: Oxford University Press for the Bibliographical Society, 1932).

54. G. Thomas Tanselle, "The Life and Work of Fredson Bowers" in *Studies in Bibliography* 46 (1993), p. 32; subsequent references will appear parenthetically in the text.

55. Hinman was Bowers's first doctoral student, completing his degree in 1941 (Tanselle, 72).

56. *Employment of Homosexuals and Other Sex Perverts in Government*, Interim Report submitted to the Committee on Expenditures in the Executive Departments by its Subcommittee on Investigations, 81st Congress, 2nd Session, Senate document 241 (Washington: U. S. Government Printing Office, 1950), gathered in *Senate Miscellaneous Documents*, vol. 11401. Subsequent references will appear parenthetically in the text.

57. John D'Emilio, *Sexual Politics, Sexual Communities: The Making of a Homosexual Minority in the United States 1940–1970* (Chicago: University of Chicago Press, 1983) p. 43; references will appear parenthetically in the text.

58. Edelman, "Tearooms and Sympathy," cited above.

59. If the virulence of this surveillance did not directly derive from the military's similar surveying of troop and recruit sexual practices and identities during the Second World War, the discourse would nevertheless have been familiar to those in the armed services. See Alan Bérubé, *Coming Out Under Fire: The History of Gay Men and Women in World War Two* (New York: Penguin, 1990).

60. In general, see Bérubé, pp. 149–74, especially 152-53; also *Employment of Homosexuals*, p. 12.

61. These sentences cite what were, of course, only the most *explicit* forms of surveillance. On the question of universities, see Robert K. Martin's discussion of the investigation (1953) and dismissal (1960) of Newton Arvin at Smith College ("Happy Days? Whitman in the 1950s," delivered at MLA, 1993), and Jay Grossman's contextualization of F. O. Matthiessen's death at Harvard in 1950 in a forthcoming essay, "The Canon in the Closet." On the links between communism and homosexuality, see David Savran, *Communists, Cowboys, and Queers: The Politics of Masculinity in the Work of Arthur Miller and Tennessee Williams* (Minneapolis: University of Minnesota Press, 1992), especially pp. 1–9; *Secret Agents: The Rosenberg Case, McCarthyism, and Fifties America*, eds. Marjorie Garber and Rebecca L. Walkowitz (New York: Routledge, 1995).

62. Fredson Bowers, "Whitman's Manuscripts for the Original 'Calamus' Poems" in *Studies in Bibliography* 6 (1954), pp. 257–265. Citations appear parenthetically in the text.

63. Walker, "Folio Text of *1 Henry IV*," p. 58.

64. Stanley King, *Recollections of The Folger Shakespeare Library* (Ithaca: Cornell University Press for the Trustees of Amherst College, 1950). The 30,000 volumes were stored secretly at Amherst from January, 15, 1942, through November 11, 1944.

65. Charlton Hinman, "The Proof-Reading of the First Folio Text of Romeo and Juliet" in *Studies in Bibliography* 6 (1954), p. 61n1. Hinman dates this footnote April 1953, and the Korean War may have been the specific impetus for concern, though thus far I haven't been able to ascertain when or where the books were moved. I'm indebted to Elizabeth Walsh and her staff at the Folger for assistance in attempting to track the moving books.

66. On the citation of this essay, see note 68 below.

67. My argument follows the account published in the university newspaper; this account was reprinted almost verbatim in the Charlottesville and Richmond newspapers. I am grateful to Eric Wilson and Steve Wilson for assistance in locating these accounts.

68. Readers of this essay will here expect, but will not find, a note citing Bibliographer B's essay, but the perceived necessity of a citation for this text and of the newspaper account of Bibliographer B's death quoted above must be seen within a larger set of citational imperatives: the competing demands of intellectual property (Bibliographer B's), scholarly accountability (mine), and the closet (his?). I have chosen not to cite B's text because to do so would have the effect of disclosing a homosexuality that I do not know he lived or identified with, and would provide too easily an answer to more complicated questions I hope this essay asks: what would it mean to "know" that Bibliographer B was gay? what would constitute knowledge of this fact—especially, but not only, in the 1950s U. S. context? To pursue such knowledge, furthermore, is to participate, however sympathetically, in the activities and discourses of detection/scandal we are analyzing. This is perhaps the place to record the larger debt of this section to the work of D. A. Miller, in particular *Bringing Out Roland Barthes* (Berkeley: University of California Press, 1992).

69. "A Classified List of Topics, Chairmen, and Speakers, 1939–1963," The English Institute, memorandum [1963?], p. 3. Walker's paper was apparently read in absentia.

70. *Areopagitica; A Speech of Mr. John Milton For the Liberty of Vnlicenc'd Printing, To the Parlament of England* (London: 1644), p. 4.

71. The exception is Margreta de Grazia's essay on the reproductive discourses of the press and imprinting in Moxon and more generally in the seventeenth century, "Imprints: Descartes, Shakespeare, and Gutenberg," forthcoming in *Alternative Shakespeares*, 2nd edition, ed. Terence Hawkes.

72. de Grazia, "Imprints."

73. My paraphrases of *OED* definitions 1 and 4–5.

74. Joseph Moxon, *Mechanick Exercises: Or, the Doctrine of handy-works. Applied to the Art of Printing*, The Second Volumne [of the *Exercises*], (London: Printed for Joseph Moxon, 1683). References will appear parenthetically in the text.

75. Pierre Bourdieu, *The Logic of Practice*, trans. Richard Nice (Stanford: Stanford University Press, 1990), p. 53. Subsequent references will appear parenthetically in the text.

76. The mechanick exercises of the compositor ("his Thoughts run no faster than his Fingers") resemble, rather than distinguish themselves from, the mechanicks of authorship; "His mind and hand went together," the actors write of another compositional process, Shakespeare's ("To the great Variety of Readers," as reproduced in *The Norton Facsimile*, sig. A3).

77. Cyrus Hoy, "The Shares of Fletcher and his Collaborators in the Beaumont and Fletcher Canon (I)" in *Studies in Bibliography* 8 (1956), pp. 129–46; Hoy, "The Shares of Fletcher and his Collaborators in the Beaumont and Fletcher Canon (III)" in *Studies in Bibliography* 11 (1958), pp. 85–106; Jonathan Hope, *The authorship of Shakespeare's plays: A Socio-Linguistic Study* (Cambridge: Cambridge University Press, 1994). For a critique of this method, see Jeffrey Masten, "Beaumont and/or Fletcher: Collaboration and the Interpretation of Renaissance Drama" in *ELH* 59 (1992), pp. 337–56.

78. Philip Edwards, "An Approach to the Problem of *Pericles*" in *Shakespeare Survey* 5 (1952), pp. 25–49; "immoral" appears at pp. 31 and 32.

79. Barbara A. Mowat, "Theatre and Literary Culture" in *A New History of Early English Drama*, eds. John D. Cox and David Scott Kastan (New York: Columbia University Press, forthcoming, 1997).

80. See Jeffrey Masten, "Textual Deviance: Ganymede's Hand in *As You Like It*" in *Field Work: Sites in Literary and Cultural Studies*, eds. Marjorie Garber, Paul B. Franklin, and Rebecca Walkowitz (New York: Routledge, 1996), pp. 153–163.

81. Fredson Bowers, "The Folio *Othello*: Compositor E," lecture delivered 1959, published 1964, and reprinted, pp. 326–58 in Bowers, *Essays in Bibliography, Text, and Editing* (Charlottesville: University Press of Virginia, for the Bibliographical Society, 1975) p. 357.

82. Richard Helgerson, "Note on the Text," *Forms of Nationhood*, p. xi.

83. Hinman, for his part, tries to close this potentially disastrous loop by appealing to apparent coincidence. Reading a list of employees of the print shop where the folios were produced, he notices that "one John Shakespeare, son of a Warwickshire butcher, was bound apprentice to William Jaggard. . . . and took up his freedom . . . in May, 1617" (*PPFFS*, 2: 513). "It is pleasant to wonder," he writes, near the end of his study, "if the man who set more than half of the Folio into type (and who also took many liberties with its text)—to wonder if Compositor B was by any chance this same John Shakespeare" (2: 513). The name seems hopefully to guarantee, within the family, a textual fidelity the rest of Hinman's project has undermined.

4

VINAY DHARWADKER

PRINT

CULTURE

AND

LITERARY

MARKETS IN

COLONIAL

INDIA

I. PRINT CULTURE AND EARLY MODERN INDIA

THE FIRST PRINTING press arrived in India from Lisbon in the summer of 1556, with a group of Jesuits who set it up at their College of Saint Paul in Goa, the principal Portuguese colony on the western coast of the peninsula. For the next 250 years Catholic and Protestant missions from Europe, working along the margins of the mainland, dominated the technology of the printed book on the subcontinent. By 1578 the Jesuits had installed a press at Quilon, on the Malabar coast; between 1706 and 1715 the Danish Lutheran Mission, in conjunction with the Society for the Promotion of Christian Knowledge, established a press, a type foundry, and a paper mill at Tranquebar, near Madras; and in the following decade the Dutch East India Company and the mission of the Dutch Reformed Church jointly set up the Hollander Press in Colombo, Sri Lanka. Although the spread and growth of printing was sporadic for many decades, by the end of the eighteenth century—around the time that "a well-developed print society" emerged in England—the map of the subcontinent was dotted with about forty printing presses in a dozen towns and cities.[1]

Throughout this period, the publication of Christian and secular works in India was intricately woven into the fabric of capital, technological innovation, religious institutions, and cultural production stretching across the metropolitan centers of Europe. The first book containing texts in Indian languages—Thamiz and Tamil, printed in Roman characters—appeared in Lisbon in 1554, while the first with Malayalam in Roman characters was published in Amsterdam in 1678. The first two books containing the Devanagari script—used to transcribe Sanskrit, Hindi, Marathi, Dogri, and Nepali—appeared in Europe in 1743 and 1771, respectively, and the first book composed entirely in the Malayalam language and printed in the Malayalam script was manufactured in Rome in 1772.[2] In the seventeenth and eighteenth centuries European designers, craftsmen, and metallurgists working in Europe and India experimented with wood, metal, and stone, attempting to invent a technology adequate to the complexities of Indian alphabetical script systems in the new age of mechanical reproduction. Foundries in Amsterdam, Halle (near Leipzig in Germany), Rome, and London punched or cast the first metal types for several Indian scripts used in Europe, and also supplied the types used for printing European as well as Indian languages in India. Most of the paper for the early imprints on the subcontinent was produced by European paper mills, but some of it also came from China since Quilon, among various cities on the Malabar and Coromandel coasts, was a major port of call on the old Chinese sea route for trade with the Arabs.[3] The developments that linked the Indian languages to print culture thus were not confined to the subcontinent, and the developments within India were connected intimately to those in Europe and Asia. As I have suggested elsewhere, although the movement and interdependence of capital, technology, and resources have become more complicated since the end of the eighteenth century, Indian print culture, taken in all its aspects and relations, remains as multilingual, crosscultural, and transnational an enterprise in the past two hundred years as it was in its first two and a half centuries.[4]

The English began trading with India late in the reign of Elizabeth I, shortly after a group of investors formed the East India Company in London on the last day of the sixteenth century. In the military, diplomatic, and commercial war for the colonization of India, they won finally against the Portuguese, the Dutch, and the French, but came surprisingly late to the battle for the control of print culture on the subcontinent, establishing their first press—which they confiscated from the French as war booty—in Madras only in 1761.[5] When the East India Company acquired the right to collect the revenue of Bengal in 1757, its charter prohibited Christian missionaries from operating in its territories, for fear that their evangelical, educational, and publishing activities might incite Indians to revolt against religious conversion and foreign rule which would, in Gauri Vishwanathan's words, "cause trouble for England's commercial ventures."[6] The initial government monopoly on print in British India ended within a couple of decades, however, when in 1777 James Hicky, an irrepressible English entrepreneur, set up a press in Calcutta and started his *Bengal Gazette*, the first newspaper to be published in any language on the subcontinent. In the next thirty years print culture mushroomed in British India, with three kinds of participants, other than the colonial government, entering the economy: private English and European printers, with about twenty-five presses in and around Calcutta by the end of the eighteenth century; English missionaries, operating out of European missions technically outside English territory, protected by Indian princes and European governments and trading companies; and private Indian printers and publishers, the first of whom set up his press in Calcutta in 1807.[7]

In 1800 two momentous cultural interventions changed this situation, transforming not only India but also other parts of Asia and altering Europe's self-understanding as well as its understanding of the East. One was Lord Wellesley's establishment, in April 1800, of Fort William College in what is now southern Calcutta, for the professional education of the company's officials, including their training in Indian languages. The college created the first professors of Arabic, Persian, Sanskrit, Bengali, Hindi-Urdu, Marathi, and other languages, and a curriculum in the literatures, histories, and cultures of a dozen major regions of India, a full twenty-eight years before an English university created the first professor of English language and literature. The college press published some of the first introductory and advanced textbooks, grammars, and dictionaries in Arabic, Bengali, Burmese, Chinese, Hindustani [Hindi–Urdu], Kannada, Marathi, Oriya, Punjabi, Persian, Sanskrit, and Telugu.[8] Although it was clearly a colonialist enterprise, Fort William College remains a remarkable institution in the history of empire because of its contrast to colonial practices elsewhere: as late as 1812, for example, the Portuguese concluded a Holy Inquisition in Goa, and Bishop Manuel de San Godinho prohibited Goanese children from speaking Konkani in schools.[9]

The other memorable cultural intervention of the time was the Serampore Mission Press, funded by Baptist churches and founded in January 1800 in Serampore (Srirampur, north of Calcutta), under the protection of the Danish mission in a politically independent pocket within British India. Over the first two decades of the nineteenth century, the mission became the site for the largest and most specialized press and type foundry in Asia. Between 1800 and 1840 it printed 212,000 items in forty languages, including books in thirty Indian languages and dialects, as well as books in Arabic, Armenian, Burmese, Chinese, Javanese, Malay, Maldivian, Persian, Singapuri, and Thai.[10] Its foundry was run by Panchanan Karmakar, a Maratha immigrant in Bengal, and his son-in-law Manohar, both of whom were Hindu metalsmiths by birth. Panchanan had been trained at the company's press at Hooghly by Charles Wilkins—metallurgist, engraver, founder, printer, pioneering English translator of the Sanskrit *Bhagavad-gita* (1785), and great-nephew of gem engraver Robert Bateman Wray—for whom he had cut the first complete fount of Bengali, with 600 characters, and the first Devanagari type in India. Panchanan and Manohar cut and cast founts for Indian and foreign languages for use at the Serampore Mission Press, as well as for sale to other presses in India and various parts of Asia.[11] The press, managed by Joshua Marshman and William Ward, was led intellectually by William Carey, a Baptist minister who is now criticized for his residual Orientalism, Eurocentrism, and even racism, but who served as professor of Sanskrit, Persian, Bengali, and Marathi at Fort William College, learned fifteen Indian languages, and with several collaborators translated directly from Greek and Latin into twenty-nine Asian languages. In the course of its existence the Serampore press published the Bible in forty-five languages in all; translations into thirty-eight of these languages were produced by scholars working in Serampore and Calcutta.[12] In retrospect, the Calcutta region, as it must have been between about 1760 and 1830, seems to be the single most important site in the histories of Indo-European and general linguistics; of the translation of Asian languages from the media of voice, palm-leaf, and scroll to the medium of print; and of the mediated transposition of print culture from Europe to Asia.

2. THE EFFECTS OF PRINT
ON NINETEENTH-CENTURY INDIA
(A) THE BIRTH OF MODERN PROSE
AND THE COLONIAL SUBJECT

The multifarious culture of the print-medium that came into existence on the subcontinent by the beginning of the nineteenth century
was a historical phenomenon unprecedented on a global scale. It was
the first fully formed print culture to appear outside Europe and North
America, and it was distinguished by its size, productivity, and multilingual and multinational constitution, as well as its large array of Asian
languages and its inclusion of numerous non-Western investors and
producers among its active participants.[13] In the course of the century,
this culture radically transformed society in and around British India
with a chain-reaction of unpredictable causes and effects.

One of the most far-reaching effects of print between about 1800
and 1835 was the more or less simultaneous invention of modern prose
in various languages, including Bengali, Hindi, Marathi, Tamil, Telugu,
and Urdu. Some of these had older indigenous traditions of prose writing that went back several centuries and were connected in different ways
to canonical prose in Sanskrit, Arabic, and Persian. Nonetheless, all these
languages discovered an unexpected potential for innovation and reno-
vation in the medium of print, and shifted quite dramatically to new
lexicons and grammars, new principles of punctuation and syntax, new
discursive forms and styles, and even an "unlimited range" of new subject matters and fields of application. Like the formation of the subcontinent's print culture as a whole, the invention of modern Indian prose was
a multilateral, cross-cultural, and interdisciplinary enterprise, in which
Europeans and Indians worked independently and together in response
to the "new set of intellectual, social, and economic requirements" that
the medium of print had imposed on writing and cultural production.[14]

The interpenetration of print and prose, in turn, had immediate and
powerful consequences of its own. As Sisir Kumar Das has demonstrated
in detail, several Indian languages passed rapidly through three distinct
phases of development at this time, creating a broad historical and cultural paradigm for the other languages for the next one hundred years or
so. The first phase involved the "production of pedagogic materials" in
printed prose form, which provided a new material and textual basis for

the education of Indians in their own mother tongues. In the second phase, usually beginning a few years later, the publication of "religious tracts and works on social problems" in Indian-language prose stimulated a widespread debate among Indians about reforms in their society. The third phase, often overlapping with the second, focused on the establishment of print journalism in the Indian languages, with newspapers and news and entertainment magazines emerging as its principal forms.[15] By about 1835 the evolving multiplex of writing, print, prose, journalism, education, and social and religious reform had become the locus of a long revolution in everyday Indian life, one which occurred, as Partha Chatterjee notes, "*outside* the purview of the [colonial] state and the European missionaries."[16] One particular intersection of modes, mediums, and domains of representation within this metamorphosing multiplex had irreversible consequences for the life of the empire on the subcontinent. This intersection metaphorically defined the space in which writing, print, and education converged to constitute the Indian colonial subject.

Despite intense discussion in recent years, theories of subject formation, colonialism, and culture still do not explain adequately the historical features and cultural complexities of the process at work in British India. Gayatri Spivak's treatment of colonialism, for example, as Henry Louis Gates observes, suggests that "there is nothing outside (the discourse of) colonialism" and, in an even stronger form, that "all discourse is colonial discourse." Such a perspective implies that the Indian colonial subject constituted on the ground of print would reproduce the autonomous, rational subject of the European Enlightenment, or what Spivak herself calls "the subject of the West, or the West as Subject." In fact, her argument goes so far as to claim that the Indian subaltern subject, especially the gendered subaltern, does not and cannot exist in discourse, and hence cannot "speak."[17] Along a different line of reasoning, Benedict Anderson's account of nationalism implies that the Indian colonial subject constituted on the ground of print would tend to mimic the characteristics of the subject of print capitalism and romantic nationalism in modern Europe. In this perspective, anticolonial nationalisms in the non-Western world seem to be belated afterimages of European imperialistic nationalisms that give rise only to a "derivative discourse" of postcolonial nationhood. Or, as Partha Chatterjee puts it, "nationalisms in the rest of the world have to choose their imagined community from certain 'modular' forms already made available to them by Europe and the Americas."[18]

Such arguments have to assume, at least tacitly, that print is controlled completely by its origins, transcends the specificity of cultural (re)location and historical (dis)articulation, and therefore homogenizes all the objects it encounters. What is missing from theories that "play up," in Gates' phrase, "the absolute nature of colonial domination"—thereby "negating the subjectivity and agency of the colonized"—is the crucial fact that the print culture that emerged on the subcontinent by the beginning of the nineteenth century was a hybrid, multicultural formation actively involving a large population of Indian investors, producers, distributors, and consumers.[19] The ineluctable and uncontainable hybridity of this print culture, without precedent in the West or elsewhere, ensured that it did not and could not replicate in India the conditions, processes, and outcomes of the Enlightenment, print capitalism, or romantic nationalism of Europe. The numerous historical connections between Europe and India and the obvious continuities of print and related technology across different cultural settings have created a series of similarities and approximate translations between European print culture and its Indian counterpart, but these connections and continuities, though necessary, have not been sufficient to render the two cultures homogeneous or identical. The colonial subject formed at the intersection of writing, print, and education on the subcontinent therefore had to be and is significantly different from the "sovereign subject" of Europe, and also possesses, to invoke Gayatri Spivak's metaphor but not her argument, the power "to speak." In fact, unlike the self-centering and self-centered European master-subject, in the course of the nineteenth and twentieth centuries the Indian subject of colonial rule split up into four sharply distinguished, fragmentary, and mutually antagonistic subject-positions in the field of discourse, each of which has charted a different course through subsequent Indian political and literary history. These are the positions of resistance, collaboration, cosmopolitanism, and revivalism, the first three of which I shall discuss at some length in the rest of this section.

(B) THE BIRTH OF RESISTANCE

The first subject-position to appear on the historical horizon was that of resistance to colonial rule, defined explicitly in the domains of writing and print as early as the 1810s and 1820s. Sir John Malcolm, the administrator of the Central Provinces, subsequently the Governor of the Bombay Presidency, and one of the principal older liberal architects of British India as it was stabilized in the first quarter of the nineteenth century, gives us a vivid thumbnail sketch of this position. In a letter to a colleague written on April 8, 1821, Malcolm confesses that he dreads "no human being," "certainly no Nabob or Maharajah,"

> half so much as an able Calcutta civilian, whose travels are limited to two or three
> hundred miles, with a hookah in his mouth, some good but abstract maxims in his
> head, the Regulations in his right hand, the Company's Charter in his left, and a
> quire of wire-woven foolscap before him.[20]

In Malcolm's miniature drama of confrontation, the Bengali activist-intellectual's strategy of resistance is simple but extremely effective. He observes, records, and analyzes the actions of the colonial administration, and demonstrates when and where its performance deviates from the colonial contract ratified by King and Parliament, or from the policies and procedures laid down by the Company's Board. He demands a complete consistency between contract, policy, procedure, and performance, wishes to debate the general principles of colonial government, and is ready to defend his position by quoting chapter and verse from a large number of canonical English authorities, ranging from Francis Bacon and William Shakespeare to Edmund Burke. He deploys his resistance by closely reading the printed texts of the Company's Charter and Regulations—which are published in England as well as the colony as part of the liberal system of checks and balances against the potential abuse of power—and, what is more important, by writing frequently and at great length to his colonial masters.[21]

Malcolm dreads the encounter because he understands, as we do in retrospect, that this "able Calcutta civilian" has completely internalized, in Edward Said's words from another context, "the literal truth of the universalist sentiments propounded by the European Enlightenment."[22] Viewed through a different historical and theoretical lens, he appears to have fully grasped, and challenges the colonizer to bring into play in the colony, the principles of civil society and the public sphere that had emerged in western Europe by the middle of the eighteenth century. As

Jürgen Habermas and his followers have argued, the bourgeois public sphere opens up a space between society and the state, in which members of "the educated strata," whose lives as subject-citizens are shaped and sustained by print culture, form a "literate public" that "expresses critical opinions and judgments in writing."[23] But such a public can mediate successfully between society and the state only when its paraphernalia of publicity—newspapers, periodicals, editorials, letters to the editor, books, pamphlets, broadsheets, white papers, reviews, critiques—is able to translate public opinion into manifest political representation. Malcolm dreads the Bengali subject precisely because the latter's literate resistance reveals clearly how, in the process of colonization, the British (and Europeans in general) inadvertently have transplanted onto Indian soil some of the social conventions and technological instruments of the public sphere, but none of its crucial political preconditions. His resistance also underscores the fact that the peculiarities of the transplantation specifically preclude the process of political representation from being set in motion as promised by the original European institutions. In fact, the civilian's resistance publicizes one of the basic internal contradictions of liberalism which Malcolm, in guilty self-knowledge, cannot bear to face: that the liberal who lives by "the pen" at home ends up wielding "the sword" in the colony. Or, as Abdul JanMohamed discovers along parallel lines in the late-twentieth-century South African context, "The English culture that cherished the values of liberalism and democracy . . . had produced in its colonial government social structures that were antithetical to its own avowed values."[24]

But the stereotyped portrait of the early Indian subject of resistance that Malcolm outlines so deftly in 1821 is not merely a phantasm of the guilt-ridden liberal-colonial imagination. It is also an astute delineation of the new kind of Indian that print culture had actually engendered in the middle- and upper-class Hindu community in Calcutta and, at the same time, a representation of startling political foresight. The subject-position that Malcolm identifies here closely foreshadows the position that Indian "moderates" and "reformers" were to occupy in the second half of the nineteenth century, when they attempted to mobilize their political agency in an ideology of anticolonial nationalism and in an institution like the Indian National Congress (launched in 1885).[25] It is also a prototype of the subject-position that Mahatma Gandhi was to

elaborate in his work in South Africa and British India in the early twentieth century, when he began to practice moral suasion, civil disobedience,
and nonviolent resistance as much in the domain of mass agitation as
in the domains of writing and print.[26]

What is historically and theoretically striking, however, is that in
Malcolm's vignette the Indian subject of resistance turns out to be very
different from the resisting colonial subject that Frantz Fanon, for
instance, constructs for mid-twentieth-century Africa, with the help of
the Hegelian dialectic of master and slave, the phenomenology of self
and other, and the Marxist theory of revolutionary practice.[27] "In Fanon's
world," Edward Said observes, "change can come about only when the
native . . . decides that colonization must end," and it "is set in motion
. . . by the native's violence," which is a "cleansing force" that "pits colonizer against colonized directly." As Fanon himself says, "The violence
of the colonial regime and the counter-violence of the native balance
each other in an extraordinary reciprocal homogeneity."[28] The Fanon-
like revolutionary colonial subject appears in the Indian print world
only a couple of decades after the civil resister, when the position of
resistance splits ideologically into the moderate and the militant, and
even then (especially after the unsuccessful "Mutiny" of 1857) occupies primarily the extremist margins of resistance. To an always
surprising extent, the Manichean binarism of violence and counter-
violence that seems so central to the African experience of colonialism
is deferred and displaced often in the Indian situation, where the print
culture that houses the Indian colonial subject postpones repeatedly—
but not always successfully—the eruption of resistance into bloodshed.[29]

(C) THE BIRTH OF COLLABORATION

The second main subject-position that print culture, and specifically the
intersection of writing, print, and education, delivered in and around
early-nineteenth-century British India was that of collaboration with
the colonial order. Although individual collaborators as well as complicitous groups (such as the *pandits*, *munshis*, and *banians* in Bengal) had
appeared among Indian scholars, bankers, landowners, and princes by the
middle of the eighteenth century, the *comprador* intelligentsia, as a distinct
class of professionals who mediate between a colonial state and a colonized
people from subservient nodal positions in the state apparatus—to adapt

Kwame Anthony Appiah's formulation—came into being on the sub-continent after 1835.[30]

In February of that year Thomas Babington Macaulay, who had recently joined the East India Company's board in Calcutta as its resident law member, completed the Minute on Indian Education in which he dreamt that a new system of company-sponsored English education for Indians would create "a class of persons, Indian in blood and color, but English in taste, in opinions, in morals, and in intellect," to help run the empire at the lower levels of the bureaucracy, the judiciary, and the police, as "interpreters between us and the millions whom we govern."[31] Although Macaulay strongly criticized the Utilitarians on many key issues earlier and later, he developed his policy recommendations in the Minute by combining the authoritarian Utilitarian program for India, conceived by Jeremy Bentham and blueprinted by James Mill, and the universalistic Evangelical critique of India, prepared and promoted aggressively by Charles Grant.[32] Juxtaposing these ideological positions without the explicit Christian elements of the latter, Macaulay formulated an Anglicist universalism that mocked the cautious cultural relativism of Fort William orientalists such as Horace Hyman Wilson, and proclaimed England's indisputable cultural superiority over the East, which guaranteed "the imperishable empire of our arts and our morals, our literature and our laws."[33] Like Malcolm's guilt-ridden vision of the agent of Indian resistance, Macaulay's phantasm of the socially engineered collaborator proved to be a self-fulfilling prophecy. The rhetoric of his Minute was quickly translated into law by the Indian Education Act of 1835, which required the company to invest a substantial sum of money in the English education of some of its Indian subjects. Starting in the late 1830s, company-sponsored education began to produce several thousand voluntary Indian collaborators each year who became career functionaries of the British imperial order, initially only in India but a few decades later also in British territories elsewhere, especially Africa.

Over time, however, Indians found the subject-position of complicity and collaboration the hardest to sustain. Contrary to what Gauri Vishwanathan appears to imply, the Macaulayan system of education was relatively small and selective (though socially prestigious), and had to compete, as both Anil Seal and Partha Chatterjee have shown, with extensive and influential networks of schools and colleges run by Indians outside the cultural control of the colonial state.[34] While the Indian institutions offered instruction in English and European languages as well as Indian languages, and developed pedagogic styles and curricula ranging from the modern Western to the traditional Hindu, Muslim, or Jain (among other religions), increasingly after the third quarter of the nineteenth century they produced an educated Indian subject whose desire for a secure livelihood in the Raj was deeply ambiguated by nationalist resistance. More importantly, by the final decades of the century numerous Indians had concluded from experience—like the Bengali writer Bankimchandra Chattopadhyay—that the Macaulayan promise of rewards for collaboration was a sham. In practice, until the end of the Raj in 1947, the Indian collaborator could not enter the colonial system easily, did not rise in the hierarchy in proportion with his intelligence, professional skills, or length of service, and was always humiliatingly subject to the Englishman's (and later also the Englishwoman's) racism, ignorance, prejudice, and social snobbery.[35]

Both the resister and the collaborator in colonial India were historically the products of hybridized Enlightenment institutions of mass literacy and education that mediated and were mediated by the technology of print, as these institutions and this technology evolved into an unprecedented, multifaceted culture of reproduction peculiar to the subcontinent. After the middle of the nineteenth century, the willing collaborator frequently became the scribe and scribal repository or archive of the empire or, more visibly, the subject of colonial mimicry. He—rarely she—subsequently entered the world of print primarily as an object of representation rather than as its subject, most often only to be savaged by a long line of satirists. In Bengali prose, for instance, the Indian collaborator was embodied in the figure of the *babu* (the petty bureaucrat in colonial administration) and became a target for Bankimchandra Chattopadhyay's "vitriolic" mockery as early as the 1870s. In Indian-English fiction, the enthusiastic Bengali imitator of Englishness, his thought and speech dysfunctional with bookish quotations from the Bard and the classics of Macaulay's canon, became the butt of G. V. Desani's still-neglected master-satire, *All About H. Hatterr*, as far back as 1948. Most recently, the collaborator has served as the metamorphic central trope in Salman Rushdie's *The Satanic Verses* (1988), where Saladin Chamcha, the mimic with a thousand voices, personifies the unregenerate postcolonial "spoon" or toady of the empire, now relocated as an immigrant in the heart of the metropolis.[36]

In contrast, since about 1820 the Indian resister (whether moderate or militant) has written against the empire from within and outside it, and has participated in Indian and Western print culture as both the subject and the object of representation, as much in a discursive as in a political sense. As the producer of discourse in print, he—and quite often she—has powerfully shaped modern Indian education, the unending debate over "revival" and "reform" in Indian society and religion, and the enormous body of Indian journalistic reportage, commentary, and criticism in some forty languages.[37] As the object of representation in the medium of print, the subject of resistance (male as well as female) has been the idealized protonationalist and nationalist protagonist of fiction, poetry, and drama in virtually all the major modern Indian literatures.[38] To a large extent, print was the ground on which the resisting subject was fashioned, fashioned himself or herself, and acted as an agent of historical change, even when the colonizer seemed to control or dominate the medium and its culture.

Contrary to some current commonplaces, then, print culture in colonial India did not give birth only to colonial mimics, subalterns who could not speak, and socially engineered clones of European subjectivity. With its burdens of incompletely translated and substantially hybridized Enlightenment activism, quasi-civil society protocols, and protopublic-sphere conventions, nineteenth- and early twentieth-century Indian print culture succeeded in engendering a large number of historical actors whose agency may have been severely curtailed in specific political regimes, but who nevertheless retained the power or counterpower, as Karl Marx had hoped idealistically, to change the conditions of their existence.[39]

(D) THE BIRTH OF AMBIDEXTERITY

Resistance and collaboration, like domination and subordination or coercion and persuasion, constitute a tidy binary opposition. Like the terms in the other pairs, they continue to structure arguments regarding modern Indian cultural history, such as those offered by the scholars associated with the Subaltern Studies project.[40] But, in spite of their neatness and utility, resistance and collaboration do not exhaust the subject-positions that Indians occupy in nineteenth-century print culture. A third position, which also appears in the 1810s and 1820s and differs significantly from the first two, characterizes the "hybrid" modern Indian writer and intellectual.

Hybridity, as Homi Bhabha reminds us, "is never simply a question of the admixture of pre-given identities or essences"; rather, it is "the perplexity of living as it interrupts the representation of the fullness of life."[41] Bhabha's conception of hybridity and its functions, however, grows out of a broad cultural thematics, rather than a rigorous historicization, of the nation and the nation-state in the period after decolonization, specifically of the nation in Europe as it would like to reconceive itself now. In this thematization, what Bhabha satirizes as "the fullness of life" is the "authenticity of being" found, for instance, in the so-called "ties of blood and earth" about which Heidegger fantasized earlier this century, when he constructed the image of a *Volk* whose "destiny" would be embodied in the cleansed and homogenized nation of National Socialism.[42] Against the fullness of authenticity Bhabha poses "the perplexity of living" which erupts iteratively into individual lives as well as collective existence, moves from the margins and interstices of the nation toward its center, manifests itself in the doubling and ambivalence of cultural difference within the nation, and leads to the splitting of the sovereign subject into the familiar, the foreign, and the fragmentary. Drawing on Rushdie's politics of "purity" and "mongrelization" in *The Satanic Verses*—which is also spelled out in some of his essays in *Imaginary Homelands*—Bhabha calls for an aggressive disruption of authenticity by hybridity, primarily in the contest for the empowerment of the minorities, the immigrants, and the marginalized who have now gathered, after being scattered, in the (post)colonial (anti)metropolis.[43]

The methodological question is whether Bhabha's cultural logic can be applied without modification either to nations whose histories do not mimic those of European models and "modular forms," or to historical periods, such as the colonial one, in which the conditions of cultural production may have been radically different. In the nineteenth century, "India" already consisted of hundreds of distinct societies that were loosely interlocked by a long history of mutual economic dependence and cultural interaction, but were divided up among a few unequal

European powers (mainly England, France, and Portugal) and some 600
separate Indian state-formations that had yet to accept, uniformly, the
principle of British paramountcy.[44] In this heteromorphous multiverse,
hybridity did not need to disrupt a territorially or culturally unified whole
(which did not exist then), but instead had to attempt constructively to
conjoin what was already fragmented, scattered, and perplexed. That is,
in what is reductively called "colonial India," hybridity performed a historical and cultural function that is exactly the opposite of the one it
has—in Bhabha's account—in postcolonial England and the European
nations today. So when Indian subjects began to occupy hybrid intellectual or literary positions in early-nineteenth-century print culture on the
subcontinent, they defined roles for themselves in the colonial order that
were, in contrast to both nationalist resistance and colonialist collaboration, syncretistically interdisciplinary, cross-cultural, and transnational.

This constructive colonial hybridity, as distinguished from Bhabha's
deconstructive postcolonial hybridity, is evident in the work of a large
number of nineteenth- and twentieth-century Indian writers, ranging
from, say, Rammohun Roy, Henry Derozio, Michael Madhusudan Dutt,
and Toru Dutt to Bankimchandra Chattopadhyay, Rabindranath Tagore,
Subramania Bharati, Mahadevi Verma, and Munshi Premchand.[45] But
it may be most clearly exemplified in the little-known nineteenth-century *pandit-kavis* or brahman scholar-poets of British India, who played
prominent local and regional roles in reshaping Indian literary culture
in the medium of print. To apply a metaphor invoked recently by
Partha Chatterjee, the average *pandit-kavi* remained much further
"inside" Indian linguistic, scholarly, and religious traditions than any of
the more Westernized, nationally visible hybrid writers mentioned
above, but he nevertheless acquired a comparable degree of interdisciplinary and cross-cultural competence.[46]

A striking instance of this type of hybridized subject is a *pandit-
kavi* like Krishnashastri Chiplunkar (1824–1878), who spent all his life
in Poona (Pune) in the Bombay Presidency. He was a master at the
Pune Pathshala (the city's high school), the Principal of the city's
Training College for Indian scholars, and a translator, editor, and cultural commentator, besides being a poet. He studied Sanskrit, Marathi,
and English, and specialized in the *shastras* (disciplines) of *alamkara*
(poetic and rhetorical figures), *nyaya* (logic), *dharma* (religion, law, ethics),

artha (economics), and *manas* (humanistic studies), only the last of which was a modern rather than a traditional discipline in the mid-nineteenth-century Indian intellectual world. The thematic range of the books he published suggests the sheer richness of the hybridity he achieved, in the interstices of the empire rather than at its nodes: *Socratisache charitra* (1852), a study of Socrates; *Vicharalahari* (1852), personal essays on philosophy and religion; *Arthasastra-paribhasha* (1855), principles of economics; *Sanskrit bhasheche lahan vyakaran* (1859), short grammar of Sanskrit; *Arabi bhashetil suras va chamatkarik gosthi* (1861), enjoyable and wondrous tales from the Arabic; *Padyaratnavali* (1865), Marathi verse, including translations from the Sanskrit, most notably his classic rendering of Kalidasa's "Meghaduta"; *Rasselas* (1873), a translation of Samuel Johnson's "Oriental Tale" (completed by Krishnashastri's more famous and influential son, Vishnushastri Chiplunkar); and a posthumous collection of essays and reviews (1893), covering grammar and literature in several languages.[47] As it emerges in print chiefly over the third quarter of the nineteenth century, Chiplunkar's hybrid identity turns out to be quite different from that of, say, Michael Madhusudan Dutt, who is sometimes treated as an archetype of all modern Indian hybrids.[48] This suggests that hybridization, like resistance and collaboration, was itself a heterogeneous phenomenon, to be defined as a cluster of subject-positions rather than as a single, monolithic stance.

Contrary to Bhabha's reductive representations of hybridity and ambivalence, a writer like Chiplunkar does not linger liminally between two cultures but stands quite firmly in both of them. He is likely to be ambivalent about each of the cultures he inhabits, but his ambivalence is subsumed by his *cultural ambidexterity*, an equal or commensurate facility in two or more cultural systems concurrently. If the resister acts out of a subaltern culture against a dominant other culture, and the collaborator acts in a subaltern culture for a dominant culture, then the ambidextrous subject acts simultaneously in two or more cultures without making unmixed, unilateral choices or commitments. That is, if the resister and the collaborator, in contrary ways, display a "positive capablity" with regard to one particular culture in relation to another, then the ambidextrous subject may well display a "negative capability" equally toward two or more cultures, possibly keeping himself suspended, as John Keats puts it, "in uncertainties, mysteries, doubts, without any irritable reaching after fact and reason" and without seeking what he perceives to be the handicapped extremes of resistance and collaboration.[49] Or, again, if the resisting subject sacrifices a dominant culture in favor of a subaltern one, and the complicitous subject sacrifices a subaltern culture in favor of a dominant one, then the ambidextrous subject tries to maintain a critical distance toward two cultures so that he can act in both without sacrificing either.

In the nineteenth- and twentieth-century Indian print world, the ambidextrous subject appears most often as the bilateral cosmopolitan—as in the texts of Gopal Krishna Gokhale, M. G. Ranade, and B. R. Ambedkar, for instance—who translates Indian and Western cultures into each other, reforming and modernizing both.[50] He or she is the subcontinental equivalent of the ambidextrous colonial subject in the Caribbean, represented by a writer-activist like C. L. R. James who, as Edward Said remarks, "stubbornly supported the Western Heritage at the same time that he belonged to the insurrectionary anti-imperialist movement which he shared with Fanon, Cabral, and Rodney." As James himself put it in a late interview,

> How am I to return to non-European roots? If it means that Caribbean writers today should be aware that there are emphases in their writing that we owe to non-European, non-Shakespearean roots, and the past in music that is not Beethoven, that I agree. But I don't like them posed there in the way they have been posed either-or. I don't think so. I think both of them.[51]

The position of the ambidextrous subject in relation to the colonial order thus cannot be reduced to either collaboration or resistance, and also cannot be adduced as merely a combination of those two positions.

3. COLONIAL MARKET CONDITIONS: OWNERSHIP, CENSORSHIP, AND HEGEMONY

The synoptic history of print and the effects of the medium on Indian subjects and cultures that I have sketched thus far are circumscribed by the specific political conditions that regulate colonial print markets. As I have already indicated, in nineteenth-century British India the domain of print was divided up as property among colonial government institutions, missionary presses, private Anglo-Indian and European presses, and Indian-owned presses. These presses were owned and operated in an economy that carried the ghostly vestiges of a free-market system and were regulated by a series of (often harsh) company acts and actions. After heated skirmishes in the 1770s and 1780s between company officials and private Anglo-Indian printers over malicious rumor, defamation, and provocation, the colonial government imposed restrictions on printed matter regarding libel, sedition, and incitement to violence, particularly in ordinances promulgated in 1799 (under Lord Wellesley) and 1823 (under Lord Amherst).[52] In practice, these ordinances served as disincentives to Indian as well as European individuals and institutions wishing to invest in print culture in the private sector. In 1835, shortly after Lord Bentinck's departure, Sir Charles Metcalfe, one of the paternalistic liberals of John Malcolm's generation and subsequently Governor of Jamaica (1839–42) and Governor-General of Canada (1843-45), used his interim Governor-Generalship at Calcutta to rescind the press ordinance of 1823. Interestingly enough, Metcalfe acted on his own convictions and also at the urging of Macaulay, who stood with him against the Benthamite radicals on this occasion, even though he had supported their authoritarian program of controls in his Minute on Indian Education some months earlier.[53] As a direct consequence of Metcalfe's liberalization, the next thirty years saw an exponential growth in English as well as Indian entrepreneurship in print culture, leading to a virtual explosion in Indian-language publishing in many different genres.[54]

After the widespread, violent uprising against the East India Company in 1857, and after the subsequent dismantling of the company and the formal establishment of the British Raj in 1858, in which London began to govern India directly, the surveillance of print in India became a pressing colonial issue. It brought to a head once more the oldest and deepest contradictions in England's imperial enterprise: the empire was founded on an ideology of free trade, but free trade was forcefully curtailed in the colony; the English cherished freedom at home but practised repression abroad; the Utilitarians believed in the greatest good for the greatest number, but not for their loyal Indian subjects; and while many of the masters of the empire admired the French Revolution, they travestied its slogan of liberty, equality, and fraternity in their own practice on the subcontinent.[55] In 1867, as a pragmatic compromise between *laissez faire* and authoritatian rule, the imperial government passed the Books and Periodicals Registration Act, requiring every publication to carry the names and addresses of its printer and publisher, and to be deposited for the record with a national registrar. After the events of the violent "Mutiny" of 1857, the government, irreparably alienated from its subjects, also instituted the practice of preparing weekly English summaries of the Indian-language press, especially of political discourse, to be scrutinized locally and nationally, all the way up to the office of the Viceroy. Since the Books and Periodicals Registration Act of 1867 did not give the English enough preemptive control over the Indian press, in 1878 they passed the Vernacular Press Act, which imposed strict censorship rules on journalism and publications in the Indian languages. But the new act drew such strong protests from the organized Indian literary and political spheres, as well as English liberals in England and India, that it had to be repealed four years later.[56] The formation of the Indian National Congress in 1885 and the strengthening of a countrywide nationalist movement in the final years of the nineteenth century rapidly changed the circumstances in which the empire could be and had to be ruled. The power of the imperial government to censor newspapers, magazines, political pamphlets, and books, as well as theater and public performance, remained intact until 1947, but it often had to be used cautiously in remedial situations and could no longer be exercised without severe political repercussions, some of them violent.[57]

The significance of the pattern of ownership and operation in the domain of print in the nineteenth century, and of the legislative framework within which the medium had to function in British India, is clearest in the case of journalism. In the course of those one hundred years, helped especially by the liberalization of press laws between 1836 and 1867, Indians and non-Indians together published a total of about 14,000 newspapers and periodicals in some forty languages.[58] Most of these failed soon after being launched, but hundreds survived for impressive lengths of time and even reached large regional and national audiences, while several dozens of them continued into the twentieth century, and some remain active down to the present.[59] Even the most marginalized groups in Indian society succeeded in entering print culture at this time; for instance, the untouchables, traditionally the lowest of the low in Hindu caste society and systematically denied literacy for 2,000 years or more, managed to acquire or find the education, money, and presses needed to launch more than one hundred newspapers for themselves between 1850 and 1950, often with patronage and encouragement from Christian missions and the colonial government, both of which, though racist and segregationist themselves, opposed caste discrimination.[60] Given the sheer volume and linguistic diversity of nineteenth-century journalism, it is no surprise that the colonial state remained perpetually tense about the intentions of the Indian-language press and its power to shape public opinion through representations in print.

As the post-Independence period also demonstrates, the multilingualism and political resilience of Indian culture have consistently produced an avalanche of heterogeneous discourse in modern times, and no government can survive it without at least prudentially tracking all the varieties of free speech in its backyard, frontyard, and neighborhood streets; in 1983, for instance, the Ministry of Information and Broadcasting in India registered 20,758 newspapers, with a total declared circulation of over 55 million copies across the linguistic spectrum.[61] The English colonial system of surveillance in the late nineteenth century was aimed mainly at political criticism of the Raj, and hence was directed toward potentially dangerous dissent and incipient insurgency as shadowed in journalistic publications. But it also extended directly to texts in performance in public places (regulated by the Dramatic Performances Control Act of 1876), and to those print forms that reached large or influential audiences, such as contemporaneous prose fiction and poetry.[62] The market for print in the Raj was thus very far from free in theory or practice: some kinds of speech may have been in demand or in supply but simply could not be marketed, and the life of anti-British writing was easier to lead either in other colonial havens, such as the French city of Pondicherry, or in the smaller native states, which may have accepted the paramountcy of the British but did not actively collaborate to preserve the latter's imperial interests.[63] The peculiar paradox of the empire in all this was that its press acts and regulations, including the most repressive ones, did not and could not prevent Indians from thinking their own thoughts, cultivating oppositional or subversive opinions, voicing them in any language they chose (including English), or even acting on them. Increasingly after 1836, and exponentially after 1867, Indians learned to manage their political and literary public spheres with all the sophistication of citizens in a civil society, thus ensuring, as Ranajit Guha has argued persuasively from a different angle, that English rule in India remained an excercise in "dominance without hegemony."[64]

NOTES

1. Early printing in India and in the Indian languages is discussed in B. S. Kesavan, *History of Printing and Publishing in India: A Story of Cultural Reawakening,* vol. 1: *South Indian Origins of Printing and its Efflorescence in Bengal* (New Delhi: National Book Trust, 1985); see especially pp. 13–17. Also see Dennis E. Rhodes, *The Spread of Printing. Eastern Hemisphere: India, Pakistan, Ceylon, Burma, and Thailand,* ed. Colin Clair (Amsterdam: Vangendt, 1969), pp. 11–78. Print culture in England is discussed in Alvin Kernan, *Samuel Johnson and the Impact of Print* (Princeton: Princeton University Press, 1987); refer especially to pp. 1–8, 48–90; the quotation is from p. 48. See the map of India in Rhodes, pp. 8–9; and the lists of Calcutta printers in Rhodes, p. 31, and Kesavan, p. 196.

2. The first imprints in various Indian languages are identified in Kesavan, pp. 16, 28–29; and in Amaresh Datta and Madan Lal, eds., *Encyclopedia of Indian Literature,* 6 vols. (New Delhi: Sahitya Akademi, 1987–94), vol. 4, pp. 3340–59.

3. On types, typography, and paper, see Kesavan, pp. 31–36, 55–56, 205–7; Rhodes, pp. 11–19; and Datta and Lal, vol. 4, pp. 3345, and 3351.

4. Contemporary Indian and other postcolonial literary markets and print cultures are discussed further in my "Afterword: Modern Indian Poetry and its Contexts" in *The Oxford Anthology of Modern Indian Poetry,* eds. Vinay Dharwadker and A. K. Ramanujan (Delhi: Oxford University Press, 1994), pp. 185–206; and my "The Internationalization of Literatures," in *New National and Post-Colonial Literatures: An Introduction,* ed. Bruce King (Oxford: Clarendon Press, 1996), pp. 59–77.

5. Kesavan, p. 62; and Rhodes, p. 33, n. 1.

6. Gauri Vishwanathan, *Masks of Conquest: Literary Study and British Rule in India* (New York: Columbia University Press, 1989), p. 36.

7. Hicky and the emerging economy of print in India are analyzed in Kesavan, pp. 189–229; and Rhodes, pp. 21–31. Also refer to Sisir Kumar Das, *A History of Indian Literature, 1800–1910. Western Impact: Indian Response* (New Delhi: Sahitya Akademi, 1991), p. 426.

8. On Fort William College and its press, see Kesavan, pp. 391–404. Also consult David Kopf, *British Orientalism and the Bengal Renaissance: The Dynamics of Indian Modernization, 1773–1835* (Berkeley: University of California Press, 1969); and R. S. McGregor, *Hindi Literature in the Nineteenth and Early Twentieth Centuries,* vol. 8, fasc. 2 of *A History of Indian Literature,* ed. Jan Gonda (Wiesbaden: Otto Harrassowitz, 1974). On English literary studies, see Franklin E. Court, "The Social

and Historical Significance of the First English Professorship in England," in *PMLA* 103 (1988), pp. 796–807.

9. Das, *History 1800–1910*, p. 431.

10. See Kesavan, pp. 237–46, 381–88; and Das, *History 1800–1910*, 32–33. On the linguistic diversity of India in the post-Independence period, which places the nineteenth-century situation and the accomplishments of the Serampore Mission Press in perspective, consult Paul R. Brass, *The Politics of India since Independence*, pt. 4, vol. 1 of *The New Cambridge History of India* (1990; Cambridge: Cambridge University Press, 1991), ch. 5; and A. K. Ramanujan, *Folktales from India: A Selection of Oral Tales from Twenty-Two Languages* (New York: Pantheon, 1991), pp. xiv–xviii. Useful linguistic maps appear in Ramanujan, *Folktales*, xvii, and in Brass, p. 148. A list of thirty-three languages covered by the 1971 Census of India is given in Brass, pp. 137–39; compare with the languages used at the Serampore Press, in Kesavan, pp. 254, 381–88. On Indian languages and scripts in general, see K. S. Singh and S. Manoharan, *Languages and Scripts,* vol. 9 of *People of India, National Series* (Delhi: Anthropological Survey of India and Oxford University Press, 1993), which reached me after I had completed this essay.

11. On Wilkins, see Kesavan, pp. 205–7. On Panchanan, see Kesavan, pp. 191–92; and Datta and Lal, vol. 4, pp. 3341 and 3346.

12. See Kesavan, pp. 237–63; and Rhodes, pp. 29–30.

13. Compare, for instance, with Africa in Albert Guerard, *African Language Literatures: An Introduction to the Literary History of Sub-Saharan Africa* (Harlow, Essex: Longman, 1981); and with Japan in Donald Keene, *Dawn to the West: Japanese Literature in the Modern Era*, 2 vols. (New York: Holt, 1984).

14. Das, *History 1800–1910*, pp. 67–75; Das quotes the last phrase from Muhammad Sadiq, *A History of Urdu Literature* (Delhi: Oxford University Press, 1974), p. 291.

15. Das, *History 1800–1910*, pp. 73–75; also see Datta and Lal, vol. 1, pp. 3384–3425.

16. Partha Chatterjee, *The Nation and Its Fragments: Colonial and Postcolonial Histories* (Princeton: Princeton University Press, 1993), p. 7. Also see the excellent local, regional, and subcontinental surveys and case studies in Kenneth W. Jones, ed., *Religious Controversy in British India: Dialogues in South Asian Languages* (Albany: State University of New York Press, 1992), chs. 1–3, 6, 8–10.

17. Henry Louis Gates, Jr., "Critical Fanonism," in *Critical Inquiry* 17 (1991), p. 466; and Gayatri Chakravorty Spivak, "Can the Subaltern Speak?" in *Colonial Discourse and Postcolonial Theory: A Reader*, eds. Patrick Williams and Laura Chrisman (New York: Columbia University Press, 1994), p. 66.

18. See Benedict Anderson, *Imagined Communities: Reflections on the Origin and Spread of Nationalism* (1983; London: Verso, 1987). The phrase "derivative discourse" comes from Partha Chatterjee, *Nationalist Thought and the Colonial World: A Derivative Discourse* (1986; Minneapolis: University of Minnesota Press, 1993). The quotation is from Chatterjee, *Nation and Its Fragments*, p. 5.

19. Gates, p. 462.

20. Eric Stokes, *The English Utilitarians and India* (1959; Delhi: Oxford University Press, 1989), p. 20.

21. Such a reading of Malcolm's vignette draws obviously on Rammohun Roy's activities in Calcutta after 1815; see Stephen Hay, ed., *Sources of Indian Tradition*, vol. 2, *Modern India and Pakistan*, 2d ed. (New York: Columbia University Press, 1988), pp. 15–35.

22. Edward W. Said, *Culture and Imperialism* (New York: Knopf, 1993), p. 246.

23. Susan Maslan, "Resisting Representation: Theater and Democracy in Revolutionary France," *Representations*, No. 52 (Fall 1995), p. 29; also see p. 48, n. 12. Habermas's analysis appears in *The Structural Transformation of the Public Sphere: An Inquiry into a Category of Bourgeois Society*, trans. Thomas Burger (1989; Cambridge: M.I.T. Press, 1992); see esp. chs. 2–3.

24. Abdul R. JanMohamed, *Manichean Aesthetics: The Politics of Literature in Colonial Africa* (Amherst: University of Massachusetts Press, 1983), pp. 112–13.

25. On nineteenth-century Indian moderates and reformers, see the sections on M. G. Ranade and G. K. Gokhale in Hay, pp. 102–20. An overview also appears in Sumit Sarkar, *Modern India 1885–1947* (1983; Madras: Macmillan, 1990), pp. 70–100. In addition, consult M. G. Ranade, *The Miscellaneous Writings of the Late Hon'ble Mr. Justice M. G. Ranade* (1915; New Delhi: Sahitya Akademi, 1992); and Stanley A. Wolpert, *Tilak and Gokhale: Revolution and Reform in the Making of Modern India* (1961; Delhi: Oxford University Press, 1989).

26. See Hay, pp. 243–73. Other interpretations of Gandhi appear in Chatterjee, *Nationalist Thought*, ch. 4; and in Shahid Amin, "Gandhi as Mahatma: Gorakhpur District, Eastern U.P., 1921–2" in *Selected Subaltern Studies*, ed. Ranajit Guha and Gayatri Chakravorty Spivak (New York: Oxford University Press, 1988), pp. 288–348.

27. Gates, pp. 457–70; and Homi Bhabha, "Remembering Fanon: Self, Psyche, and the Colonial Condition" in Williams and Chrisman, pp. 112–23, especially p. 114.

28. Said, pp. 270–71; Fanon's words, from *The Wretched of the Earth*, trans. Constance Farrington (1961; New York: Grove, 1968), p. 88, are quoted in Said, p. 271.

29. The Indian revolutionary subject (the militant resister) appears in the texts of nationalists and extremists ranging from Bankimchandra Chattopadhyay, Bal Gangadhar Tilak, Aurobindo Ghose, and Lala Lajpat Rai, to Vinayak Damodar Savarkar, Manabendra Nath Roy, Subhas Chandra Bose, and Balraj Madhok; see the sections on these figures in Hay, pp. 128–72, 289–315, and 359–65. On the opposition between "reform" and "revolution," also see the brilliant passage from Charles Trevelyan, *The Education of the Indian People* (1838), reproduced in Stokes, pp. 46–47. The situation of militant resistance, violent subversion, and revolutionary insurgency, and its relation to the print medium and to colonial mechanisms of repression, are more complicated than I have managed to indicate here; see especially the various works by Ranajit Guha, Partha Chatterjee, and Sumit Sarkar cited above and below.

30. On eighteenth-century collaborators, see Philip D. Curtin, *Cross-Cultural Trade in World History* (Cambridge: Cambridge University Press, 1984), pp. 172–76; and C. A. Bayly, *Indian Society and the Making of the British Empire*, pt. 2, vol. 1 of *The New Cambridge History of India* (1988; Cambridge: Cambridge University Press, 1990), ch. 2. On the *comprador* class, see Kwame Anthony Appiah, "Is the Post- in Postmodernism the Post- in Postcolonial?" in *Critical Inquiry* 17 (1991), pp. 336–57, especially p. 348. The article is reprinted as "The Postcolonial and the Postmodern" in Appiah's *In My Father's House: Africa in the Philosophy of Culture* (New York: Oxford University Press, 1992), pp. 137–57.

31. Thomas Babington Macaulay, *Minute on Indian Education*, 2 February 1835; quoted in Stokes, p. 46.

32. Stokes, pp. 29–47, 57–58; and Das, *History 1800–1910*, pp. 85–88. Also note the discussion in Homi Bhabha, "Signs Taken as Wonders: Questions of Ambivalence and Authority under a Tree outside Delhi, May 1817" in *Critical Inquiry* 12 (1985), pp. 144–65.

33. Macaulay's phrase, from his speech to the House of Commons on July 10, 1833, is quoted in Stokes, p. 45. On the Anglicist-Orientalist controversy of the 1820s and 1830s, see Kopf; and on Macaulay's satirical strategies, see my "The Future of the Past: Modernity, Modern Poetry, and the Transformation of Two Indian Traditions" (Ph.D. diss., University of Chicago, 1989), ch. 1. On the roles of English nationalism and Christianity in early constructions of colonialism, see Aparna Dharwadker, "Nation, Race, and the Ideology of Commerce in Defoe" in *The Cultures of Early English Nationalism*, ed. Joel Reed (forthcoming).

34. See Anil Seal, *The Emergence of Indian Nationalism* (Cambridge: Cambridge University Press, 1971); and Chatterjee, *Nation and Its Fragments*. Late-nineteenth-century documents on education in India include the rich accounts in Ranade, pp. 248–329. A partial but excellent summary of the effects of modern education in nineteenth-century India also appears in Sarkar, pp. 65–67. In addition, consult Partha Chatterjee, "The Disciplines in Colonial Bengal," and Tapti Roy, "Disciplining the Printed Text: Colonial and Nationalist Surveillance of Bengali Literature," in *Texts of Power: Emerging Disciplines in Colonial Bengal*, ed. Partha Chatterjee (Minneapolis: University of Minnesota Press, 1995), pp. 1–62; these two essays deal resonantly with many of my themes, but they reached me several months after I had completed this essay.

35. Tapan Raychaudhuri, *Europe Reconsidered: Perceptions of the West in 19th Century Bengal* (1988; Delhi: Oxford University Press, 1989), ch. 3, especially pp. 114–22; and Sarkar, pp. 22–24.

36. Bankimchandra is discussed in Raychaudhuri, ch. 3; see especially p. 197. On Desani, consult M. K. Naik, *Mirror on the Wall: Images of India and the Englishman in Anglo-Indian Fiction* (New Delhi: Sterling, 1991); and my review in *World Literature Today* 67 (1993), pp. 234–35. Analyses of Rushdie appear in Gayatri Chakravorty Spivak, *Outside in the Teaching Machine* (New York: Routledge, 1993), pp. 217–41; and Homi K. Bhabha, "DissemiNation: Time, Narrative, and the Margins of the Nation" in

Nation and Narration, ed. Homi K. Bhabha (London: Routledge, 1990), pp. 291–322. Naipaul's notion of collaborators as "mimic men" is discussed in Said, p. 272.

37. Susie Tharu and K. Lalita, eds., *Women Writing in India: 600 B.C. to the Present*, 2 vols. (New York: Feminist Press at City University of New York, 1991); Chatterjee, *Nation and Its Fragments*; and Das, *History 1800–1910*, chs. 3, 5, 8.

38. Among notable examples are the first Indian-English short story, Kylas Chunder Dutt's futuristic "A Journal of Forty-Eight Hours of the Year 1945" (1835), discussed in Das, *History 1800–1910*, p. 80; and Bankimchandra Chattopadhyay's classic Bengali novel, *Anandamath* (1882), analyzed in Raychaudhuri, pp. 119–20, 132–34, and in Das, *History 1800–1910*, pp. 213–14.

39. Marx sounds the optimistic note especially in "Theses on Feuerbach" and "The Eighteenth Brumaire of Louis Bonaparte" in Karl Marx and Frederick Engels, *Selected Works*, vol. 1 (1969; Moscow: Progress, 1973), pp. 15, 398.

40. See Ranajit Guha, "Dominance without Hegemony and Its Historiography," in *Subaltern Studies VI: Writings on South Asian History and Society*, ed. Ranajit Guha (Delhi: Oxford University Press, 1989), pp. 210–309. Said complicates both collaboration and resistance, especially in ch. 3, secs. 2 and 5.

41. Bhabha, "DissemiNation," p. 314; my criticism here should also apply broadly to "Remembering Fanon" and "Signs Taken for Wonders," where again Bhabha thematizes ambivalence, hybridity, and mimicry without rigorously historicizing the texts and issues involved.

42. See the discussion of Heidegger in Thomas Sheehan, "A Normal Nazi" in *The New York Review of Books* 40, nos. 1–2 (1992), pp. 30–35.

43. See "The New Empire Within Britain" and "In Good Faith" in Salman Rushdie, *Imaginary Homelands: Essays and Criticism 1981–1991* (New York: Viking, 1991), pp. 129–38, 393–414; refer especially to p. 394. Also consult "Movements and Migrations" in Said, pp. 326–36.

44. The complexity of the fragmentation of the "native states" outside British India is best indicated in the long footnote in Jawaharlal Nehru, *The Discovery of India* (1946; Delhi: Oxford University Press, 1985), pp. 527–28. Also consult the map of late-eighteenth-century India in Ralph Russell and Khurshidul Islam, *Three Mughal Poets: Mir, Sauda, Mir Hasan* (Cambridge: Harvard University Press, 1968), p. 27; and the map of India in 1836 in Percival Spear, *A History of India*, vol. 2 (Harmondsworth: Penguin, 1979), pp. 136–37.

45. See Das, *History 1800–1910*, on the first seven writers on my list here; on the last two, see Sisir Kumar Das, *A History of Indian Literature 1911–1956. Struggle for Freedom: Triumph and Tragedy* (New Delhi: Sahitya Akademi, 1995). Consult these two volumes by Das, along with Datta and Lal's encyclopedia, for basic information on most of the individual Indian writers mentioned throughout this essay. On Bankimchandra, also see Raychaudhuri, ch. 3; and on Bharati, see Kesavan, pp. 107–112.

46. Chatterjee, *Nation and Its Fragments*, 6.

47. See my "Future of the Past," ch. 1; and Kusumavati Deshpande and M. V. Rajadhyaksha, *A History of Marathi Literature* (New Delhi: Sahitya Akademi, 1988), pp. 45–71.

48. R. Parthasarathy, ed., *Ten Twentieth Century Indian Poets* (Delhi: Oxford University Press, 1976), p. 4.

49. Quoted in M. H. Abrams, *A Glossary of Literary Terms*, 5th ed. (Fort Worth: Holt, 1988), pp. 112–13.

50. See Wolpert; Ranade; and Hay, pp. 102–20 and 324–48.

51. Said, p. 248; emphases in original.

52. Refer to Kesavan, pp. 210–17. Also consult Rammohun Roy's "memorial" to the Supreme Court on the 1823 ordinance, which required "all newspapers to be licensed under terms laid down by the [British colonial] government," in Hay, pp. 29–31.

53. Stokes, p. 239; Das, *History 1800–1910*, 463; and Kesavan, pp. 210–17.

54. Das, *History 1800–1910*, 541; and Kesavan, pp. 210–17.

55. Refer to the discussion of the *Bengal Hurkaru*'s criticism of James and John Stuart Mill in 1828 in Stokes, p. 60; and of Ranajit Guha, *The Rule of Property for Bengal: An Essay on the Idea of Permanent Settlement* (The Hague: Mouton, 1963), in Said, p. 250. Also see JanMohamed.

56. Das, *History 1800–1910*, p. 541; Kesavan, pp. 210–17; and Raychaudhuri, p. 133.

57. Das, *History 1911–1956*, pp. 8–9; and Kesavan, pp. 214–17.

58. Estimated figures provided in summer 1992 by James Nye, South Asia Bibliographer, Joseph Regenstein Library, University of Chicago, based on an ongoing Indo–U.S. archival microfilm project. Nye's approximation of 14,000 newspapers in all languages for the entire nineteenth century is placed in perspective by the official figures for the number of newspapers in post-Independence India summarized usefully in Brass, p. 146: in 1960 India had 8,026 newspapers, while by 1983 the total had risen to 20,758.

59. Das, *History 1800–1910*, pp. 168–70.

60. See my "Future of the Past," ch. 2; and my "Dalit Poetry in Marathi" in *World Literature Today*, 68 (1994), pp. 319–24. Also see Eleanor Zelliot, "Dalit Sahitya: The Historical Background" in *Vagartha* 12 (1976), pp. 1–10.

61. Brass, p. 146.

62. Das, *History 1800–1910*, pp. 192–93; and Raychaudhuri, pp. 119–20.

63. See, for example, the entries on Aurobindo Ghose and Subramania Bharati in Datta and Lal, vol. 1, pp. 271–73, and vol. 5, pp. 4190–92.

64. See Guha, "Dominance without Hegemony." I wish to thank John Brenkman for an ideal opportunity to write this essay; Marjorie Garber and Barbara Johnson for their encouragement; and Aparna Dharwadker, Jeffrey Masten, Peter Stallybrass, and Nancy Vickers for their friendship and their stimulating comments and criticism.

SCREENS

MARY ANN DOANE

5

SCREENING TIME

WHEN WALTER BENJAMIN writes, with respect to Baudelaire's poetry, "In the spleen, time becomes palpable: the minutes cover a man like snowflakes,"[1] he is not isolating an attitude unique to Baudelaire. One could argue more generally that at the turn of the century time becomes palpable in a quite different way—one which is specific to modernity and intimately allied with its new technologies of representation (photography, film, phonography). Time is indeed *felt*—as a weight, as a source of anxiety, and as an acutely pressing problem of representation. Modernity is perceived as a temporal demand. In 1903 Georg Simmel linked the precision of the money economy to the precision "effected by the universal diffusion of pocket watches." Simmel associated this new obsession with temporal exactitude to the heightened tempo and the "intensification of nervous stimulation" of urban life—"Thus, the technique of metropolitan life is unimaginable without the most punctual integration of all activities and natural relations into a stable and impersonal time schedule."[2] The acceleration of events specific to city life is inseparable from the effects of new technologies and a machine culture made possible by developments within modern science. Within the realm of physics and beyond, the refinement of the second law of thermodynamics (the law of entropy) engendered a conceptualization of time as the tightness of a direction, an inexorable and irreversible linearity.

In this context, the cinema emerges as a privileged machine for the representation of temporality. Its decisive difference from photography was its ability to inscribe movement through time. As Tom Gunning has pointed out, much of the fascination of the earliest screenings was generated by beginning with a projected still photograph (a form of representation thoroughly familiar to the spectator) and subsequently propelling it into movement so that the temporal work of the apparatus could be displayed as a spectacle in its own right.[3] The cinema engages multiple temporalities and it is helpful, at least temporarily, to disentangle them. There is the temporality of the apparatus itself—linear, irreversible, "mechanical." And there is the temporality of the diegesis, the way in which time is represented by the image, the varying invocations of present, past, future, historicity. And finally, there is the temporality of reception, theoretically distinct but nevertheless a temporality which the developing classical cinema attempted to fuse as tightly as possible to that of the apparatus, conferring upon it the same linear predictability and irreversibility. It is possible to look away or to exit momentarily, but in the process something is lost and felt as such.

My aim here is to investigate the temporalities of the early cinema, to try to recover something of their historical and representational novelty as well as their destabilizing potential. The excesses of the discursive rhetoric which greeted the cinema, its invocation of the grandiose tropes of life, death, waste, and eternity as well as its elicitation of both fascination and antipathy indicate the traumatic nature of its cultural/representational intervention. Space precludes a discussion of the temporality of the apparatus and its links to the temporality of reception. Here, my main concern is with the cinematic image as a representation *of* time, focusing on the cinematic construction of the event as the most condensed and semantically wealthy unit of time, but also as the site of intense internal contradictions.

In contrast to the security and certainty of the irreversible flow of time incarnated in the projector's relentless forward movement, there is, I will argue, an intolerable instability in the image's representation of temporality (where one might be led to expect, in fact, a grounding referentiality). This instability is linked to the early cinema's predilection for the contingent and the resistance the contingent offers to any notion of structuration. Most of the earliest films were, in fact, "occasional" films, dealing in a documentary fashion with an incident, a place, an activity—the stuff of everyday life. The overwhelming hegemony of narrative in the later Hollywood cinema of the classical era led earlier film historians to construct a teleology which organized silent films and hierarchized them according to their ability to anticipate the dominant narrative function and "invent" or "discover" its most salient signifying strategies. More recently, film historians such as Charles Musser and Tom Gunning have pointed out that this teleological approach tends to mask the fact that the dominant genre of the early silent cinema was the actuality or topical film which dealt with current events or incidents of general interest (the demolition of buildings, fires, the aftermath of natural disasters such as floods, prize fights as well as family scenes, work scenes, and travelogues or scenics). Although there is some debate about the precise timing of the transition, it is clear that sometime between 1902–3 and 1907, the popularity of actualities declined and narrative films began to take precedence in the various studios' productions. This transition indicates a crucial representational shift. But for a brief period of time, the cinema seemed to be preoccupied with the minute examination of the realm of the contingent, persistently displaying the camera's aptitude for recording.

This predilection for the contingent is yoked to the photographic base of the cinema. Historical analyses of photography consistently demonstrate photography's inclination toward the contingent, the particular, the detail. For Peter Galassi, photography is simply the culmination of a movement in the history of art away from the general and schematic and toward the precise, the partial, the transient and embodied view. In the two centuries preceding the birth of photography, artistic representation strove "to present a new and fundamentally modern pictorial syntax of immediate, synoptic perceptions and discontinuous, unexpected forms. It is the syntax of an art devoted to the singular and contingent rather than the universal and stable. It is also the syntax of photography."[4]

It is a theme which continually recurs in discourses on photography. In "A Small History of Photography" (1931), Benjamin claims that "No matter how artful the photographer, no matter how carefully posed his subject, the beholder feels an irresistible urge to search such a picture for the tiny spark of contingency, of the Here and Now, with which reality has so to speak seared the subject . . . "[5] Writing in 1927,

Siegfried Kracauer examines the role of the detail, the accessory in photography and argues that the photograph "must be essentially associated with the moment in time at which it came into existence."[6] Such an appeal to the indexicality of the photograph grounds Roland Barthes's more recent investigation of photography in *Camera Lucida* and underwrites the very category of the "punctum" (the unstructured, unanticipated detail which fascinates the individual spectator).[7]

But the analysis of photography's alliance with contingency is predicated upon the acknowledgment that photography freezes a moment in time (Kracauer's "essential" association with the "moment in time in which it came into existence"). In a sense, as Barthes has argued, the photograph is imbued with an immediate "pastness." In the cinema, the appeal to contingency is from the start saturated with temporality. Filmic duration is the factor that leads Barthes to posit the absoluteness of the gap between photography and film as modes of representation; their temporal references are distinct and opposed. While photography is inevitably in the past tense, evoking the recognition of a *"having-been-there,"* the cinema makes an inexorable appeal to the present tense—a *"being-there* of the thing."[8] Yet, Barthes is wrong or, at the very least, incomplete. For there are always at least two temporalities at work in film. Accompanying the spectatorial experience of the present tense of the filmic flow is the recognition that the images were produced at a particular time, that they are inevitably stained with their own historicity. This is what allows film to age—quickly and visibly—in a way similar to that of the photograph. Not only does the technology itself become "dated" (the use of black and white, Cinemascope, film noir lighting) but the contents of the image inevitably bear the traces of the moment in time at which they were produced (fashion, cars, interior design, architecture). As André Gaudreault points out, unlike literature, a fiction film is "necessarily compelled to give an account of some sort of reality—that is, the one that appeared in front of the camera—even though it has been disguised in a fiction in order to be recorded" and "it is indeed by using portions of historical time that cinema builds up *fictional* time, hence the always-already-given historiographical character of cinematographic time."[9] In this respect, the cinema's alliance with contingency, like that of photography, would appear to be irreducible.

The plethora of actualities produced between 1895 and 1904–5 testifies to the strength of such a recognition. Seemingly *anything* could constitute the occasion for a film—most famously, perhaps, the simple activity of workers leaving a factory, the arrival of a train, a snowball fight, children swimming, feeding a baby, etc. The cinema was assigned the task of producing a record of time which allowed for the spontaneous and unexpected—a look at the camera, a shadowy figure passing in front of the lens. What was intended as "event" could, at least theoretically, be overshadowed. This is not to suggest, however, that actualities were uncomposed or unstructured, that they did, in fact, constitute simply a transparent record. As Thomas Elsaesser points out,

> Actualities obliged the film-maker to create, even as he [sic] records an event, a specific sequential or spatial logic, which becomes in some sense the event's (intensified) abstracted representation, as opposed to reproducing its (extensive) duration.[10]

However, Elsaesser's claim here is haunted by the difficulties and contradictions which always seem to adhere to the concept of the event. The event precedes its record—it possesses its own duration which can, in a subsequent moment, be intensified or abstracted. The argument enacts a theoretical (and popular) tendency to situate the event as the site of residence of the contingent (a tendency to which I will later return). Nevertheless, it would be more accurate to note that the cinema, together with other technologies of modernity, is instrumental in producing and corroborating an investment in events, in dividing temporality to elicit eventful and uneventful time. The confusion of construction and contingency around the concept of the event is crucial in the historical elaboration of a cinematic syntax. At the turn of the century, contingency is both lure and threat, and this double valence is played out in the rapid representational transformations of the cinema. The embarrassment of contingency is that it is everywhere and that it everywhere poses the threat of an evacuation of meaning. The concept of the event provides a limit—not everything is equally filmable—and reinvests the contingent with significance. The contingent is, in effect, tamed.

In this respect, the short-lived genre of the actuality provides a particularly fertile field of investigation since it harbors the contradictory dream of re-presenting the contingent. What I would like to focus on here is the inscription of the contingent in two early actualities (one on the scene of the event, the other re-enacted) and the implications of that inscription for the conceptualization of the cinema's relation to time, its status as a quite precise type of technology of temporality. The films are *Electrocuting an Elephant* (Edison, 1903) and *Execution of Czolgosz with Panorama of Auburn Prison* (Porter/Edison, 1901). Both films inhabit the particularly popular subgenre of the execution film, which included titles such as *Execution by Hanging* (Mutascope/Biograph, 1905), *Reading the Death Sentence* (Mutascope/Biograph, 1905),[11] *Execution of a Spy* (Mutascope/Biograph, 1902), *Beheading the Chinese Prisoner* (Lubin, 1900), and *The Execution of Mary Queen of Scots* (Edison, 1895). The subgenre manifests an intense fascination with the representation of death, or the conjunction of life and death (contemporary sources describe the paradox of the image of death in a medium which makes represented bodies so "life-like"[12]). Death and the contingent have something in common insofar as they are both situated as that which is unassimilable to meaning. Death would seem to mark the insistence and intractability of the real in representation.

Electrocuting an Elephant utilizes authentic footage of the execution of an elephant who had killed three men. The film begins as the elephant is led toward the camera. The camera pans to the right to keep the elephant in frame and the elephant effectively walks into a close-up. There is then a jump cut (probably caused by a camera stoppage to elide the time necessary to attach the animal to the electrocuting apparatus). In the following shot, the elephant stands facing the camera, tied down, with two of her feet attached to wooden sandals. A sign in the background advertises Luna Park as the "Heart of Coney Island." Suddenly, smoke rises from the elephant's feet and envelopes her as she stiffens and collapses forward. A shadowy figure passes in front of the camera which holds on the scene a while longer as the elephant produces a few more jerks and twitches. *Electrocuting an Elephant* was released on January 12, 1903. The *New York World* of January 5 reported the incident: "While fifteen hundred persons looked on in breathless excitement, an electric bolt of 6,000 volts sent Topsy, the man-killing elephant, staggering to the ground yesterday afternoon at Luna Park, Coney Island. With her own life [she] paid for the lives of the three men she had killed . . . It was all over in a moment."[13] The reference to the fifteen hundred persons looking on "in breathless excitement" indicates that the elephant's death constituted a spectacle for the Coney Island audience as well. The crucial difference is that the film managed to reach an audience not physically present at the scene as well as to act as an indexical record of Topsy's death. And while the newspaper account reached its audience faster, the film allowed the spectator to see with his/her own eyes the exhibition of an elephant's death throes. Hence the nickname given to the early cinema—the "visual newspaper."[14]

Execution of Czolgosz also exploits an interest in current events. On September 6, 1901, while President McKinley was visiting the Pan-American Exposition in Buffalo, he was shot by the Cleveland anarchist, Leon Czolgosz, and died eight days later. Czolgosz was tried, found guilty, and executed on October 29. Edison exploited interest in the assassination by producing the reenactment of the assassin's execution, whose complete title was *Execution of Czolgosz with Panorama of Auburn Prison*. It is clear that Edison would have liked to film the actual execution or at least Czolgosz entering the death chamber, but in the absence of permission to do so, the crew had to settle for a panorama of the prison walls taken the morning of the execution joined with a reenactment of the electrocution which the company labeled "a realistic imitation of the last scene in the electric chair."[15] The film begins with a pan following a train moving in front of the prison walls. There is a jump cut (possibly indicating only missing footage) to the same type of pan moving along a stationary train and ending after the last empty car. The next shot is a pan, also moving to the right, over the massive prison walls, ending with the image of bare trees in the prison yard. There is a dissolve to the next shot, in which Czolgosz waits in his cell. Prison guards stand motionless on the right side of the frame and begin to move toward the cell several seconds after the initiation of the shot. As they approach, Czolgosz shrinks back. The guards lead him from the cell and exit frame right. In the second interior shot, the electric chair is prominently centered in the frame and the State Electrician, wardens, and doctor are making a final test of the electricity with a bank of electric light bulbs. The bulbs are removed and

Czolgosz is escorted into the frame from the right. He stumbles briefly as he is seated in the chair and is strapped in. The warden gives the signal, the electric switch is pulled, and Czolgosz heaves three times and is still. The warden and doctor confirm that he is dead.

The two films have a great deal in common. Both exhibit a marked fascination with electricity as a conveyor of death. In the 1880s the electric chair had become the socially acceptable form of execution, and at the turn of the century electricity was still an intriguing phenomenon in its own right. Electricity signifies not only a technological form of death but a compression of time and process as well. For electricity seems to effectively annihilate delay, the distance between cause and effect, and to evoke the idea of the instantaneous.

A second attribute shared by the two films is their status as the orchestration of guilt and punishment around the concept of a criminality understood in relation to otherness. Czolgosz is tinged with the threat of the foreign, the immigrant, the unfamiliar. Topsy's name ineluctably reverberates with the racial politics of *Uncle Tom's Cabin* as well as with the colonialist aspirations distilled in the representational repertoire of the circus. Benjamin claimed that Atget's work demonstrated the close allegiance between the space of photography and the scene of a crime.[16] The transformation of the contingent into evidence allies it with a legal hermeneutics. When any detail can become the sign of a crime, can make legible guilt or innocence, photographic and cinematographic evidence enables the subordination of the contingent to the rule of law, ultimately imbued with a power over life and death. Electrocution simultaneously provides a "clean" way, an efficient and punctual method for dealing with such tainted criminality and a forum for the exhibition of technological prowess. In its own fashion it also involves a taming and structuring of the accidental: the idea of electrocution allegedly emerged from the witnessing of accidental electrical death (a man being killed instantly by a live wire).[17]

While *Electrocuting an Elephant* and *Execution of Czolgosz* both activate curiosity about electricity and the lure of witnessing an electrical death, there is one difference between the two films which to today's spectator of film, photography, and television would seem to far outweigh any similarities. For the relations to time sustained by the two films are quite different, if not opposed. In *Electrocuting an Elephant*, the camera operator is actually present at the scene of the execution and the death recorded is a "real" death. There are various textual assurances of this fact: the camera operator's presence is marked by the pan which follows the movement of the elephant into close-up, the break in the footage or camera stoppage functions to elide time but is not concealed as a rupture (the implication being that it is a pragmatic break which simply excises "uneventful" time), the image is composed in depth (as opposed to the flatness of staged productions), and its contents are not entirely predictable (a shadowy figure passes in front of the camera after the elephant collapses). None of this, of course, guarantees that the image is acually documentary, but certain stylistic traits had already been attached to the on-the-scene actuality, giving it a rudimentary form and recognizability.

The question of the epistemological status of the image is less certain with *Execution of Czolgosz*, which was a reenactment and advertised as a "realistic imitation." In a reenactment, the time of the image does not coincide with the time of the event signified. The construction of the Czolgosz film is evidence of an awareness of that disjunction and of an attempt to rectify it. As Charles Musser has pointed out, the film is a hybrid, joining the panorama with the dramatic reenactment.[18] The opening pans of Auburn Prison were taken on the day of Czolgosz's execution, thus providing the spectator with images whose temporality did, in fact, coincide with that of the actual event being represented. Nevertheless, once the film circulates as a product, that temporality becomes illegible, effaced from the image which is disengaged from its origins. In the absence of outside information about their origin, the temporality of the pans receives specification internally, as a function of their juxtaposition with the reenacted scene of the execution and their own duration on the screen.

Given the representational history of the panorama, it is not surprising that the pan in the cinema would first be activated in the on-the-scene footage of the actuality which fully exploited the realistic effect associated with its photographic base. Here, the illusionistic virtuosity is a function not of the skill of the camera operator (whose task has been largely appropriated by the automatism associated with the machine) but of simply being there at the right time. The accumulation of historical detail was one of the assumed properties of the apparatus, and the unpredictability of the random movement of figures within the frame consolidated the impression of the real. The cinematic pan, like the panorama, constituted a denial of the frame as boundary, and hence promised access to a seemingly limitless vision.

Since the pan in the early cinema signified a certain presence in relation to the event, the stylistic disjunction of *Execution of Czolgosz, with Panorama of Auburn Prison* is quite striking. The "event," inside the prison, is filmed with a static camera, on a set which has no hint of depth. The camera movement which ought to guarantee the authenticity of the footage, its license to re-present, is allied with a shot of a space where nothing happens but which has at least a metonymic link to the site in question. It is almost as though the filmmakers hoped that the panoramas' temporal coincidence with the event would somehow bleed over into the restaged scenes and contaminate them with their veracity or authenticity. The pans of Auburn Prison act as an alibi (in the etymological sense of invoking "another place") or an excuse which entails being elsewhere.

Nevertheless, there is no attempt to deceive the spectator who is forewarned that this is a "realistic imitation." In fact, *Execution of Czolgosz* fits readily into the well-accepted category of the dramatic reenactment, a subgenre which lost its currency around 1907.[19] These films modeled themselves on important current events and often used newspaper accounts as pretexts. They were advertised as "faithful duplications," "reproductions," "dramatic representations of current events." The anomalous category of the dramatic reenactment seems to grasp simultaneously at two contradictory temporal modes of the cinematic image. On the one hand, the reenactment exploits the temporal specificity of the image, its ability to record a quite precise temporal event and hence to be "timely" or topical. Thus, the "visual newspaper" rushes to represent the most newsworthy current events, the more quickly the better. On the other hand, the very acceptability of the reconstruction of an event constitutes an acknowledgment of the atemporality of the image, the fact that it does not speak its own relation to time. Here, the temporal aspirations of the cinema would seem to be contained in the notion of making the event "present" to the spectator. David Levy argues quite convincingly that the re-enactment was a kind of transitional object between the actuality and the narrative film, that techniques developed in relation to the changing conditions in shooting actualities (pans, shooting in depth, non-eye-level angles, etc.) were taken up by narrative films to enhance their realism.[20] It seems to me equally plausible (and not necessarily in contradiction to such a hypothesis) to argue that narrative functioned as a displacement of unanswerable questions about the ontology of the image. What comes to be known eventually as "deception" in the reenactment is made harmless as "illusion" in the narrative film. Clearly, the progressive domination of the industry by narrative is overdetermined (culturally, economicaly, technologically), but from this point of view, narrative would constitute a certain taming or securing of the instability of the cinematic image. In the same way, narrative becomes the model for the apprehension of the legal unity of film.[21]

From this perspective, *Electrocuting an Elephant*, which postdates *Execution of Czolgosz* by two years, would appear to be the more "primitive" film. The time and space of the image coincide with the time and space of the referent; the spectator is positioned as an "onlooker" with a stable spatial viewpoint. The camera simply substitutes for the spectator who cannot manage to be at Coney Island at the appropriate moment. Hence, the film spectator sees nothing that the Coney Island spectator does not see. But this account is not quite true. For the film spectator sees both less and more. His or her vision is limited by the frame and the access it allows to the execution—when the camera pans, that vision shifts. Yet, the film spectator also sees something which the Coney Island spectator cannot see—a break in the film where the camera is stopped and then started again. Because this break constitutes an elipsis, it is arguable that the film spectator again or in another way sees less, but I want to focus on the sight of the break itself, which is by no means concealed. This is in contrast to a later execution film, *Execution by Hanging* (1905), in which a camera stoppage is the condition of possibility of the representation of a death. In this reenactment of an execution, a woman is led up to the stage, a black hood is placed over her face and a noose is placed around her neck. At this point, there is a barely perceptible break in which, evidently, the actors freeze in position, the woman is removed, and a dummy is substituted for her so that the execution can continue unimpeded. When the film is screened, the break is all but invisible. Such a strategy is a denial of process and insures the spectator's experience of continuous time. In *Electrocuting an Elephant*, there is no attempt to conceal the break or to deny its existence. That break functions to elide time that is seen to be "uneventful"—the work of situating the elephant and binding her in the electrical apparatus. The disruption is itself a signifier of a certain closeness to the real.

In an actuality, the time which is excluded or elided is constituted as "dead time"—time which, by definition, is outside of the event, "uneventful." But such an explanation assumes that the event is simply "out there" and dead time a byproduct of grasping the event's clear-cut and inherent structure. It would be more accurate, I think, to assume that an understanding of "dead time"—time in which nothing happens, time which is in some sense "wasted," expended without product—is the condition of a conceptualization of the "event." From this point of view the documentary event is not so far from the narrative event. The event may take time but it is packaged as a moment—time is condensed and becomes eminently meaningful. Such a conceptualization of time as punctual is fully consistent with the fascination with electricity. Part of the lure of electricity is the lure of an escape from process, duration, work. This conjunction of cinematic time and a temporality owing much to an understanding of electricity is suggested by Benjamin's notion of giving the moment a posthumous shock.[22]

In *Electrocuting an Elephant*, time is certainly condensed and abstracted but it also bears the stamp of an authenticity which is derived from the technological capabilities of the camera. Since the camera could not "be there" at the moment of the execution in *Execution of Czolgosz*, the film borrows the aura of technological authenticity by connecting the temporality of the pan (already a prime signifier of the actuality) and the temporality of the event. But the effectivity of taking the panorama shots on the day of the execution is lost unless the spectator has external knowledge about their origin, for the image is not self-sufficient in this respect; its own temporal history is not legible. In the earliest years of the cinema, this requirement of external spectatorial knowledge is not atypical but, rather, constitutes something of a norm. The spectator was often expected to have knowledge of another text (newspaper accounts of a current event that was being reenacted, for example, a familiar story [the passion plays, Jack and the Beanstalk, etc.] which the films alluded to or illustrated but did not fully develop).

Or, in many cases, the lecturer would act as an external source, pointing out aspects of the image whose readability might be a function of external information. Conditions of exhibition were grounded in an acknowledgment that the image was not self-sufficient.

In the actuality, the time of the image is determined to a large extent externally—ideally the time of the image and the time of the referent would coincide. The camera would act purely as a recording device. The dramatic reenactment of current events aspires to that temporal relation. But actualities, which dominate film production up until 1903, gradually lose ground with the ascendancy of narrative. Around 1907, the dramatic reenactment disappears as a genre despite the persistence of isolated examples.[23] The subordination of documentary to a marginal mode within the cinematic institution is simultaneous with the inscription of temporality as an internal attribute. Even within the realm of narrative, temporality attains a new level of significance. Narrative constructs its own coherent and linear temporality, enhancing the autonomy of the film and the self-sufficiency of its own projected spectator. The initial centrifugal momentum of film exhibition—in which the spectator is thrown outward from the viewing situation to other texts, other sources of knowledge, is halted. As André Gaudreault points out, ". . . an insistence on temporality [in narrative film] is a phenomenon which grows in importance during 1907. By the following year, many themes will emphasize story elements tied to temporality."[24] Gaudreault notes in particular the growing emphasis upon clocks in the mise-en-scène and on suspense as a structuring agent. Because the time flow is now an imaginary one, situated in the realm of fiction and mimicking a sense of ordinary everyday time, it cannot be tested against an external measure, thus contributing to the stabilization of a potentially deceptive or disruptive image.

From this point of view, the pans in *Execution of Czolgosz* constitute a type of hinge phenomenon since their temporality is readable as a function of both external and internal determinants. While the spectator would need external knowledge to verify the fact that the pans were taken on the day of the execution, there are other, internal signals of simultaneity drawn from a narrative imaginary—the dissolve which links the panoramas to the reenacted scenes, the resulting construction of an opposition between inside and outside which situates the pans as establishing shots, and the succession of shots which yokes the pans to a precisely timed story. In other words, the film exploits both the technology's relation to time (that of recording) and the technology's ability to construct a time which has the imaginary coherence of "real time," everyday time. It hedges its bets.

It would be inaccurate to suggest that the first relation to time (that of the actuality) is abandoned. Rather, it is rewritten in such a way that contingency and unpredictability are reduced as a part of the process, reemerging as the signified. The pan, resolutely linked to the real in the early days of the cinema, is also, in comparison with the panoramas of the early and mid-nineteenth century, a way of mechanizing and regulating the subject's relation to time. The cinema participates in the rationalization of time characterizing the industrial age. "Economy" is a fundamental value of the developed narrative film, and the efficiency of electricity is paralleled by the efficiency of narrative. Resolute linearity, efficiency, and economy are also crucial goals of scientific management in its attempt to deploy the human body in labor with a maximum reduction of wasted time. "Dead time" is, again, anathema. As Michael Chanan has argued,

It is this fixing of our experience of time which constitutes the dominant ideological form of time in commoditized society . . . . You could also say that the two processes—"scientific" management and "mass culture"—have in common the practice of *time economy* insofar as they both structure the flow of time.[25]

This analysis is consistent with Kracauer's understanding of mass culture in the 1920s as, at least in part, the negation of unorganized, unstructured time. In this context, boredom becomes the "only proper occupation," if not a radical resistance to the media's incessant production of images and sounds.[26] Mass culture seeks to annihilate the possibility of boredom, of dead time, of a monochrome, unpunctuated time. Modernity, in contrast, becomes the persistent production of events.

From this point of view, the inevitable historiographic tendency of cinema, its ability to record "real" time and its duration, poses critical difficulties for the early cinema. Cinema's time is surely referential—it is a true record of time with the weight of indexicality. But its time is also always characterized by a certain indeterminacy, an intolerable instability. The image is the imprint of a particular moment whose particularity becomes indeterminable precisely because the image does not speak its own relation to time. Film *is*, therefore, a record of time, but a nonspecific, nonidentifiable time, a disembodied unanchored time. The cinema hence becomes the production of a generalized experience of time, a duration. The unreadability or uncertainty concerning the image's relation to temporality and to its origin are not problems which are resolved—they are, in fact, insoluble. But they are displaced through the elaborate development of structures which produce the image of a coherent and unified "real time" that is much more "real" than "real time" itself. The resulting cinema delicately negotiates the contradiction between recording and signification.

It is striking that these dilemmas concerning the cinematic representation of time should emerge so starkly in films depicting executions. If cinematic narrative develops in part as a structuring of contingency (and hence its reduction as such), the most intractable contingencies would seem to be those having to do with the body and death. Early actualities exploit the cinema's apparent predilection for the contingent, its capacity to record whatever happens to be there at the moment. As highly structured as these actualities were, they left a space open for the unpredictable, the spontaneous—that which would differentiate the cinema from all previous forms of signification precisely because it appears to reject the very idea of meaning. Death is perhaps the ultimate trauma insofar as it is situated as that which is unassimilable to meaning (for Benjamin, "shock" named that which was unassimilable in experience, a residue of unreadability). Freud consistently emphasized that what the subject could never fully accept or grasp was the fact of his/her own death.

Perhaps the execution films circulate around the phenomenon of death, striving to capture the moment of death, in order to celebrate the contingency of the cinematic image, a celebration which is always already too late since the contingent, in the face of the cinematic apparatus, has already received a "posthumous shock." In the cinema, the fascination with depicting death, presenting it in a direct and unmediated way for the gaze of the spectator, lasts for only an extremely brief period of film history and a period which is also bound up with speculations about the new technology itself (what it is for, what it can do).

Just as electricity could be activated as a technological control over life and death, the cinema must have seemed to offer the same promise in the field of representation. Topsy and Czolgosz are kept alive through the representations of their deaths. Technology's veiled assurance of compensating for the limitations of the body, i.e., its finitude, would be synonymous with a hope of conquering death. But to the extent that the spontaneous and the unpredictable seemed to invade the image of the actuality, to the extent that that image cannot speak its own relation to temporality, narrative proved to be a more effective and sure means of assimilating the unassimilable by conferring on death a meaning. The direct presentation of death to the spectator as pure event, as shock, was displaced by its narrativization. Technology and narrative form an alliance in modernity to ameliorate the corrosiveness of the relation between time and subjectivity.

Perhaps death functions as a kind of cinematic ur-event because it appears as the zero degree of meaning, its evacuation. With death we are suddenly confronted with pure event, pure contingency, what ought to be inaccessible to representation (hence the various social and legal bans against the direct, nonfictional filming of death). Such a problematic is possible only where contingency and meaning, event and structure are radically opposed. The extreme instance of such a formulation is familiar to us in a more recent historical incarnation—that of structuralism. In "Structure, Sign and Play in the Discourse of the Human Sciences," Derrida opens a discussion of Lévi-Strauss's structuralism with a reference to the incompatibility of the concepts of structure and event, where the event emerges as a concept which is intolerable within a structuralist epistemology (to the extent that it is precisely that which is supposed to escape structure): "Perhaps something has occurred in the history of the concept of structure that could be called an 'event,' if this loaded word did not entail a meaning which it is precisely the function of structural—or structuralist—thought to reduce or suspect."[27] And Lévi-Strauss himself does, indeed, explicitly and extensively activate the opposition between structure and event, particularly in "The Science of the Concrete."[28] Unalloyed contingency is constituted as a danger, as the site of semiotic failure. Structuralism as a movement, in order to produce knowledge, evicts the event from its epistemological domain; it disdains the contingent. The event, within structuralism, is unthinkable, or, perhaps more accurately, the event can only be thought as rupture or catastrophe, as a kind of time or non-time between, marking the lack of a causal or developmental explanation for the historical change from one structure to another.

Structuralism should be historically out of place in this discussion of early cinema. But I would argue that it effectively consolidates an opposition between structure and event which at the turn of the century is emergent and, in many respects, less stable. The pressure of resolving the contradiction between the two seems more intense, and staking out a meaningful place for contingency becomes paramount. This is particularly striking in the work of Freud, who struggled incessantly, throughout his career, with the oppositions between constitution and event, fantasy and the real. But this struggle in and around the concept of the contingent is also visible even earlier, in the efforts of Baudelaire to come to terms with the trauma of modernity. I would like to examine briefly the way in which the opposition between structure and event (and its variants: the general and the particular, constitution and event, the necessary and the contingent) plays itself out in the work of these two figures before returning to the process through which the cinema grapples with this problematic.

It could be said that Freud's entire project is a battle against contingency, an attempt to violently yoke it to meaning. In *The Interpretation of Dreams* and *The Psychopathology of Everyday Life* no detail is immune from significance, and meaning is located where one would most expect opacity, unreadability. But it is the theory of the screen memory that condenses most strikingly Freud's confrontation with the concept of the contingent.[29] For the screen memory is a detail, a contingency which is nevertheless richly vivid and sensuous in its cognitive opacity. It stands out in a scene and constitutes itself as the marker of specificity itself. The trivial, the indifferent, the contingent comes to act as a veil, covering over significance—"an unsuspected wealth of meaning lies concealed behind their [the screen memories'] apparent innocence."[30] The detail—that which stands out in a scene—becomes a *screen*. Itself emptied of content, the screen memory attains value through a relation, a spatial and temporal connection; it is in the "neighborhood" of meaning. The screen memory becomes legible through this connection and is ultimately subordinated to a more significant psychical scenario.

The Psychopathology of Everyday Life is an extended demonstration of the impossibility of the concepts of chance or meaninglessness in psychical life. Every moment of forgetting, every gesture, every slip of the tongue is legible. But toward the end of this work, Freud becomes somewhat nervous about the extensiveness of the implied determinism and devotes a chapter to "Determinism, Belief in Chance and Superstition," in which he attempts to defend himself against charges of superstition. The superstitious person differs from the psychoanalyst (i.e., Freud) insofar as he/she projects meaning outward, onto "external chance happenings" or "real events." Freud claims, "he [the superstitious person] interprets chance as due to an event, while I trace it back to a thought," and "I believe in external (real) chance, it is true, but not in internal (psychical) accidental events."[31] With this gesture, Freud effectively relegates contingency to the event, defined as external, nonpsychical, "real." Perhaps this is why Freud resisted the cinema; chained to the domain of the visible, to the external surface of events, the cinema must have struck Freud as a veritable reservoir of meaninglessness. Nevertheless, the distinctions Freud struggled to maintain at the end of The Psychopathology—between psychoanalysis and superstition, structure and event, the internal and the external—were always fragile and subject to collapse in the course of his own analyses. And at times he actively attempted to dismantle them. Contingency haunted Freud as the mark of interpretive failure, and frequently his texts bear witness to a troubled and uneasy relation to the category of the event.

In Baudelaire, the opposition is cast in somewhat different terms. The logic of the essay, "The Painter of Modern Life," is structured by the tension between the general and the particular, the eternal and the contingent, oppositions whose deployment ultimately hinges on the figure of the woman. For Baudelaire, modernity is "the ephemeral, the fugitive, the contingent, the half of art whose other half is the eternal and the immutable."[32] His endeavor is to collapse the opposition between the two, to situate the contingent as the only possible means of access to the eternal, to "distill the eternal from the transitory" (12). Any attempt to relinquish the contingent, to attain pure and unadulterated access to eternal and immutable beauty, courts danger and can only be figured as a confrontation with a gaping hole, an abyss which is figured in its turn as originary and timeless female beauty.

This transitory, fugitive element, whose metamorphoses are so rapid, must on no account be despised or dispensed with. By neglecting it, you cannot fail to tumble into the abyss of an abstract and indeterminate beauty, like that of the first woman before the fall of man. (13)

The first woman is naked and exposed, and it is fashion which, for Baudelaire, is the very site of contingency and acts as a defense against this abyss. It is the woman's clothing—the "muslins, the gauzes, the vast, iridescent clouds of stuff in which she envelops herself" (30)—which protects the man against the blinding abyss of the abstract, the indeterminable and, ultimately, against meaninglessness. It is the contingent which, in Baudelaire as in Freud, comes to bear the weight of meaning. Yet, Baudelaire, like Freud, vacillates. Although Baudelaire was certainly drawn toward the ephemeral, the fleeting, the effervescent which he associated with modernity, his nostalgia for the eternal is also quite apparent. He strives to maintain a precarious balance between structure and event.

The last half of the nineteenth century witnesses the growth of the perception of contingency as both threat and lure. And both could be said to be linked to its tenuous and unstable relation to meaning. The cinema emerges in this context as a technology which appears to be capable of *representing* the contingent, of providing the ephemeral with a durable record. This capability is the source of both fascination and anxiety. For the idea of representation without meaning involves the forfeiture of limits and hence of semiotic control. The cinema is forced to confront the episteme wherein structure and event both oppose and tantalize one another. The polarization of structure and event that underwrites structuralism is less tenable at the turn of the century, and Freud, Baudelaire, and the cinema all contest, in some manner, its logic.

The cinematic image's privileged relation to the contingent renders it unstable. As certain as the spectator may be that this image is a record of a real duration, a unique temporality, that temporality is unspecifiable and unverifiable. This temporal instability is dealt with historically in two ways. The first can be traced in the movement from the actuality, with its allegiance to the ephemeral and the contingent, to narrative as a tightly structured web of manufactured temporalities. In both, it is the event which comes to bear the weight of meaning—the event, where time coagulates and where the contingent can be readily imbued with meaning through its very framing *as* event. The elision of time that structures *Electrocuting an Elephant* actively undercuts the dissipation of the contingent, the "riot of details" feared by Baudelaire, to produce simultaneously the event and its significance. In *Execution of Czolgosz*, a transitional form between actuality and narrative, the contingency which seems to be specific to the medium is subjected to a temporal domain where it is transformed into a second-order signifier of the real. The internal lack of temporal specificity of the opening pan is retrospectively endowed with historical certainty by the highly structured narrative of Czolgosz's death, at the same time that the pan lends to the narrative the authority of the contingent. At what point does the shadowy figure who passes in front of the camera in *Electrocuting an Elephant* cease to be a marker of instability, of potential spontaneity, and become the signifier of a medium's power to access the real?

The second attempt to deal with the temporal instability of the image involves not the taming of the contingent but its denial. Like the event, spectacle effects a coagulation of time, but in its effort to evoke an "abstract and indeterminate beauty" it courts the outcome feared by Baudelaire—that of tumbling into the "abyss" of femininity. The event bears a relation to time, spectacle does not. Spectacle is, as Laura Mulvey has pointed out, fundamentally atemporal, associated with stasis and the antilinear.[33] And it is not accidental that Mulvey's influential attempt to delineate the production of sexual difference in the cinema is forged through the crucial categories of narrative (as a chain of *events*) and spectacle. In a film, the event furthers and supports narrative progression while the spectacle halts it in a protracted stare. Spectacle is not a self-evident category in the early cinema and it, together with its allied fetishistic and voyeuristic spectator, have been analyzed as a relatively late formation, synonymous with the development of the classical system.[34] Nevertheless, I would argue that it emerges sporadically much earlier, as a crucial component of the representational struggle with contingency. Spectacle functions to localize desire, fantasy, and longing in a timeless time, outside of contingency. In this respect, spectacle, in contrast to the event, is epistemologically reactionary, and decidedly *unmodern* (in the terms outlined by Baudelaire). For, the spectacle of female beauty becomes the nostalgia for pure structure—a world without contingency.

The cinema's struggles with contingency repeat in the field of representation what Ian Hacking has termed the "taming of chance" in sociology, philosophy, and the sciences during roughly the same time period.[35] And, as he points out, the growing acknowledgment of and acceptance of chance and indeterminism did not imply chaos or a loss of control. To the contrary, it consolidated the law–like regularities of statistics and probability and encouraged the growing numerical quality of knowledge. The idea of the normal produced in such a context implied an even greater control over that situated as deviant, aberrant, other. The cinema's predilection for the contingent was accompanied by the threat of excess and representational indeterminacy. In many respects, this was most evident in its capacity to record/represent a duration, unanchored and potentially without limits. Temporality hence became the site of the critical control and regulation of cinematic meaning. The cinema had a stake in not allowing the event to fall outside the domain of structure. In the cinema, as in much theoretical writing of the period, it would be more accurate to say that the event comes to harbor contingency within its very structure.

NOTES

1. Walter Benjamin, *Illuminations*, trans. Harry Zohn, ed. Hannah Arendt (1968; reprint, New York: Schocken Books, 1969), p. 184.

2. Georg Simmel, "The Metropolis and Mental Life" in *The Sociology of Georg Simmel*, ed. and trans. Kurt H. Wolff (London: Collier-Macmillan, 1950), pp. 412–13.

3. Tom Gunning, "An Aesthetic of Astonishment: Early Film and the (In)credulous Spectator" in *Art and Text* 34 (Spring 1989), p. 35.

4. Peter Galassi, *Before Photography: Painting and the Invention of Photography* (New York: The Museum of Modern Art, 1981), p. 25.

5. Walter Benjamin, *One Way Street and Other Writings*, trans. Edmund Jephcott and Kingsley Shorter (London: Verso, 1985), p. 243.

6. Siegfried Kracauer, *The Mass Ornament: Weimar Essays*, trans. and ed. Thomas Y. Levin (Cambridge: Harvard University Press, 1995), p. 54.

7. Roland Barthes, *Camera Lucida: Relections on Photography* (New York: Hill and Wang, 1981), pp. 40–43.

8. Roland Barthes, *Image, Music, Text*, trans. Stephen Heath (New York: The Noonday Press, 1977), p. 45.

9. André Gaudreault, "The Cinematograph: A Historiographical Machine" in *Meanings in Texts and Actions: Questioning Paul Ricoeur*, eds. David E. Klemm and William Schweiker (Charlottesville: The University Press of Virginia, 1993), p. 95.

10. Thomas Elsaesser, "Early Cinema: From Linear History to Mass Media Archaeology" in *Early Cinema: Space, Frame, Narrative*, ed. Thomas Elsaesser (London: British Film Institute, 1990), p. 17.

11. *Execution by Hanging* and *Reading the Death Sentence* are clearly segments of the same film. In line with the practices at this time, the exhibitor was given the option of buying the parts as separate entities.

12. Charles Musser, *Before the Nickelodeon: Edwin S. Porter and the Edison Manufacturing Company* (Berkeley: University of California Press, 1991), p. 187.

13. Cited in *Before Hollywood: Turn-of-the-Century Film from American Archives* (New York: The American Federation of the Arts, 1986), p. 109.

14. Musser, pp. 162–67.

15. Musser, p. 187.

16. Benjamin, "A Small History of Photography," p. 256.

17. Tim Armstrong, "The Electrification of the Body at the Turn of the Century" in *Textual Practice* 5 (Winter 1991), p. 315.

18. The exhibitor was given the option of buying the narrative section with or without the opening panoramas. See Musser, p. 188.

19. David Levy, "Re-constituted Newsreels, Re-enactments and the American Narrative Film" in *Cinema 1900/1906: An Analytical Study*, ed. Roger Holman (Brussels: Fédération Internationale des Archives du Film, 1982), p. 248.

20. Levy, p. 243–58.

21. See, for instance, André Gaudreault, "The Infringement of Copyright Laws and its Effects (1900-1906)" in *Early Cinema: Space, Frame, Narrative*, pp. 114–122.

22. Benjamin, *Illuminations*, p. 175. Benjamin is referring to still photography here but later he designates "shock" as a formal principle of film.

23. Levy, p. 254.

24. André Gaudreault, "Temporality and Narrativity in Early Cinema, 1895–1908" in *Film Before Griffith*, ed. John L. Fell (Berkeley: University of California Press, 1983), p. 326.

25. Michael Chanan, *The Dream that Kicks: The Prehistory and Early Years of Cinema in Britain* (London: Routledge & Kegan Paul, 1980), p. 41.

26. *The Mass Ornament*, pp. 331–34.

27. Jacques Derrida, "Structure, Sign and Play in the Discourse of the Human Sciences," *Writing and Difference*, trans. Alan Bass (Chicago: University of Chicago Press, 1978), p. 278.

28. Claude Lévi-Strauss, *The Savage Mind* (Chicago: The University of Chicago Press, 1966), pp. 1–34.

29. For a related and extremely provocative reading of Freud's concept of the screen memory, see Naomi Schor, *Reading in Detail: Aesthetics and the Feminine* (New York: Methuen, 1987), pp. 71–78.

30. Sigmund Freud, "Screen Memories" in *The Standard Edition of the Complete Psychological Works of Sigmund Freud*, vol. III, trans. James Strachey (London: The Hogarth Press and the Institute of Psychoanalysis, 1962), p. 309.

31. Sigmund Freud, *The Psychopathology of Everyday Life*, trans. Alan Tyson, ed. James Strachey (New York: W.W. Norton & Company, Inc., 1965), p. 257.

32. Charles Baudelaire, *The Painter of Modern Life and Other Essays*, trans. and ed. Jonathan Mayne (New York: Da Capo Press, 1964), p. 13. Subsequent references are given as page numbers in the text.

33. Laura Mulvey, "Visual Pleasure and Narrative Cinema" in *Visual and Other Pleasures* (Bloomington: Indiana University Press, 1989), pp. 14–28.

34. See, for instance, Miriam Hansen, *Babel and Babylon: Spectatorship in American Silent Film* (Cambridge: Harvard University Press, 1991).

35. Ian Hacking, *The Taming of Chance* (Cambridge: Cambridge University Press, 1990).

6

MARSHA KINDER

I. REFRAMING EISENSTEIN'S
ANALOGIES

SCREEN WARS

TRANSMEDIA

APPROPRIATIONS

FROM EISENSTEIN

TO *A TV DANTE* AND

CARMEN SANDIEGO

Only by a critical comparison with the more
basic early forms of the spectacle is it possible
to master critically the specific methodology of
the cinema.

—Eisenstein, "A Course in Treatment," 1932

A good old text always is a blank for new things.

—Phillips, *A TV Dante*, 1988.

IN HIS 1929 ESSAY, "The Cinematographic Principle and the Ideogram,"
Sergei Eisenstein contrasts the Japanese
method of teaching drawing with that
used in the west, claiming that the former provides a wonderful model in cinema for "the most fascinating of optical
conflicts: the conflict between the frame
of the shot and the object."[1] He
observes that whereas in the western
approach students are given a four-cor-
nered piece of white paper and then
asked to "cram onto it" some object
artificially placed in the center, in Japan
they are shown the branch of a cherry-
tree and then asked to cut out "compositional units" from this whole object,
with a square, circle, or rectangle, as if
"hewing out a piece of actuality with
the ax of the lens" (see Figure 1). By
appropriating this analogue from
Japanese culture, Eisenstein not only
helped defamiliarize his own approach
to cinematographic montage (making it appear a more radical departure
from other Soviet and American alternatives) but he simultaneously
made it seem universal (since it had analogues in other cultures and art
forms). It was not just the conflict between the object and its framing

that provided a new resource for dialectic montage but also the way he framed this conflict through a *comparison* across contextualizing media, cultures, and periods, a process that generated a productive analogy between framing and adaptation. Having demonstrated that frame and object are positions which can be occupied by a wide range of signifiers, he remained open to new analogies, for (like new technologies

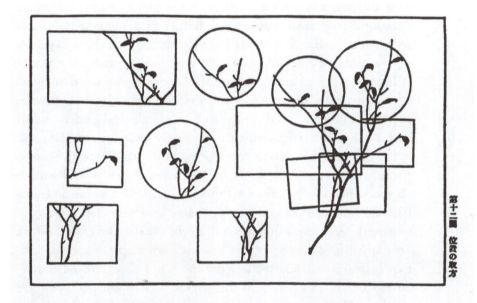

Fig. 6.1   An illustration of the Japanese method of teaching drawing from Eisenstein's *"The Cinematographic Principle and the Ideogram."*

such as sound and color) they provided raw material for expanding dialectic montage.

This strategic mode of analogic argumentation frequently comes under attack in the discourse on Eisenstein's theory, most recently in David Bordwell's *The Cinema of Eisenstein* (1993). Accusing him of being "intellectually promiscuous" and attacking his "often diverse and obscure formulations" in which "digressions abound, and argument by analogy is much in evidence,"[2] Bordwell (like J. Dudley Andrew two decades ear-

lier) tries to prune him down to a neo-Aristotelian purity.[3] In the process
Eisenstein is stripped of his dialectics and transformed into a Bordwellian
whose main contribution is "an empirical poetics of cinema" (114).

In contrast, this essay will build on Eisenstein's "promiscuous" use of
analogies by reframing it as an ongoing process of transmedia adaptation, in which earlier works are appropriated as a "screen" through which
artists and audiences perceive and thereby shape a new medium. While
the designated "pair" in the analogy is a temporary point of collision
with historical and cultural specificity, it provides access to other multi-
directional comparisons that lead us farther afield temporally, spatially,
and culturally and thereby destabilize a topography of center and periphery—a strategy that is analogous to the decentered, multilinear structures
of hypertexts that increasingly characterize our own postmodernist period.

For example, Eisenstein's comparison between Japanese drawing
and Soviet cinema could lead us to Chinese classical gardens, which
have a conception of framing that is closely analogous to that found
in the Japanese approach to drawing—a move that would give greater
resonance to Eisenstein's choice of the cherry branch as his illustrative
object. When one enters an architectural structure within a classical
Chinese garden, one frequently finds four diversely shaped windows
to gaze through, each facing in a different cardinal direction. Like the
variously shaped cuttings of the Japanese drawing paper, each window
frames the outer landscape in a distinct way and thereby generates a
different dialectic conflict. Moreover, the four landscapes themselves
are also deliberately cultivated to maximize the differences. Thus, when
the spectator turns from one window to another, she experiences a
complex montage effect that is analogous to cinema—particularly if
that perception has been filtered through a reading of Eisenstein.

One can also extend Eisenstein's analogy by exploring its morphological connections with the structure of the essay in which it
appears. This passage occurs within a long (six-page) digression on
the shot, which is positioned slightly off-center in the middle of a
seventeen-page essay and begins, "Let us be allowed the luxury of a
digression—on the matter of the shot, to settle the debated question
of its nature, once and for all" (36). Paradoxically this luxurious digression becomes the heart of the essay (its main object like the cherry
branch), transforming the so-called main body into a frame. In his later

essay, "Dickens, Griffith, and the Film Today" (1944), Eisenstein marvels at Dickens's use of the same formal strategy in *Cricket on the Hearth*, where he "wedges . . . a whole digression . . . in the *very center*" of his story to express his "own 'treatise' on the principles of this montage construction . . . which he carries out so fascinatingly."[4] Aware of the power dynamics implicit in adaptation, Eisenstein notes that this formal strategy "passed into the style of Griffith" but without mentioning that he had appropriated it himself in "The Cinematographic Principle and the Ideogram." By revealing Griffith's indebtedness to Dickens, Eisenstein strategically naturalizes his own indebtedness to Griffith while positioning himself higher on the chain of appropriation, which gives him greater mastery over the drive toward the future. As he puts it,

> I understand quotations as outrunners to the right and left of the galloping shaft horse. Sometimes they diverge, but they help to speed the imagination by their broadening, reinforcing parallel run. As long as one does not let go of the reins![5]

This essay will pursue Eisenstein's galloping transmedia appropriations, first briefly moving backward beyond Dickens to the early development of the English novel, a hybridized genre that reinscribed conventions borrowed from earlier forms, and then leaping forward to television, a medium that has come to mediate our understanding and consumption of virtually all other forms of cultural production, including those newly emerging multimedia hyptertexts.

The explicit comparison between Eisenstein and Dickens evokes a virtual analogy with Henry Fielding, primarily for two reasons. First, his novels provide the structural link between digression and montage that Eisenstein attributed to Dickens. As in the example of the Chinese garden, they are latent intertexts that lie hidden behind the direct allusion. Not only did *Joseph Andrews* and *Tom Jones* directly influence Dickens, but their authorial narrators acknowledge that they in turn learned the structural principle of digression and the "art of contrast" from Cervantes and Homer. Moreover, Fielding uses these structural devices to achieve two of the same epistemological goals that Eisenstein pursued through his montage—a broader comprehensiveness in scope and a greater mastery in reinscribing quotations and perceptions.

Second, there is an uncanny parallel in the way Eisenstein and Fielding used their early experimentation in the theater to conceptualize the cinema and novel respectively. In his 1934 essay, "Through Theater to Cinema," Eisenstein describes how experiments designed to overcome the technical limits of the stage in plays like *The Mexican* and *Gas Masks* ultimately led to a theory of montage, which he could develop more fully once he turned to cinema. Paradoxically, this movement from theater to cinema did not make his films more theatrical; on the contrary, it made them more cinematic, for they emphasize the differences between the two media.

Precisely the same dynamic occurs in the case of Fielding. Before helping to launch the English novel, he wrote twenty-six plays, including four experimental works: *The Author's Farce* (1730), his first burlesque; *The Tragedy of Tragedies* (1731), his best-known play; *Pasquin* (1736), his biggest contemporary success; and *The Historical Register* (1737), the satire which motivated the 1737 Licensing Act that forced Fielding out of the theater. In these four plays he experimented with five main devices: a hybridization of forms, a play within a play, an on-stage author who commented on the action, an on-stage spectator whose reactions could be mocked, and a comparative structure that promoted digressions and verbal irony.[6] These devices achieved a more comprehensive scope and a tighter control over audience response, qualities difficult to attain through ordinary dramatic conventions. Once Fielding left the stage, these experimental devices were easily transferred to the novel where they could be pushed much further. As in the case of Eisenstein, this movement from theater to fiction did not make his novels more theatrical; on the contrary, it made them emphasize precisely those qualities that were ordinarily lacking in theater.

Despite the distance between Fielding and Eisenstein in period, culture, and media, their careers both support Walter Benjamin's observation that

> One of the foremost tasks of art has always been the creation of a demand which could be fully satisfied only later. The history of every art form shows critical epochs in which a certain art form aspires to effects which could be fully obtained only with a changed technical standard, that is to say, in a new art form.[7]

This process of accommodation carries a threat of obsolescence for the older art form functioning as screen—a threat that was largely disavowed in the discourse of authorial mastery performed by Fielding and Eisenstein.

II. *A TV DANTE* AS HYPERTEXT

This threat reemerged with a vengeance in the decentered hypertexts of postmodernism, particularly as theorized by George Landow:

> One *should* feel threatened by hypertext, just as writers of romances and epics should have felt threatened by the novel and Venetian writers of Latin tragedy should have felt threatened by the *Divine Comedy* and its Italian text. Descendants, after all, offer continuity with the past, but only at the cost of replacing it.[8]

Or as Michael Heim puts it: "Over the ten years of the 1980s . . . an estimated 80 percent of written language began existing in digital form. Computers swallowed the cultural heritage of English-speaking countries."[9] Although theorists like Landow and Heim focus on the displacement of the page by the screen (what Sven Birkerts calls "the reading wars") and the threat that it poses for literature, all three ignore the relationship between hypertext and television, a medium that uses its position in the home to mediate all other forms of cultural production.

Rather than focus on the early days of television when the primary rivalry was with prior media like radio and cinema, I will select a few examples from the 1980s and 90s when the main threat is coming from the digitized future—from multimedia computers. With the massive restructuring of communication and information technologies and the increasing fetishization of convergence and connectivity, no medium can afford to stand alone; like a lego piece it acquires new meanings and functions in each new corporate merger and network that is built, deconstructed, and made over. The driving question is which medium will absorb or "swallow" the other, even if both are transformed in the process. Although television (like cinema and the novel before it) still frequently adapts texts from prior media (as if mobilizing the past to forestall the threat of obsolescence), it also increasingly simulates futuristic rivals by masquerading as a multimedia hypertext.

In his groundbreaking book, *Hypertext: The Convergence of Contemporary Critical Theory and Technology*, Landow defines hypertext as

An information medium that links verbal and nonverbal information. Electronic links connect lexias "external" to a work—say, commentary on it by another author or parallel or contrasting texts—as well as within it and thereby create text that is experienced as nonlinear, or, more properly, as multilinear or multisequential. (4)

The television work that this definition immediately brings to mind is *A TV Dante*, an ambitious miniseries based on *Dante's Inferno* which was commissioned by Michael Kustow in the 1980s for Channel 4 (London). Though originally conceived as encompassing the whole poem and involving the participation of many artists, the work that was actually broadcast in Britain in July 1990 consisted of eight ten-minute episodes created in collaboration by Tom Phillips, the visual poet/composer/critic who translated an illustrated version of the *Inferno* in 1983 and who is best-known for his "treated" book, *A Humument*, and filmmaker Peter Greenaway, who is best known for movies like *The Draughtsman's Contract* (1982), which enabled him to cross over from avant garde video and filmmaking to mainstream production, and *The Cook, the Thief, His Wife and Her Lover* (1989), whose notoriety achieved a surprising commercial success.[10]

Having variously been described as "a thinking person's pop video" (AFI Video Festival catalogue), a "translation" from the language of the book to the language of video (Tracy Biga), and "a video palimpsest" that marks the cultural transition from "the dominance of the word to ...the dominance of the sound-word-image" (Nancy Vickers), *A TV Dante* reveals a chain of complex relations between a series of art forms and media which extend backward to cinema, photography, and poetry as well as forward to computer animation, high-definition television, and multimedia technology.[11] Paradoxically, this extraordinary hypertext material is all easily absorbed within the ordinary repetitive segmentation of commercial television along with its usual dialogic combinations of literary adaptations, nature documentaries, erotic spectacle, talking heads, banal chatter, and commercial breaks.

The cantos are mediated not only through a series of narrators (including Dante and Virgil from within the poem, as well as "naturalist" David Attenborough, "classicist" David Rudkin, and coauthor Tom Phillips, who gloss the text with various degrees of omniscience) but also through the inset screens or "windows" in which their authoritative "talking heads" appear. Besides appearing as an ingenious way of visualizing footnotes and of transforming a potentially linear narrative into a hypertext, these "windows" evoke the Microsoft programs that enabled PC computers first to rival and then threaten Macintosh with extinction, thereby making Bill Gates one of the richest, most powerful men in the world. Thus the series is structured around serial appropriation—Greenaway's and Phillips's appropriation of Dante, Dante of Virgil, Attenborough of nature, and Bill Gates of the information superhighway—all involving rapid movement across spatial, temporal, cultural, generic borders.

Just as Eisenstein naturalized his own borrowings from Griffith by exposing the latter's borrowings from Dickens, Greenaway and Phillips make their own appropriation of Dante part of a series, but the effect is very different. For in this postmodernist context where such appropriations are commonplace, it is our perception of Dante's practice (rather than that of Greenaway and Phillips) that undergoes the most dramatic transformation. As Phillips proclaims at the opening of canto one in direct address (a convention derived from poetry that is pervasive in television yet traditionally avoided in cinema), "A good old text always is a blank for new things." Dante suddenly becomes postmodernist and televisual—a metamorphosis that is accomplished through television's seemingly unlimited power to appropriate anything that appears on its screen. And this perception of cooptive power helps forestall television's own appropriation by multimedia computers.

In canto one this power is extended to Greenaway's own original medium, independent video, as the privileged screen that mediates between past, present, and future, between poetry and cinema, and between broadcast television and computers. Nancy Vickers has brilliantly detailed how the series reinscribes the corpus of Eadweard Muybridge and its technological passage from photography to cinema, particularly through the depiction of humans (that mass of writhing naked flesh) and animals in motion. As she puts it, "Muybridge, like Dante, takes on 'new life' through video 'translation.'"[12] Yet there is a further irony in the way the television medium surpasses Muybridge by blatantly harnessing the cutting-edge powers of computer animation to manipulate and layer the image, so that it can rival the density of the classic arts of poetry and painting.

As we hear the opening lines of the first canto in voice-over, we see a stone tablet containing the graphic representation of the words. A window appears containing a group of naked sinners, as if in a crowded elevator, descending through numbered circles of hell, punctuating the poetry with their screams of torment. The images of the naked crowds are varied stylistically, through their diverse colors, actions, and movements, a constructed set of functional differences that *neutralize* the naked flesh (in the Eisensteinian sense), transforming it into an element of montage that is eventually contrasted with Beatrice's fiery circle of the soul.

This opening immediately introduces the dominant technique of layering both on the visual and audio registers, with images emerging through dissolves like stacks of hypercards, numerically cataloging levels and cantos and hybridizing past and present, word and image. Out of the orchestrated background of urban cacophony, a woman's musical laughter periodically rings out followed by percussive noises of reflexive mechanisms that register the passage of time and image. As Dante describes "the dark wood" that appears "half way through the journey of our life," we see a cityscape and hear urban sounds as background to the poetry, juxtapositions that provide an implicit gloss on the verse and that redefine his "wild, harsh forbidding world" as our own urban dystopia.

The most startling rupture comes from broadcast television rather than the poetics of video—that moment when the first numbered "window" pops up on screen with David Attenborough commenting on Dante's leopard. This moment usually evokes laughter, perhaps as much from the pleasure of recognizing the familiar generic conventions of the TV nature documentary as from the incongruity of the surrealistic jolt. In telling us the leopard was thought to be "the offspring of the union of a lion and a panther . . . sprung from two different parents," Attenborough calls attention to the hybridization that was already present in Dante's poem and that is central to this postmodernist adaptation. He also demonstrates the serial interpretation that is pervasive in both writerly texts, evoking the kind of layered, pluralistic readings that Barthes performed in *S/Z*. When Dante says, "I turned and turned," we see boxed images of the leopard against the background of a spotted field, images flopped not only to echo that act of repetitive turning but also to violate the cinematic conventions of con-

Fig. 6.2   In *A TV Dante* the poet's "trinity of beasts" is presented as a hypertextual form of triptych.

tinuity editing. At this point the layering becomes so extreme that it is difficult to distinguish between the various layers of the spotted leopard or between background and foreground.

When Dante mentions the "lion" we are reminded that the visual representations are chosen from a paradigm of cultural images of that beast—for we see a realistic lion from a documentary charging at the camera, which is juxtaposed with images of domesticated circus lions leaping through burning hoops in the background within the window that boxes (and thereby domesticates) Attenborough, an image that prefigures the fiery circle of the soul in which the beatific face of Beatrice will later appear.

When Phillips glosses Dante's "trinity of beasts" (leopard, lion, and hound), we see an illustrative triple-layered stack of animal images that evokes a hypertextual form of triptych. (See Figure 2.) Not only does this establish a morphological analogy between form and content, it also demonstrates how the meaning of each poetic phrase is altered or extended by the visual imagery with which it is juxtaposed; images are selected not to illustrate the words but rather to destabilize their meanings.

Another example of this dynamic occurs when processed, colored images of the hound appear over aerial footage of bombed cities, evoking World War II. This association is amplified by Phillips as he lists the historic figures ("Napoleon, Mussolini, Gramsci, and Garabaldi") who have used various names for the hounds—a catalog that extends the list of referenced battles further backward to include the Napoleonic wars, the Risorgimento, and (with the next gloss to Virgil) the Trojan War. What is evoked is a Gramscian hegemonic struggle for the position of historic referent as well as for the foreground of the screen, an instability of signification that is rendered in concrete formalist terms while retaining its full ideological resonance.

It is difficult to tell which medium is appropriating the other, for not only is Dante's *Inferno* being "screened" through television and computers, but television is also being filtered through Dante's vision. Just as Dante is praised for "wielding" his own language into "a poetic instrument," we watch Greenaway and Phillips wielding video into a "poetic language." Specifically, we see how to use televisual verticality productively, how to make footnotes work on screen, and how to transform TV's endless flow of chatter into a "generous stream of poetic speech"— strategies that seem more compatible with independent video than with broadcast television. As Vickers astutely observes, "the series certainly resists any familiar notion of television as an ephemeral flow of programming; its dense intertextual field virtually demands a VCR." (267).

By coupling Dante's poetry with the banality of television, the series infuses both of them with new life. This effect is made literal when we see the actor playing Dante "materialize" out of the death mask of the poet through a dissolve, and we watch the familiar face of Sir John Gielgud literally become animated from a still image to live action. Rather than being boxed like the noted scholars and naked sinners, these famous faces (the primary source of that "generous stream of poetic speech") float freely in televisual space. Moreover, the contemporary star power of Gielgud is balanced against the cultural resonance of Beatrice, both transformed into oracular talking heads who (like PeeWee Herman's Genie, the Power Rangers' Zordon, and

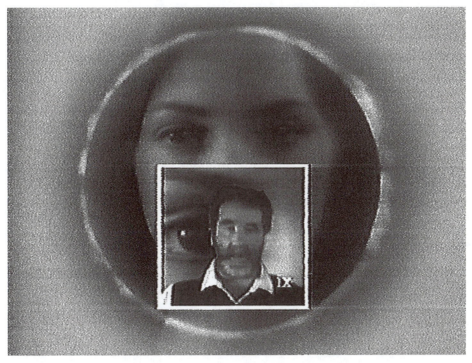

Fig. 6.3   In *A TV Dante* the boxed head of Tom Phillips is superimposed over the encircled face of Beatrice who substitutes for the free-floating head of Virgil.

CBS's Dan Rather) occupy full screen, balancing that writhing mass of victims who are doomed to naked anonymity. When Phillips introduces Beatrice as the one who "substitutes" for Virgil, his own talking head is temporarily superimposed over hers, thereby extending the chain of serial substitutions—from the free-floating head of Virgil, to the encircled face of Beatrice, to the boxed insert of Phillips—a virtual trinity of graphically modulated guides. (See Figure 3.) These talking heads make us see TV's "guiding stars" in a new light—the news anchors who nightly narrate the trials and tribulations of those in limbo and those certified experts who (like Fielding's narrators) authoritatively gloss images from poetry and nature. They help us realize that serial television is the hypertext medium most appropriate for adapting poetry, not cinema, which, according to Greenaway, is a "dying" medium, rapidly becoming as retro as literature.

While Landow argues that hypertext is as central to critical theorists like Derrida, Barthes, and Bakhtin as to computer scientists like Theodor H. Nelson (who coined the term in the 1960s), Greenaway and Phillips demonstrate that it is also constituent to broadcast television. This characterization applies not only to music videos and radical experimental works like their own *A TV Dante* (with its traces of high modernism and residual "high art" status) but also to the medium's ordinary operations through its so-called "lowest" forms such as news, soaps, talk shows and Saturday morning cartoons.[13]

III. *WHERE ON EARTH IS CARMEN SANDIEGO* AS REVISIONIST HISTORY

Nowhere is this convergence between television and hypertext more apparent than on Saturday morning television, which transforms post-structuralist conceptions of textuality into child's play as it reproduces postmodernist subjectivity. As Landow points out, "the convergence of textuality and electronic embodiments of it" sometimes has embarrassing consequences.

> Hypertext creates an almost embarrassingly literal embodiment of a principle that had seemed particularly abstract and difficult when read from the vantage point of print ... this more literal presentation promises to disturb theoreticians, in part, of course, because it greatly disturbs status and power relations within their field of expertise. (43)

While one might be willing to tolerate such an embodiment in a complex writerly hypertext like *A TV Dante*, it may seem downright humiliating when they are found in Saturday morning kiddie shows like *Muppet Babies* and *Power Rangers*. Another consequence of this shift to a "simpler" context is that it is easier to perceive the ideological implications of these textual strategies, which might even make Landow's utopian fervor an embarrassment. As Carolyn Marvin observes, it is "in the uncertainty of emerging and contested practices of communication that the struggle of groups to define and locate themselves is most easily observed."[14]

I have argued elsewhere that Saturday morning television teaches kids a complex form of media literacy—one that may be as sophisticated a method of reading as is found in Barthes's *S/Z*.[15] It teaches them how to use television to read all forms of popular culture intertextually. Partly because of television's position in the home and its ability to provide young children with their first entry into narrative, television mediates sensory perceptions and proposes a set of cognitive categories for organizing memories. In this way, it maps the world and the viewer's position within it. Calling attention to intertextuality and direct allusions, it teaches kids how to master the broader historical/cultural field against which all texts are decoded and to feel empowered in the process. Yet at the same time it commodifies that cognitive process by linking it to consumerism, establishing brand names (like Nike and Gap), commercial networks (like Nintendo and Sega), and licensed figures (like the Power Rangers and Teenage Mutant Ninja Turtles) as generic categories. In the process, it teaches kids how to buy into the system. Like *A TV Dante*, children's television frequently comments on other media both from the past and the future, as if to ensure that television will not be replaced by the new interactive multimedia which are also increasingly available to youngsters in the home and at school. One way to do this is to simulate interactivity and assimilate the computer screen.

Although these dynamics function systemically rather than being limited to a specific network, genre, or series (a position I have demonstrated in my previous work on CBS, the Fox network, and Nickelodeon), I will focus here on a single example, *Where on Earth Is Carmen Sandiego*, a television adaptation of Broderbund's successful educational computer software which was introduced in 1985 and by 1992 had sold over 2.5 million copies, with six variations of the game that have been widely adopted in schools nationwide. The original *Carmen Sandiego* software generated many spinoffs, but none so successful as the animated series on Fox.[16]

First aired on the Fox Children's Network in February 1994, *Where on Earth Is Carmen Sandiego* quickly became the first educational show in TV history to succeed on a commercial network (ranking number one in its Saturday morning time slot). Although its ratings have subsequently declined and some have attributed its initial success to its privileged position within the Fox lineup, its achievement is still historic. The original computer game was designed to teach geography and history by having players track the mysterious Carmen Sandiego, a former spy-turned-thief, across space and time in order to restore stolen treasures. Usually sandwiched between two male-oriented action series (such as *X-Men* and *Mega Man*), the Fox series features a pair of young brother-sister detectives, Ivy and Zack, chasing Carmen. The show is attentive to gender issues, encouraging both boys and girls to use computers, but it teaches a lot more besides.

In the 1994 season premiere (broadcast on September 17), Ivy and Zack track Carmen back to the American colonies in the eighteenth century, where she threatens Paul Revere's warning of American rebels that the British are coming, Ben Franklin's harnessing of electricity with his kite, and the Liberty Bell's survival. Despite the show's emphasis on cutting-edge technology, the narrative strives to preserve the traditional version of American history, defending it against any revisionist override.

The episode restores a colonizing discourse within a postcolonial sphere—celebrating the postcolonial independence of the United States (which Revere helped to win), its superior technology particularly in the field of electronic communications (which Franklin's harnessing of electricity helped to launch), and its democratic ideology (which is represented by the visual icon of the Liberty Bell). Thus, along with history and geography, the episode teaches kids a national discourse on American supremacy—which Europeans (like Carmen Sandiego) were trying to reverse. In 1994 that supremacy was centered on the trade status of America's second leading export, its movies and television shows, particularly in the G.A.T.T. talks where European nations were trying to curtail our domination of the global market. Although Carmen (like the EC) claims that "Time is on her side," Ivy and Zack as American patriots are determined to "get history back on track" in order to protect our nation's cultural hegemony. This reading supports Marvin's contention that "old habits of transacting between groups are projected onto new technologies that alter, or seem to alter, critical social distances" (5).

Although this globe-trotting narrative makes youngsters feel comfortable in an international setting, they are constantly being reminded of their national identity—especially in the weekly lead-in to the show where they are posed against the Statue of Liberty as they hold a miniaturized globe in the palm of their hand, exercising their privileged position of freedom and mobility. Ivy and Zack are empowered to travel freely through space and time like nomadic tourists, colonizing figures from the past, who (like people of underdeveloped nations) are

Fig. 6.4   In *Where on Earth is Carmen Sandiego* commercials are framed by this image of a unisex player in front of a computer screen.

stuck in a single zone. Whenever their technology breaks down (in this episode their time machine temporarily malfunctions), these American heroes are threatened with the prospect of getting stuck in one place— back in history or sitting passively in front of their screen, which is precisely where we television viewers are positioned, even though we are directly addressed as active players within the fiction.

As if to counter that predicament, the series frames all of its commercial breaks with a recurring image of a unisex player seated in front of a computer screen with back to camera, as if to facilitate identification for a wider range of viewers of both genders. (See Figure 4.) In the upper left corner of the room we see a sports pennant with the word "Go," a familiar mantra chanted not only by fans in sports arenas but also by action heroes in westerns and other popular American movie genres from *The Wild Bunch* to *Pulp Fiction*. The pennant points like an arrow to a large facial close-up of the Statue of Liberty in the upper right corner. These icons connote mobility and freedom respectively, a combination that evokes the kind of interactivity that is promised not only by computer games but also by the American system of corporate democracy that is increasingly endorsed both by the Left and the Right.

Although the series is frequently praised for its gender and ethnic diversity, it still casts the empowered adult female as the villain and doubly codes her ethnicity as Hispanic, not only through both her names (Carmen Sandiego) but also through her jet black hair (which contrasts sharply with the strawberry blond tresses of the heroic Anglo siblings, Ivy and Zack) and her bright red trench coat and fedora. The color coding in this series is no more elaborate than that in the Teenage Mutant Ninja Turtles myth or the Power Rangers cult that replaced it, for they all empower young players through the cognitive pleasures of mastery and decoding. Carmen's red color coding also links her to danger and the stop sign, associations which emphasize her narrative function (in the Proppian sense) as the character who has to be stopped and the one who is set in symbolic opposition to that jolly green giantess, the Statue of Liberty who (with her Go pennant) rallies our spirits like a cheerleader, urging American players to go beat Carmen and her team of treacherous international thieves. The red coding also evokes Carmen's past as a former spy who (we soon discover) speaks flawless Russian and who got her hardware from the Soviet Union—a backstory that helps recuperate the Cold War paradigm. Perhaps this explains why this particular episode on American colonial history opens in Arctic Russia, with Carmen stealing a "Top Secret" time-travel machine from our old Cold War rivals, which enables her to attempt to reverse the outcome of the American Revolution. Thus the story follows a route that parallels the trajectory of this essay—first poaching a time-travel mechanism in Russia and then going back to the eighteenth century to change our vision of television in the postmodernist present.

In the scene where Ivy and Zack finally recover the time machine, we see how the viewer is mobilized as an active player who supposedly pushes the buttons and supplies definitions (like the experts in *A TV Dante*) and who can supposedly communicate directly both with the young heroes and the villain. Not only does the plot increasingly poach on *Back to the Future*, but Ivy and Zack appropriate an ordinary commercial billboard as a screen for displaying the talking head of their authoritative chief, who (despite his temporary British accent that results from Carmen's reversal of history) is visually linked with Albert Einstein in this advertisement for American know-how. When Zack picks up the time-travel gadget, he holds it in his hand and tries to think of a more familiar object to compare it with, pausing just long enough for us to come up with our own analogue—a TV remote-control. Although Zack finally compares it to a garage door opener, the trope of the TV joystick proves more resonant, particularly when we realize how proficient television is as a time machine that can represent any period through the appropriation of other media both from the past and future: the low-tech classroom medium of the slide show, which segues our heroes back to the eighteenth century, and the simulated cutting-edge computer screen, which provides an illusory sense of interactivity and control. The episode shows us that the battle over screens is really a struggle between rival media and their competing versions of history.

Not surprisingly, the tone in this series is very different from that found in *A TV Dante*, a difference analogous to the one Landow perceives between poststructuralist theory and its embodiment in electronic hypertexts (as well as between Birkerts's dystopic perspective and Landow's own utopian vision):

> Whereas terms like *death, vanish, loss,* and expressions of depletion and impoverishment color critical theory, the vocabulary of freedom, energy, and empowerment marks writings on hypertextuality . . . Critical theorists . . . continually confront . . . the exhaustion of the culture of print . . . . Writers on hypertext, in contrast, glory in possibility, excited by the future of textuality, knowledge, and writing. (87)

While Greenaway and Phillips quietly appropriate computer software to demonstrate television's superior abilities in recuperating an exhausted poetic classic about death, *Carmen Sandiego* brazenly appropriates cutting-edge educational software and its illusory promises of freedom and empowerment. Yet the TV series, like the software, also focuses on the past, using its plot to preserve a version of history in which American television still reigns supreme, safe from the revisionist challenges posed by other nations, technologies, and media.

Yet, in these "reading wars" television's hegemony is not going unchallenged. Media both from the past and the future frequently resist its domination. You can find such resistance in the opening paragraph of a brilliant hypertextual novel like *If On a Winter's Night a Traveller*, where television is used as a synecdoche for the intrusive outside world.

> You are about to begin reading Italo Calvino's new novel, *If on a winter's night a traveler*. Relax. Concentrate. Dispel every other thought. Let the world around you fade. Best to close the door; the TV is always on in the next room. Tell the others right away, "No, I don't want to watch TV!" Raise your voice—they won't hear you otherwise—"I'm reading!"[17]

It can also be found in *Club Kidsoft*, a kids software catalog masquerading as a magazine, which contains a consumer guide article titled "Mighty Morphin' Power Computers" promoting the latest multimedia hardware from Apple and Compaq.

> Have you ever thought about using your computer as . . . a TV set? With these machines you can do some pretty cool stuff, like watch TV on the computer screen at the same time as you finish your homework! You see your homework appearing in one window on screen, and the TV show running in another. Or if someone else takes over your TV set on Saturday mornings, just turn on your computer to watch your favorite cartoons.[18]

Besides literalizing the cliched trope of "edutainment," this provocative passage accentuates the difference between the reception modes of two generations—the cutting-edge kids being directly addressed who will think these dual windows (like those in *A TV Dante*) are "cool stuff" and the horrified retro parents who may be paying for both the hardware and the subscription but who are reminded in the ad on the back cover of *Club Kidsoft* of their disempowered position:

> You bought the computer. You even sprung for the printer. The kids are jazzed. But you don't know beans about software . . . Join the Club!

This kind of strategic transgenerational address (that is, reaching two distinct generations of consumers by exaggerating the differences between them) has already proved central to the success of children's television programming on several stations (especially the Nickelodeon Children's Cable network). It is also essential to this article's real thematics—the replacement of television by the next generation of multimedia computers. Not only do the promoters of these computers appropriate for the title of their article and featured products the name of the most popular kids show on television, *The Power Rangers* (an American adaptation of a Japanese TV series which has already generated movie and video game spinoffs as well as thousands of licensed products), but they demonstrate the superior morphing power of the computer by showing how it can subordinate its older arch rival television to an inset window (the way *A TV Dante* boxed Attenborough) and to the bottom of a list of ancillary functions (just as parents are relegated to the back cover of *Kidsoft*).

IV. A REFLEXIVE EDUCATIONAL EPILOGUE

In light of the screen wars I have been describing, I began to wonder whether it might be possible to become more actively involved in using multimedia hypertexts to recuperate or at least demarginalize media threatened with obsolescence or extinction in the global marketplace— a project that is in some ways analogous to the one pursued in *A TV Dante* and in opposition to the nationalist goals in *Carmen Sandiego*. This project seemed particularly appropriate for the world of higher education where (despite the creeping conservatism of university presses) web sites, CD-ROMs, and computer screens are increasingly challenging books, journals, videotapes, and laserdiscs as a medium of critical commentary and a mode of publication. Having written a book on the marginalized cinema of Spain, *Blood Cinema: The Reconstruction of National Identity in Spain* (1993) which dealt with issues of transcultural and transmedia reinscription, I decided to extend that process by producing a companion CD-ROM that would present brief excerpts from fifteen films (most of which were otherwise difficult to obtain in the United States) with written and audio commentaries in English and Spanish. I was able to obtain permission to use these excerpts because I was *not* competing with the films themselves (since video compression cannot rival the visual quality of a 35 mm print). Rather, my hypertext was designed to help promote these foreign films in the

United States where they are usually perceived as peripheral. In this way, I was reopening closed texts (my own book as well as the films being excerpted), converting them into hypertexts that could be read interactively in diverse ways. The design of the interface encourages users to pursue their own interests by watching the excerpts in any order they please (with or without hearing or reading the commentaries or consulting the various overviews and glosses) and by recording their own comments on a notepad that can be saved and shared with others. Like Eisenstein's Japanese drawing students, users are encouraged to control the temporary collisions of frames and objects that appear on the computer screen. But unlike Eisenstein and Fielding, I had to relinquish the reins, for my own authorial role diminished —in the collaboration both with users and with Charles Tashiro (who designed the screens) and Barry Schneider (who designed the interface). Like Landow, I found that "hypertext as a writing medium metamorphoses the author into an editor or developer" (100).

By now it may be apparent (especially from the endnotes) that this essay reflexively traces the trajectory of my own career, which began thirty years ago with a dissertation on Fielding's experimentation in the theater in relation to his novels, and then turned in succession through an ongoing process of "promiscuous" analogic thinking to movies, television, video games, CD-ROMs, and other forms of popular culture. While each new project was screened or reframed through my previous objects of study, they all remain deeply engaged with the ongoing process of transmedia appropriation and transcultural reinscription.

NOTES

1. Sergei Eisenstein, "The Cinematographic Principle and the Ideogram" (1929), in *Film Form: Essays in Film Theory*, ed. and trans. Jay Leyda (New York: Harcourt Brace Jovanovich, 1949), p. 41.

2. David Bordwell, *The Cinema of Eisenstein* (Cambridge: Harvard University Press, 1993), pp. 137, 114.

3. J. Dudley Andrew, *The Major Film Theories* (New York: Oxford University Press, 1976).

4. Sergei Eisenstein, "Dickens, Griffith, and the Film Today" (1944) in *Film Form*, p. 223.

5. Sergei Eisenstein, *Immoral Memories*, trans. Herbert Marshall (Boston: Houghton Mifflin Co., 1983), pp. 185–86.

6. For a detailed argument see Marsha Kinder, *Henry Fielding's Dramatic Experimentation: A Preface to His Fiction*, Ph.D. dissertation, UCLA,1963; or my essay "The Improved Author's Farce: An Analysis of the 1734 Revisions" in *Costerus* (November 1972), pp. 35–43.

7. Walter Benjamin, "The Work of Art in the Age of Mechanical Reproduction" in *Illuminations*, ed. Hannah Arendt, trans. Harry Zohn (New York: Schocken, 1969), p. 237.

8. George P. Landow, *Hypertext: The Convergence of Contemporary Critical Theory and Technology* (Baltimore and London: The Johns Hopkins University Press, 1992), p. 103.

9. Michael Heim, *The Metaphysics of Virtual Reality* (New York and Oxford: Oxford University Press, 1993), p. xiv. Also see Sven Birkerts, *The Gutenberg Elegies: The Fate of Reading in an Electronic Age* (Boston and London: Faber and Faber, 1994).

10. For more information about the conceptualization and production of the series, see Michael Kustow, "How *A TV Dante* Came About" in *A TV Dante*, ed. Derek Jones (London: Channel 4 Television, 1990).

11. *A TV Dante* had its American premiere at the American Film Institute's National Video Festival in October 1990. For two of the most perceptive readings of the series, see Tracy Biga, "Cinema Bulimia: Peter Greenaway's Corpus of Excess" (dissertation, University of Southern California, 1994), pp. 167–171, and Nancy J. Vickers, "Dante in the Video Decade" in *Dante Now: Current Trends in Dante Studies*, ed. Theodore J. Cachey, Jr. (Notre Dame and London: University of Notre Dame Press, 1995).

12. Vickers, p. 272.

13. This view is compatible with Nick Browne's formulation of the "television (super) text," Mimi White's concept of the "referential imaginary" of American broadcast television, and my own theorization of MTV. See Nick Browne, "The Political Economy of the Television (Super) Text" in *American Television: New Directions in History and Theory*, ed. Nick Browne (Langhorne, Pa.: Harwood Academic Publishers, 1994), pp. 69–79; Mimi White, "Crossing Wavelengths: The Diegetic and Referential Imaginary of American Commercial Television" in *Cinema Journal* 25, no. 2 (Winter 1986), pp. 51–64; and Marsha Kinder, "Music Video and the Spectator: Television, Ideology and Dream" in *Film Quarterly* (Fall 1984), pp. 2–15.

14. Carolyn Marvin, *When Old Technologies Were New: Thinking About Electric Communication in the Late Nineteenth Century* (New York and Oxford: Oxford University Press, 1988), p. 5.

15. See Marsha Kinder, *Playing with Power in Movies, Television and Video: From Muppet Babies to Teenage Mutant Ninja Turtles* (Berkeley and Los Angeles: University of California Press, 1991); "Home Alone in the 90s: Generational War and Transgenerational Address in American Movies, Television and Presidential Politics" in *In Front of the Children: Screen Entertainment and Young Audiences*, eds. Cary Bazalgette and David

Buckingham (London: British Film Institute, 1995), pp. 75–91; and "Ranging with Power on the Fox Children's Network" in *Kids' Culture*, ed. Marsha Kinder (forthcoming from Duke University Press).

16. These other spinoffs include adventure books, jigsaw puzzles, CD-ROM games, and a PBS weekday quiz show called *Where in the World Is Carmen Sandiego* that is not as "faithful" to the original software as the Fox series.

17. Italo Calvino, *If On a Winter's Night a Traveler* (1979), trans. William Weaver (New York and London: Harcourt Brace Jovanovich, 1981), p. 1.

18. Kearney Rietmann and Frank Higgins, "Mighty Morphin' Power Computers" in *Club Kidsoft* 2, no. 4 (1995), p. 35.

N. KATHERINE HAYLES

7

THE CONDITION OF VIRTUALITY

VIRTUALITY IS THE condition millions of people now inhabit. What it means to be in a condition of virtuality was whimsically demonstrated with a device developed at Xerox PARC and exhibited at SIGGRAPH '95, the huge computer graphics convention where developers come to hawk their latest wares, hard and soft. From the twenty-foot ceilings of the Art Show exhibit thin red cords dangle like monstrous strings of spaghetti left behind by naughty giants who got in a food fight. Sometimes the strings hang quiescent; at other times they writhe like lively plastic snakes. Connected by transducers to data lines, the cords are sensing devices that measure the flow of information moving through the room. The more bits being sent over the wires, the more the cords gyrate. They are information weather vanes. Inside the walls of the gigantic Los Angeles Convention Center, a sprawling complex larger than many small towns, which way the wind blows has ceased to be a concern of the ordinary citizen. But how currents of information flow—who has access, at what baud rate, to which data banks—occupies on a daily basis nearly every one of the fifty thousand people who have come to this show.

Let me offer a strategic definition. *Virtuality is the cultural perception that material objects are interpenetrated by information patterns.* Note that the definition plays off a duality—materiality on the one hand, information on the other. The bifurcation between them is a historically specific construction that emerged in the wake of World War II. When I say virtuality is a cultural perception, I do not mean it is merely a psychological phenomenon. It is also a mindset that finds instantiation in an array of powerful technologies. The perception facilitates the development of the technologies, and the technologies reinforce the perception.[1] The analyses that constructed information and materiality as separable and discrete concepts developed in a number of scientific and technical fields during the 1940s and 1950s. The construction of these categories was far from arbitrary. The negotiations that produced them took into account existing technologies and accepted explanatory frameworks and the needs of emerging techno-scientific industries for reliable quantification. If the categories are not arbitrary, however, neither are they "natural." Whatever "nature" may be, it is a holistic interactive environment, not a reenactment of the constructed bifurcations that humans impose to understand it better.

One of the important sites for the construction of the information/materiality duality was molecular biology. In the contemporary view, the body is said to "express" information encoded in the genes. The content is provided by the genetic pattern; the body's materiality articulates a preexisting semantic structure. Control resides in the pattern, which is regarded as bringing the material object into being. The idea that reproduction might be governed by an informational code was suggested by Erwin Schrodinger in his influential 1945 book, *What Is Life? The Physical Aspect of the Living Cell*.[2] In his analysis of the discourse of molecular biology as "rhetorical software," Richard Doyle has shown how, in the decades following Schrodinger's book, the gene was conceived as the originary informational pattern that produces the body, even though logically the gene is contained within the body, not the other way around.[3] This "impossible inversion," as Doyle calls it, is aptly illustrated by a popular science book of the 1960s that Doyle discusses, George Gamow's *Mr. Tompkins Inside Himself*.[4] On a visit to his doctor, Mr. Tompkins is sitting in the waiting room when he hears a sucking sound and feels a strange sensation of constriction. Somehow he is drawn into a hypodermic needle and then injected inside his own body. This mind-bending scenario reenacts the same manuever that is carried out in more stolid fashion in the scientific discourse, when DNA is conceptualized as the genotypic pattern that produces the body as its phenotypic expression. Doyle's point is that this conceptual inversion is a rhetorical rather than an experimental accomplishment. It is in this sense that the discourse functions as rhetorical software, for it operates as if it were running a program on the hardware of the laboratory apparatus to produce results that the research alone could not accomplish.

By the 1970s, this vision reaches rhetorical apotheosis in Richard Dawkins's *The Selfish Gene*.[5] Although Doyle does not discuss Dawkins's text in detail, it provides a perfect illustration of his argument. In Dawkins's rhetoric, the genes are constructed as informational agents who control the "lumbering robots" that we call human beings. Virtually every human behavior, from mate choice to altruism, is treated by Dawkins as if it were controlled by the genes for their own ends, independent of what humans might think. Although he frequently issues disclaimers that this is merely a colorful way of talking, the metaphors do more than spice up the argument. As I have argued elsewhere, they function like discursive agents who *perform* the actions they describe.[6] Through this discursive performativity, informational pattern triumphs over the body's materiality—a triumph achieved by first distinguishing between pattern and materiality and then privileging pattern over materiality. The effect of this "impossible inversion" is the same, whether it occurs in Gamow's cartoons, Dawkins's metaphors, or the lavishly funded Human Genome Project. *It constructs information as the site of mastery and control over the material world.*

It is no accident that molecular biology and other sciences of information flourished during the immediate post–World War II period. The case can be made that World War II, more than previous global events, made the value of information real. The urgency of war highlights the fact that information is time-dependent. It matters little what information one has if a message can move only as fast as a horse can run, for by the time it arrives at its destination, its usefulness has often passed. Shakespeare's history plays are full of messages that arrive too late. Only when technological infrastructures have developed sufficiently to make rapid message transmission possible does information come into its own as a commodity as important to military success as guns and infantry. From this we can draw an obvious but nonetheless important conclusion. *The efficacy of information depends on a highly articulated material base.* Without such a base, from rapid transportation systems to fiber-optic cables, information becomes much more marginal in its ability to affect outcomes in the material world. Ironically, once this base is in place, the perceived primacy of information over materiality obscures the importance of the very infrastructures that make information valuable.

Nowhere is the privileging of information over materiality more apparent than in Hans Moravec's *Mind Children*.[7] Moravec argues that human beings are essentially informational patterns rather than bodily presences. If a technology can replicate the pattern, it has captured all that really matters in a human being. To illustrate, he offers a fantastic scenario in which "you" have your consciousness downloaded into a computer. Although the technology could be envisioned in any number of ways (since it is imaginary in any case), he significantly has the robot surgeon conducting the operation physically destroy your brain in the process. As "you" are transferred into a computer, the trashed body is left behind, an empty husk. Once "you" are comfortably inside your shiny new body, "you" effectively become immortal. For when that body wears out or becomes obsolete, "you" can simply transfer your consciousness to a new model.

I will not bother to lay out all the reasons why this vision, in addition to being wildly implausible, is wrong-headed and dangerous. Let me instead point out a correlation that helps to explain the appeal of this fantasy (for those who find it appealing). In Moravec's text, and at many other sites in the culture, *the information/matter dichotomy maps onto the older and more traditional dichotomy of spirit/matter.* The underlying premise informing Moravec's scenario is the belief that an immaterial essence, which alone comprises the individual's true nature, can be extracted from its material instantiation and live free from the body. As this wording makes clear, the contemporary privileging of information is reinforced by religious yearnings and belief that have been around for a long time and that are resonant with meaning for many people. There are, of course, also significant differences between a mindset that identifies human being with the soul and one that identifies it with information. Spirituality is usually associated with mental and physical discipline, whereas the imagined escape of the soul-as-information from the body depends only on having access to the appropriate high technology. For Moravec, the difference means the problem of mortality has been rationalized so that it is possible to make steady progress toward achieving a solution rather than flailing around in mystical nonsense. This construction of the situation obscures the fact that his text is driven by a fear of death so intense it mystifies the power of the very technologies that are supposed to solve the problem.

To probe further the implications of constructing information and materiality as discrete categories, let us return to the period immediately following World War II. In addition to molecular biology, another important site for articulating the distinction was information theory. In 1948 Claude Shannon, a brilliant theorist who worked at Bell Laboratories, defined a mathematical quantity he called information and proved several important theorems concerning it.[8] Lacan to the contrary, a message does not always arrive at its destination. In information theoretic terms, no message is ever sent. What is sent is a signal. The distinction information theory posits between signal and message is crucial. A message has an information content specified by a probability function that has no dimensions, no materiality, and no necessary connection with meaning. It is a pattern, not a presence. Only when the message is encoded in a signal for transmission through a medium— for example, when ink is printed on paper or electrical pulses are sent racing along telegraph wires—does it assume material form. The very definition of information, then, encodes the distinction between materiality and information that was also becoming central in molecular biology during this period.

Why did Shannon define information as a pattern rather than a presence? The transcripts of the Macy Conferences, a series of annual meetings where the basic principles of cybernetics were hammered out, indicate that the choice was driven by the twin engines of reliable quantification and theoretical generality.[9] Shannon's approach had other advantages that turned out to incur large (and mounting) costs when his premise interacted with certain predispositions already at work within the culture. Abstracting information from a material base meant that information could become free-floating, unaffected by changes in context. The technical leverage this move gained was considerable, for by formalizing information into a mathematical function, Shannon was able to develop theorems, powerful in their generality, that held true regardless of the medium in which the information was instantiated. Not everyone agreed that this move was a good idea, despite its theoretical power. Malcontents grumbled that divorcing information from context and thus from meaning had made the theory so narrowly formalized that it was not useful as a general theory of communication. Shannon himself frequently cautioned that the theory was meant to apply only to certain technical situations, not to communication in general. In other circumstances, the theory may have become a dead end, a victim of its own excessive formalization and decontextualization. But not in the post–World War II era. As we have seen, the time was ripe for theories that reified information into a free-floating, decontextualized, quantifiable entity that could serve as the master key unlocking the secrets of life and death.

How quickly the theory moved from the meticulously careful technical applications urged by Shannon to cultural fantasy can be seen in Norbert Wiener's suggestion in 1950 that it would be possible to telegraph a human being.[10] We can see here the prototype for Moravec's scenario of downloading consciousness into a computer. The proposal implies that a human being is a message instantiated within a biological substrate but not intrinsic to it.[11] Extract the information from the medium, and you have a pattern you can encode into a signal and reconstitute in another medium at the end of the channel. The fantasy has not lost its appeal as the century races toward the millennium; indeed, it now circulates so widely as to be virtually ubiquitous. Telegraphing a person to a remote location may have been a startling idea in the 1950s, but by the 1990s it has achieved the status of a cultural icon. What is "Beam me up, Scotty," but the same operation carried out with a different (imaginary) technology? Moravec's vision is extreme only in that it imagines "you" rematerialize inside a computer. If you had simply reoccupied your same body, nobody would have raised an eyebrow. Whether the enabling assumptions occur in molecular biology, information theory, or mass media, their appeal is clear. Information conceived as pattern and divorced from a material medium is information free to travel across time and space. Hackers are not the only ones who believe that information wants to be free. The great dream and promise of information is that it can be free from the material constraints that govern the mortal world. If we can become the information we have constructed, we too can soar free, immortal like the gods.

In the face of such a powerful dream, it can be a shock to remember that for information to exist, it must *always* be instantiated in a medium, whether that medium is the page from the *Bell Laboratories Journal* on which Shannon's equations are printed, the computer-generated topological maps used by the Human Genome Project, or the television tube that images the body disappearing into a golden haze when the Star Trek transporter locks onto it. The point is not only that abstracting information from a material base is an imaginary act. More fundamentally, conceiving of information as a thing separate from the medium that instantiates it is a prior imaginary act that constructs a holistic phenomenon as a matter/information duality.[12]

As I write these words, I can feel the language exerting an inertial pull on my argument, for I can gesture toward the unity that the world is only through the dichotomies constructed to describe it. Even as I point to the historical contingency of the terms, the very history that exposes this contingency reinscribes the information/materiality dichotomy I want to contest. This reinscription is complicated and exacerbated by the fact that the matter/information duality is enmeshed in a network of related dichotomies that help to support, distinguish, and define it. In order of increasing generality, these include signal/not-signal, information/noise, and pattern/randomness. Although I cannot avoid using these constructions, I want to show that they function as dialectics rather than dichotomies. In Derrida's phrase, they are engaged in an economy of supplementarity. Each of the privileged terms—signal, information, pattern—relies for its construction on a supplement—not-signal, noise, randomness. As an electrical engineer employed by AT&T, Shannon had a vested interest in eliminating noise. One of his most important theorems proves that there is always a way to encode a message so as to reduce the noise to an arbitrarily small quantity. But since noise is the supplement that allows information to be constructed as the privileged term, it cannot be eliminated from the communication situation, only compensated for in the final result.[13] We can arrive at the same conclusion through a different route by thinking more deeply about what it means to define information as a probability function. The definition implies that randomness always already interpenetrates pattern, for probability as a concept posits a situation in which there is no *a priori* way to distinguish between effects extrapolated from known causes and those generated by chance conjunctions. Like information and noise, pattern and randomness are not opposites bifurcated into a dichotomy but interpenetrating terms joined in a dialectic.

I am now in a position to restate my major theme in a different key. As I have shown, the concept of information is generated from the interplay between pattern and randomness. Similarly, materiality can be understood as being generated by a dialectic of presence and absence. In each dialectic, one term has historically been privileged over the other. When the terms are inverted, assumptions become visible that otherwise would remain transparent. Deconstruction gained theoretical leverage by placing absence rather than presence at the origin of language; the Maximum Entropy Formalism gained theoretical leverage by regarding randomness rather than pattern as the generator of information.[14] When information is privileged over materiality, the pattern/randomness dialectic associated with information is perceived as dominant over the presence/absence dialectic associated with materiality. The condition of virtuality implies, then, a widespread perception that presence/absence is being displaced and preempted by pattern/randomness.

As this displacement suggests, the impact of virtuality on literary theory and practice will be far-reaching and profound. At present, virtuality is largely *terra incognita* for the literary establishment. In *City of Bits*, William Mitchell has written insightfully about how technologies of information are forcing a reconceptualization of the city on many levels, from architecture to traffic flow and urban planning.[15] My interest lies in how these same technologies are forcing a reconceptualization of literary theory and practice. In the next section, I explore the effects on literature of the changing material conditions under which it is written and read in an information age. Part of what is at stake for me in this analysis is to show that materiality, far from being left behind, interacts at every point with the new forms that literature is becoming as it moves into virtuality.

THE VIRTUAL BOOK

We have seen it dozens of times—that moment in a film when a book is opened and the camera's eye zooms through the pages into the imagined world beyond. Once we are in the world, the page is left behind. It no longer appears on the screen, no longer frames the world we witness. The filmic convention captures a reader's sense that the imagined world of the text lives less on the page than in the scene generated out of the words by the mind's eye. Virtual books, that is, books imaged on and through computer screens, operate according to a different convention. As with film, the user is sometimes given the illusion that she is moving through the screen into an imagined world beyond. But unlike film, this imagined world contains texts that the user is invited to open, read, and manipulate. Text is not left behind but remains in complex interplay with the perceived space into which the screen opens. Technically speaking, of course, the interplay is possible because the computer is an interactive medium. My focus here is on how this interactivity is rendered through visual conventions. *Visually* it is possible because textual space is rendered as having depth—if not a full three dimensions, at least the "two and a half" dimensions of text windows stacked behind each other. Texts can play a part in the three-dimensional world of the screen image because in this interactive medium, they have similarly rich dimensionality. The correlation suggests that in electronic textuality, spatiality is of primary concern.

The changed conventions that operate with virtual texts are apparent in *Myst*, the game that ranks second on the U.S. best-seller list for CD-ROMs. At the game opens, three-dimensional Roman letters spelling "MYST" appear. Then a book tumbles out of space and comes to rest in the foreground. Imagine that you are sitting here at the keyboard with me so we can work together on solving the problems that *Myst* presents to us (a favorite way to interact with this challenging and complex game). As we peer at the screen, we notice that the same letters appear on the book. It comes closer, inviting us to enter. We plunge into it and find ourselves spinning through the air. Finally we come to rest on the island, the first of many worlds that *Myst* offers for exploration. We find that we have not left the book behind, for scattered about are pages giving important clues about the island's previous occupants. When we pick a page up (by clicking on it), it comes close enough for us to read. The significance of the pages becomes clearer when we enter the library, perhaps the island's most important structure. In addition to the books lining the walls, the library features two podiums on which rest, respectively, two books . When we open one of them (by clicking on it), we are greeted by a black rectangle inset on a white page. Inserting a nearby page into the book causes the rectangle to buzz into flickering life, and we realize it is a screen. Amid noise and static the image of a man appears on the screen. He tries to ask who we are, tries to communicate a message so broken up by static that we can catch only a few words asking us to find more blue (or red) pages and insert them into the book. When we do, the image gets progressively clearer and the messages become more intelligible.

To recapitulate: a book appears on the screen; we go through the book to the island, where we find fragments of more books. Reassembling the book in the library activates the screen inside the book; from the screen comes a message directing us back to the task of finding and reassembling the book. What are we to make of this extraordinarily complex interplay between screen and book? Here I want to point out something that is visually apparent to anyone who plays *Myst*. While the screens appear in a variety of high-tech settings, the books look archaic, with heavy leather bindings, watermarked covers, and ornate typefaces.

Moreover, the screens are usually activated by solving various numerical or coding problems, whereas the books require physical reassembly. The visual richness of the books compared to the screens, their fragmentation and archaic appearance, hint that books have become fetishized. When we open the book in the library, we do not find the information we seek imprinted on its pages. Instead we interact with a screen emphasizing that the book has become fragmented and urging us to put it back together. Books are associated with the object of desire—finding out information—but metonymically, by a glancing connection based on proximity rather than a direct gaze.

The fetishistic quality of the books in *Myst* is consistent with their representation as anachronisms. Everything about their presentation identifies them as artifacts from the late age of print. Books still exist in this virtual world, but they have ceased to be ordinary, matter-of-fact media for transmitting information. Instead they become fragmented objects of vicarious desire, visually sensuous in a way that implies they are heavy with physicality, teasing us with the promise of a revelation that will come when we restore them to a fabled originary unity. The same kind of transformations are evident at many sites where virtuality reigns. Let me give two more examples, this time from the Art Show at SIGGRAPH '95.

Roman Verostko's "Illuminated Universal Turing Machine" illustrates how the function of the book changes when its materiality is

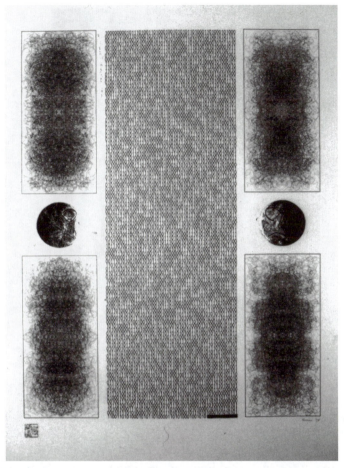

Fig. 7.1   *Illuminated Universal Turing Machine*, 1995, by Roman Verostko.

conceived as interpenetrated by informational patterns. The title alludes
to a conceptual computer proposed by Alan Turing in the 1950s.[16] The
Universal Turing Machine is simply a string of binary code that includes
instructions on how to read the code, including the code that describes
itself. Verostko appropriated the code describing the Universal Turing
Machine (which visually appears as a string of ones and zeros) and used
a computer to print it out on thick parchment, formatted as if it were
the text of a medieval illuminated manuscript. Then he fed the same
string of code into a program for a line plotter and used it to generate
the four illustrations surrounding the text, which look like not-quite-

Figure 7.2   Andy Kopra, *The Ornament of Grammar*, displayed at the SIGGRAPH Art Exhibit, August 1995, Los Angeles, California.

random nests of snaky red lines. In the center of the side margins are two gorgeous gold decals that repeat, in simplified form, one of the motifs of the line drawings; Verostko noted that he intended the decals to suggest control points for the computer. Like *Myst*, this work shows a keen interest in the physical and visual properties of the codex book, including its arrangement of space, tradition of combining text and image, and use of colored inks and gold leaf. But the book's traditional function of conveying verbal information has been given over to computer code. Just as illuminated manuscripts were used for sacred or canonical works, so Verostko uses his visually splendid work to enshrine the universal computer code that is universal precisely because it both explains and enacts its own origin. As with *Myst*, the materiality of the book is cele-

Figure 7.3   Bibliophile browsing *The Ornament of Grammar*, by Andy Kopra.

brated for its archaic and physical qualities, but it is a materiality interpenetrated by the informational patterns that generated it and that are
rendered visually incarnate in the drawings. In this work commenting
upon and exemplifying the late age of print, the book supplies image
and visual form, while the computer supplies text and signifying code.

The materiality of the codex book is also celebrated in Andre Kopra's
"The Ornament of Grammar," although the properties selected for celebration are very different than in Verostko's work. Kopra intended his
title to allude to Owen Jones's nineteenth-century text *The Grammar of
Ornament*, a collection of decorative patterns from different cultures.
Kopra's work consists of a collection of ten different texts bound in cheap
black generic paper covers, printed on inexpensive paper, and displayed

in an unpainted pine bookcase holding multiple copies of each of the ten texts. The pages of the books are filled with line drawings generated by computer programs. The drawings are laid out on a grid of thirty-six by thirty-six squares, yielding a total of forty-one different patterns. As one flips through a book, the drawings grow progressively more complex, an effect achieved by varying the parameters of the computer program generating them. Some of the books use rectilinear patterns; others feature curved lines. The patterns tease the eye, challenging the reader to discern in their visual form the algorithm that created them. Commenting on the tension between the underlying code and visual surface, Kopra wrote that the "possibility of rationalizing visual imagery is called into question by an apparent encyclopedia of the arbitrary."[17]

The material qualities celebrated in this piece include the print book's sturdiness, its relative cheapness and portability, its technological robustness and ease of use, and its potential for mass production. (When I talked with him about the work, Kopra mentioned that several of the books had been stolen by the time SIGGRAPH ended, a fact which delighted him. He said the perfect ending of the display, from his point of view, would have been to have the bookcase emptied by bibliophilic thieves). Although he focuses on different material qualities, Kopra echoes Verostko in having the book's verbal content displaced by visual forms generated from a computer. The computer's role in producing the book is highlighted by the interplay between pattern and randomness in the visual forms. This interplay at once instantiates the dialectic of pattern/randomness and draws into question the ability of computer codes to produce significance, as if recollecting for the reader Shannon's move of divorcing information from meaning. Kopra's work has an ironic undertone that reflects, he says, his growing concern that we are drowning in an ocean of information that is produced not because it is meaningful but because it can be used to generate a profit. For him the SIGGRAPH context in which the work was exhibited was significant, for over the years he has seen SIGGRAPH itself change from a coterie gathering of people who shared mutual interests to a huge commercial enterprise where millions of dollars are at stake.[18]

In an art show devoted to computer graphics, the focus on the book was remarkable. In addition to Verostko and Kopra, at least a dozen other artists produced works that were concerned with the interplay between print and algorithm. For them, the codex book functions as a crossroads in which one can see displayed the traffic between visual objects and computer programs, words and codes, images and language, fragmentation and wholeness, handwork and machine production, pattern and randomness, and rationality and numerical permutations of the arbitrary. The overarching message is that the interpenetration of materiality by informational patterns is everywhere around us, even—or especially—in the books, at once virtual and physical, that are being produced in this late age of print.

SPATIALITY AND VIRTUAL WRITING

Not all virtual books, of course, have their verbal content displaced by codes. Usually the codes work to introduce into the text's visual form a spatial dimensionality that operates in complex syncopation with language. The interplay between spatiality and text is central to electronic hypertexts. As most readers will know, hypertexts are electronic documents that are structured as networks of discrete units, or lexias, rather than as a linear sequence of bound pages. Hypertexts have encoded within them certain "hot spots" or interactive links. When a reader clicks on them, the link is activated and a new block of text comes up on the screen. As George Landow has pointed out, hypertexts are now becoming the standard way to convey information in many technical and engineering areas because they are easily updated, richly associational, and reader-directed. They can be found in everything from manuals for aircraft mechanics to electronic directories for museums. The World Wide Web is a vast hypertext, and most of the documents within it are also hypertexts. Hypertext also provides a rapidly expanding arena for literary writing, both creative and critical.

In literary hypertexts, spatial form and visual image become richly significant. For hypertexts written in Storyspace (a hypertext authoring program developed by Mark Bernstein, Michael Joyce, and Jay Bolter), the map view shows how different lexias are linked to one another. The way they are arranged in space is used to indicate logical or narrative relationships. Some lexias may nest inside others; others may have multiple connections; still others may function as autonomous units or dead ends. Color coding also indicates various kinds of relationships, from highlighted text within lexias to different-colored links and boxes. In Toolbook (another authoring program), sound can be added to enhance textual or visual effects. As a result, space in hypertexts operates as much more than an empty container into which virtual objects are placed. Rather it becomes a topography that the reader navigates using multiple functionalities, including cognitive, tactile, auditory, visual, kinesthetic, and proprioceptive faculties.

Since I am focusing here on spatiality, let us dwell for a moment on proprioception. Proprioception is the sense that tells us where the boundaries of our bodies are. Associated with inner ear mechanisms and internal nerve endings, it makes us feel that we inhabit our bodies from the inside. Proprioceptive coherence, a term used by phenomenologists, refers to how these boundaries formed through a combination of physiological feedback loops and habitual usage. An experienced tennis player, for example, frequently feels proprioceptive coherence with the racquet, experiencing it as if it were an extension of her arm. In much the same way, an experienced computer user feels proprioceptive coherence with the keyboard, experiencing the screen surface as a space into which her subjectivity can flow. This effect marks an important difference between screen and print. Although a reader can imaginatively project herself into a world represented within a print text, she is not likely to feel that she is becoming physically attached to the page itself. On the contrary, because the tactile and kinesthetic feedback loops are less frequent, less sensually complicated, and much less interactive, she normally feels that she is moving *through* the page into some other kind of space. The impression has a physiological basis. The physical stimuli the reader receives with print are simply not adequate to account for the cognitive richness of the represented world; the more the imagination soars, the more the page is left behind. This difference in the way that proprioceptive coherence works with the computer screen compared to the printed page is an important reason why spatiality becomes such a highly charged dimensionality in electronic hypertexts.

It makes sense, then, to insist as Michael Joyce does that virtual writing is also topographical writing.[19] He points to a number of assumptions that we absorb through our everyday work with electronic texts; together, they make our experience of electronic texts distinctively different from print texts. They include the following items, which I have adapted from Joyce's list and altered to suit my purposes here.

1). *Writing is inwardly elastic.* It expands and contracts; it allows the writer to work backward and forward; and it instantly adjusts the screen image to reflect these changes.

2). *The topology of the text is constructed rather than given.* Mechanisms that construct this topology include such humble devices as file names, as well as the more explicitly spatial commands used in hypertexts. As Joyce points out, file names are more powerful than they may appear. They imply that writing done at different times is the same writing if it has the same file name, and that writing stored under different file names is different, even if it was done at the same time and contains the same text. File names also imply that writing is recognized as identical with itself through labeling rather than through spatial proximity within the computer. Unlike in printed books, where the physical location of the pages coincides with labeling conventions, in electronic texts memory address and physical proximity have no necessary relation to one another. Topology is constructed by naming, not by physical assembly.

3). *Changes in a text can be superficial, corresponding to surface adjustments, or structural, corresponding to changes in topography.* Superficial changes are carried out through such formatting tools as spell-checkers and font alterations, while structural changes involve such editorial functions as cut, copy, and paste. The different way these tools are organized within the authoring program, and the different coding operations to which they correspond, embody the assumption that the text possesses both surface and depth. Alterations in the surface are of a different kind than alterations in the topography.

The power of these assumptions lies in the fact that we do not need to be consciously aware of them to be affected by them. Like posture and table manners, they implant and reinforce cognitive presuppositions through physical actions and habitual motions, whether or not we recognize that they do so. As with any ritual, to perform them is on some level to accept and believe them.[20] The materiality of these interactions is one way in which our assumptions about virtual writing are being formed. Through mechanisms and procedures whose full impact we are only beginning to understand, virtual writing is being constituted as distinctively different from print. Even when its output is printed and bound into codex books, we know from the inside that it operates according to spatial principles and a topographical logic of its own.

THE PHYSICS OF VIRTUAL WRITING
AND THE FORMATION OF THE VIRTUAL SUBJECT

With all of this emphasis on spatiality, the reader may wonder how time enters into virtual writing. To understand the interaction between time and space in this medium, it is important to know something about the way the medium works. When computers speak their native languages—assembly code, and beneath that machine language—they operate within a profoundly non-Cartesian space. Distance at this level is measured by clock cycles. The computer's CPU (central processing unit) has a characteristic clock rate. When you buy a faster computer, you are essentially buying a faster clock rate. Imagine a drummer on a Viking sailing ship, pounding out the beat for the rowers' strokes.[21] Every two beats, a rowing cycle is completed. The drummer's pace controls the rate at which the oars move, and consequently the speed at which the boat slices through the water. Similarly, inside the computer the CPU reads a byte of code every two clock cycles. The clock rate thus controls the rate at which computations occur. It follows that addresses at memory locations 1, 50, 1000, and 1001 are all equidistant. Each is exactly two cycles away if it is in local memory, and eight cycles away if it is in remote memory.

How does this non-Cartesian relation between time and space express itself at the level of the user's experience? It is relatively easy for a computer program to generate a two-dimensional array, for it simply assigns each pixel on the screen an address. But to build a three-dimensional representation, the program must layer a series of two-dimensional planes on top of one another, as if a mountain had been cut horizontally into very thin slices and was being reassembled by the computer. This means that three-dimensional representations take many more cycles to build than two-dimensional maps. Hence the user experiences the sensory richness of a three-dimensional topography as a lag in the flow of the computer's response. In *Myst*, for example, the user experiences movement through the represented three-dimensional space as a series of jumps interspersed by pauses. You click, and the computer pauses and then jumps to a point perhaps ten feet away where a flight of steps begins; you click again, and the computer pauses and jumps halfway up the steps. Distance within the screen is experienced as an inertial pull on your time as you navigate the topology. The result is an artifactual physics that emerges from the interaction of the computer clock cycle with the user's experience. In this physics born of interactivity, the more complex the screen topography, the more inertial pull is exerted on the user's flow. The exact relation between the two is determined by the structure and programming of the underlying codes. Thus these codes, which normally remain invisible to the nonspecialist, are nevertheless felt and intuitively grasped by the user, in much the same way that the earth's gravity is felt and intuitively understood by someone who never heard of Newton's laws. Apples fall down; it takes effort to climb mountains. As inhabitants of cyberspace, we similarly understand in our muscles and bones that space belongs to the computer, and flow belongs to the user.

The physics of virtual writing illustrates how our perceptions change when we work with computers on a daily basis. We do not need to have software sockets inserted into our heads (as William Gibson envisions in *Neuromancer*) to become cyborgs. We already are cyborgs in the sense that we experience, through the integration of our bodily perceptions and motions with computer architectures and topologies, a changed sense of subjectivity.

Much has been written about how the transition from orality to writing affected subjectivity. In *Preface to Plato*, Eric Havelock initiates a fascinating line of inquiry when he asks why Plato is so adamant about banishing poets from the republic.[22] Havelock suggests that poetry is associated with oral culture and consequently with a fluid, changing, situational, and dispersed subjectivity. Plato wants to establish a fixed, stable, unchanging reality, and to do this, he needs a fixed, coherent, stable subject to perceive it. So the poets have to go, for they produce through their linguistic interventions exactly the kind of subject that Plato does not want and cannot tolerate. Similarly influential has been the work of Walter Ong on the differences between oral and written culture, Elizabeth Eisenstein on the effects of printing in early modern Europe, and Marshall McLuhan on the effects of electronic technologies.[23]

We are only beginning to understand the effect of computers on culture and on subjectivity. Marsha Kinder has documented the importance of "shifting," the perception young children have watching such programs as the Power Rangers that they can morph and shapeshift into various forms;[24] Brenda Laurel and Rachel Strickland have embodied similar perceptions in their virtual reality simulation "Placeholder";[25] and Allucquère

Roseanne Stone, in *The War of Desire and Technology at the Close of the Mechanical Age,* has written about the virtual subject as a "multiple" (analogous to someone who experiences multiple personalities) warranted by the body rather than contained within it.[26] Catherine Richards and Don Idhe have focused on proprioceptive coherence, looking at the way perception of body boundaries changes through technological interactions and interventions.[27] Michael Joyce, Jay Bolter, George Landow, and David Kolb, among others, have pointed out how navigating the topologies of electronic hypertexts creates new conditions for writing and reading and thus for both producing and expressing new kinds of subjectivities.[28] Operating without any illusions about comprehensiveness or rigor, I venture below to sum up a few salient comparisons between the oral subject, the written subject, and the virtual subject.

In the transition from the written to the virtual subject, deconstruction played a significant theoretical role, for in reinterpreting writing (emphasizing its instabilities, lack of originary foundations, intertextualities, and indeterminancies), in effect it made the written subject move much closer to the virtual subject than had traditionally been the case. This process is typical of what I have called elsewhere seriation (a term appropriated from archeological anthropology), an uneven process of change in which new artifacts or ideas emerge by partially replicating and partially innovating upon what came before. Although the shape of virtual subjectivity is only beginning to emerge and is therefore difficult to envision clearly, certain features are coming into focus. Proprioceptive coherence in interplay with electronic prostheses plays an important role in reconfiguring perceived body boundaries, especially when it gives the user the impression that her subjectivity is flowing into the space of the screen. When the interface is configured as keyboard and screen, the user will perceive that space belongs to the computer, flow to the user. The symbiotic relation between humans and intelligent machines has complex effects that do not necessarily all point in the same direction. For example, it can evoke resistance and a privileging of human qualities that machines do not share, such as emotion, or it can lead to the opposite view that humans should leave to machines the things they do best, such as memory recall, and concentrate on the things humans do best, like language and complex pattern recognition. Whatever the symbiosis is taken to mean, it seems clear that the virtual subject will in some sense be a cyborg.

The Oral Subject	The Written Subject	The Virtual Subject
Fluid, changing, situational, dispersed, conflicting	Fixed, coherent, stable, self-identical, normalized, decontextualized	◆ Formed through dynamic interfaces with computers ◆ When interface is keyboard and screen, space belongs to the computer, flow to the user ◆ Body boundaries extended or disrupted through proprioceptive coherence formed in conjunction with computer interfaces ◆ A cyborg

WHAT IS TO BE DONE?

Should we respond with optimism to the products of virtual writing, or regard them (as an elderly gentlemen informed me when he heard some of these arguments) as abominations that are rotting the minds of American youth? Whatever we make of them, one thing is certain. Literature will not remain unchanged. It is sometimes difficult to convey adequately to an academic audience the very rapid pace with which computer technologies are penetrating virtually every aspect of our culture. In this respect, academia in general and literature departments in particular tend to lag far behind other sectors of the society. With some noteworthy exceptions, academia is not where it is happening as far as computer culture is concerned.

Yet academics can make, I believe, vitally important contributions to the development of these technologies. Perhaps the most crucial are interventions that provide historical contexts showing how and why the technologies developed as they did. Although certain paths of development may be overdetermined, they are never inevitable. Other paths and other interpretations are always possible. The point I want to underscore is that it is a *historical construction* to believe that computer media are disembodying technologies, not an obvious truth. In fact, this belief requires systematic erasure of many significant aspects of our interactions with computers. It is almost never used as a working hypothesis by the people who are engaged in developing the technologies, for they cannot afford to ignore the materiality of the interfaces they create or the effects of these interfaces on their customers. If we articulate interpretations that contest the illusion of disembodiment, and if these interpretations begin to circulate through the culture, they can affect how the technologies are understood and consequently how they will be developed and used. Technologies do not develop on their own. People develop them, and people are sensitive to cultural beliefs about what the technologies can and should mean.

Brenda Laurel has called recognizing the importance of embodied interaction an "endangered sensibility" that she believes the arts and humanities should fight to retain and restore. For me, this means being attentive to the materialities of the media and their implications. The illusion that information is separate from materiality leads not only to a dangerous split between information and meaning but also to a flattening of the space of theoretical inquiry. If we accept that the materiality of the world is immaterial to our concerns, we are likely to miss the very complexities that theory at its best tries to excavate and understand.

The implications of my strategic choice of definition now stand, I hope, fully revealed. Virtuality is not about living in an immaterial realm of information, but about the cultural perception that material objects are interpenetrated with informational patterns. What this interpenetration means and how it is to be understood will be our collective invention. The choices we make are consequential, for it is in the complex, doubly figured, and intensely ambiguous condition of virtuality that our futures lie.

NOTES

1. For an important collection of essays arguing convincingly that how people understand and use technology is crucial to directing technological change, see *Does Technology Drive History? The Dilemma of Technological Determinism*, eds. Merritt Roe Smith and Leo Marx (Cambridge: MIT Press, 1994).
2. Erwin Schrödinger, *What Is Life: The Physical Aspect of the Living Cell* (Cambridge: Cambridge University Press and New York: Macmillan, 1945).
3. Richard Doyle, *On Beyond Living: Rhetorical Transformations in the Life Sciences* (Stanford: Stanford University Press, 1997).

4. George Gamow, *Mr. Tompkins Inside Himself: Adventures in the New Biology* (New York: Viking Press, 1967).

5. Richard Dawkins, *The Selfish Gene* (New York: Oxford University Press, 1976).

6. N. Katherine Hayles, "Narratives of Evolution and the Evolution of Narratives" in *Cooperation and Conflict in General Evolutionary Processes*, eds. John L. Casti and Anders Karlqvist (New York: John Wiley and Sons, 1994), pp. 113–32.

7. Hans Moravec, *Mind Children: The Future of Robot and Human Intelligence* (Cambridge: Harvard University Press, 1988).

8. Claude Shannon, *The Mathematical Theory of Communication* (Urbana: University of Illinois Press, 1949).

9. *Cybernetics: Circular Causal and Feedback Mechanisms in Biological and Social Systems*, 5 vols., ed. Heinz von Foerster, [transcripts for the 6th–10th Conferences on Cybernetics sponsored by the Josiah Macy Foundation] (New York: Josiah Macy, Jr. Foundation, 1950–55). For a definition of information that, *contra* Shannon, argued it should be connected with meaning, see Donald M. MacKay, *Information, Mechanism, and Meaning* (Cambridge: MIT Press, 1969).

10. Norbert Wiener, *Cybernetics: Or Control and Communication in the Animal and the Machine* (Cambridge: MIT Press, 1948) and *The Human Use of Human Beings: Cybernetics and Society* (Boston: Houghton Mifflin, 1950).

11. Jay Clayton in "The Voice in the Machine," presented at the English Institute at Cambridge, MA in August 1995 and included in this volume, argued that the telegraph could have been interpreted in the 1880s as a disembodying technology. Significantly, however, his research indicates that during the late nineteenth century it was perceived as an odd or different kind of embodiment but not as a disembodiment. Wiener's proposal, coming seventy years later, occurred in a different cultural context that was much more inclined to construct the telegraph, along with many other technologies, as disembodying media. The comparison is further evidence for Clayton's (and my) point that perceptions of how the body related to technologies are historical constructions, not biological inevitabilities.

12. The tendency to ignore the material realities of communication technologies has been forcefully rebutted in two important works, Friedrich A. Kittler's *Discourse Networks 1800/1900*, trans. Michael Metteer (Stanford: Stanford University Press, 1990), and *Materialities of Communication*, eds. Hans Ulrich Gumbrecht and K. Ludwig Pfeiffer, trans. William Whobrey (Stanford: Stanford University Press, 1994).

13. Michel Serres plays multiple riffs upon the interconversion of noise and information in *The Parasite*, trans. Lawrence R. Schehr (Baltimore: Johns Hopkins University Press, 1982).

14. More information on this inversion can be found in *The Maximum Entropy Formalism: A Conference Held at the Massachusetts Institute of Technology on May 2–4, 1978*, eds. Raphael D. Levine and Myron Tribus (Cambridge: MIT press, 1979).

15. William J. Mitchell, *City of Bits: Space, Place, and the Infobahn* (Cambridge: MIT Press, 1995).

16. The Universal Turing Machine is conveniently described by Roger Penrose in *The Emperor's New Mind: Concerning Computers, Minds, and the Laws of Physics* (New York: Oxford University Press, 1989). Verostko drew on this description specifically in creating his work (artist's note at the Art Show, SIGGRAPH '95).

17. Artist's Note, Art Show, SIGGRAPH '95.

18. Andre Kopra, private communication.

19. Michael Joyce, *Of Two Minds: Hypertext Pedagogy and Poetics* (Ann Arbor: University of Michigan Press, 1995).

20. Paul Connerton makes this point about ritual in *How Societies Remember* (Cambridge and New York: Cambridge University Press, 1989).

21. I am indebted to Nicholas Gessler for suggesting this metaphor to me and for pointing out the significance of the CPU's non-Cartesian operation.

22. Eric Havelock, *Preface to Plato* (Cambridge: Harvard University Press, 1963).

23. Walter Ong, *Orality and Literacy: The Technologizing of the Word* (New York: Routledge, 1988); Elizabeth Eisenstein, *The Printing Press as an Agent of Change: Communications and Cultural Transformations in Early Modern Europe* (Cambridge: Cambridge University Press, 1979); and Marshall McLuhan, *Understanding Media: The Extensions of Man* (New York: McGraw-Hill, 1964).

24. Marsha Kinder, "Screen Wars: Transmedia Appropriations from Eisenstein to *A TV Dante* and *Carmen Sandiego*" presented at the English Institute, Cambridge MA, August 1995, and included in this volume.

25. The simulation is documented in a video of the same name. A discussion of how the simulation was produced and what its goals are can be found in Brenda Laurel and Rachel Strickland's essay "Placeholder" in *Immersed in Technology*, ed. Mary Anne Moser (Cambridge: MIT Press, forthcoming 1995).

26. Allucquère Roseanne Stone, *The War of Desire and Technology at the Close of the Mechanical Age* (Cambridge: MIT Press, 1995).

27. Catherine Richards's virtual reality video, "Spectral Bodies," illustrates how proprioceptive coherence can be disrupted by even such low-tech methods as massaging a blindfolded subject's arms at certain key points with an electrical vibrator. Don Idhe also discusses proprioceptive coherence in *Technology and the Lifeworld*.

28. Michael Joyce, *Of Two Minds*; Jay David Bolter, *Writing Space: The Computer, Hypertext, and the History of Writing* (Hillsdale, N.J.: E. Erlbaum Associates, 1991); George P. Landow, *Hypertext: The Convergence of Contemporary Critical Theory and Technology* (Baltimore: Johns Hopkins University Press, 1994); David Kolb, *Socrates in the Labyrinth* [hypertext diskette] (Cambridge: Eastgate Systems, 1995); and Kolb's essay by the same title in Landow (1994).

VOICE

JAY CLAYTON   8

ABELL RINGS. Another message. The voices in the machine resume their insistent chatter. So many words, streams of code, flowing through the machine on his desk. He will be doing other things, moving about his small room with the inattentive composure of a person at home in his own world, when the bell chimes. He cannot ignore it.

One morning—day had broken after another all-night session—he receives notice of a wedding to take place on the line. Sarah Orten of Pittsburgh is marrying Thomas Welch of Cincinnati, a person she has never met face-to-face, their relationship having developed on the network. Everyone on the line is invited to attend the ceremony. Most mornings at this hour the clamor is incessant, messages banging away, interrupting one another, breaking short and resuming, a chaos of

THE VOICE IN THE MACHINE
HAZLITT,
HARDY,
JAMES

signals that only an experienced hand can interpret. But today the network falls silent, waiting for the words that will unite the couple in lawful wedlock. Afterward, a chorus of good wishes pours across the wires. It makes the man in his small room feel happy. He likes knowing he is wired to a vast community of people, strangers perhaps in real life but linked by the proliferating relays of their communications network. Imagine his feelings when he reads in a trade publication some months later that Sarah Orten has been duped. Tech crimes of this sort are becoming all too common. The anonymity of the network had enabled Thomas Welch to conceal from his white, upper-middle-class wife that he was an African American and (what the paper seemed most to resent) a barber. Sarah Orten sued for an annulment, and the courts granted her request. The man shakes his head and turns the printed pages of his journal to the next story. Later, he taps out words of his own to a person on the line he has never met. He is a night telegraph operator, and the year is 1883.

The facts of *Orten v. Welch* are recorded in the November 22, 1884 edition of *The Electrical World*, and the terms I have used to retell the case are drawn from this and other nineteenth-century publications about the telegraph.[1] My purpose in turning to the prior century is to explore the first comprehensive information network, the electric telegraph, which originated more or less simultaneously in both Britain and the United States in 1837, and spread so rapidly that virtually all the towns and cities of England were linked by the end of the 1840s, a feat that foreshadows the astonishing growth of the internet over the last decade. Like the internet, the telegraph was a point-to-point system, allowing two-way communication between individuals, not a one-to-many or broadcast system such as radio, film, and television, the media most often studied in communications theory.[2] Carolyn Marvin, one of the best social historians of communications technology, claims that the modern era "starts with the invention of the telegraph, the first of the electrical communications machines, as significant a break with the past as printing before it," but few theorists of modernity have evinced any interest in this technology.[3] I became interested in this forgotten precursor to the internet for two interrelated reasons.

First, the origin of the telegraph in the 1830s and 1840s separates it from most other electric communications technologies, which only came into widespread use in the final decades of the nineteenth century. As a result, the telegraph presents a distinctive historical problem, one that complicates many common assumptions about modernity and postmodernity (including Marvin's appealing but too-simple belief that the telegraph inaugurated the modern era). In this respect, my project parallels that of Jonathan Crary, who finds in technological developments of the 1830s grounds for challenging the received history of modernist art. Crary argues that a fundamental reorganization of the observing subject takes place in the early decades of the nineteenth century and that to understand this shift one must look not merely at painting and other visual arts but also at optical devices such as the stereoscope that "operate directly on the body of the individual."[4] The telegraph, too, operated on the bodies of its users, but its effects were very different from those of optical technology. The telegraph turns out to have a surprising connection with the stereoscope, but it is the difference, not the similarity, between these two technologies that poses the greatest challenge to the history of modernity.

Second, exploring the origins of the telegraph brings to prominence a curious struggle that has run throughout the 150 years in which there have been electric data networks. This struggle is between visual and aural scanning of signals. The telegraph was the site of a prolonged debate over the comparative advantages of "sound reading" and of instruments that incorporated a recording apparatus for taking down messages in visible form. A vast array of "recording" telegraphs were patented over the course of the nineteenth century; the list anticipates (and was the inspiration for) many later printing innovations, including not only the typewriter and teletype machines but also braille embossing techniques and chemically treated paper systems. Despite this ingenuity, aural data processing won out. To the extent this struggle has been studied at all, it has generally been viewed as a conflict among rival media—phonograph, radio, and the "talkies," on the one hand; print, silent film, and the computer screen, on the other hand. The history of the telegraph, however, reveals ways in which the conflict is internal to early communications technology. This insight becomes increasingly important as advances in information delivery make it possible for the end-user at a computer terminal to transform the data stream into signals readable by any of the senses—sight and sound preeminently, but with the advent of virtual reality, touch, taste, and smell too.

The special historical problem of the telegraph, in brief, is this: although the nineteenth-century technology strikingly foreshadows later communications networks, it was experienced at the time in a very different way. The physical impact of sound in the instrument's operation contrasts with the disembodiment often thought characteristic of the modern subject's encounter with technology. My contention is not that sound is inherently more embodied than sight but that our experience of both sight and sound is historically constructed. Hence the problem concerns how different technologies relate to a conceptual framework, not the practical matter of whether one is more user-friendly than another. The absence of sound technology from most models of modernity calls into question the global applicability of the term. Raymond Williams has attempted to account for aspects of a culture that do not conform to the dominant paradigm by calling them "residual" or "emergent."[5] Since acoustic technology was on the cutting edge of scientific innovation in its day, however, it cannot be thought of as "residual," but neither can it be called "emergent," because a new social formation did not, in fact, emerge from this discrepant experience. How does one characterize phenomena that have undeniable connections to major scientific, industrial, and economic developments but that ultimately do not become part of dominant social experience? Despite its importance in the nineteenth century, the voice in the machine remains odd, a deviant experience, unassimilable to the regime of modernity.

This oddity is registered in the literature of the period. A number of interesting, largely neglected texts treat the role of sound devices in the communications network of their day, and they explicitly associate an engagement with acoustic technology with other forms of "deviance," political, social, and sexual—but chiefly sexual. The sexual association first becomes prominent in a series of sensation novels of the 1860s, such as Mary Braddon's *Lady Audley's Secret* (1862), whose plots turn on the striking effect of a telegram; then in detective fiction, particularly that by A. Conan Doyle;[6] and finally in a series of telegraph-obsessed texts from the end of the century, including Gissing's *The Odd Women* (1893), Stoker's *Dracula* (1897), and two novels I shall examine at more length, Hardy's *A Laodicean* (1881) and James's "In the Cage" (1898). In James's story the oddity surrounding the machine's voice receives another name. There, the effects produced in the telegraph office are called not "odd" but "queer."

As the story of *Orten v. Welch* illustrates, the technological vocabulary surrounding the telegraph surprisingly anticipates today's cyberbabble. "Communications network," "relays," "code," "wired," "face-to-face," "tech," even the "web"—these terms, and others equally familiar, crop up in the earlier discourse. But the familiarity of this nineteenth-century episode reaches beyond vocabulary to encompass larger social anxieties.

Marvin reports on countless articles and stories from the last century concerned with the kind of issues that are making headlines today: the dangers of sexual predation over the wires, fears of uncontrolled social mobility made possible by the anonymity of the new technology, threats to the family, new forms of white-collar crime, the possibility that communications technology would be available only to the rich, and increasing government surveillance over the lives of citizens.

Equally, the kind of utopian claims about communications technologies that one hears everywhere today were easily as prominent in the last century. Here is language from a Commerce Committee report in Congress on Samuel Morse's new invention. The telegraph, this report gushes, will

> amount to a revolution unsurpassed in moral grandeur by any discovery that has been made in the arts and sciences, from the most distant period to which authentic history extends, to the present day. With the means of almost instantaneous communication ... space will be, to all practical purposes of information, completely annihilated. ... The citizen will be invested with ... the [attributes of God], in a degree that the human mind, until recently, had hardly dared to contemplate.[7]

This Congressional Report was issued in 1837, when no practical telegraph lines had been laid in the United States and when the speed of data transmission was far from "instantaneous," even by the standards that were to prevail in the next decade.

Comparisons with the deity soon became a standard trope of the celebratory literature surrounding the telegraph. A poem published in the October 1858 issue of the *Atlantic Monthly* celebrating the (short-lived) triumph of the first Atlantic telegraph cable exhorts the shores of the new world to "hear the voice of God!"—"The angel of His stormy sky / Rides down the sunken wire," bringing a message of peace.[8] "Close wedded by that mystic cord" the continents will clasp hands "beneath the sea," spelling the final end of human conflict, "The funeral shroud of war!" This message of brotherhood is fused with imperialist rhetoric common in nineteenth-century technological discourse:

> Through Orient seas, o'er Afric's plain,
>   And Asian mountains borne,

The vigor of the Northern brain
  Shall nerve the world outworn.

Prescott's history of the electric telegraph (1860) boasted that the peoples of every Christian nation could answer in the affirmative the question God put to Job: "Canst thou send lightnings, that they may go, and say unto thee, Here we are?"[9] In *The Ocean Telegraph to India* (1870), Parkinson compares the engineers on the Great Eastern, which laid the cable through the Persian Gulf, to Moses standing on Mount Sinai.[10]

The congruence between the birth of the telegraph and the coming of the information age is strong. Vocabulary, anecdotes, and social responses separated by more than a century and a half seem eerily alike. As a step toward thinking about this historical conjuncture, let me draw attention to a little-known essay about early nineteenth-century communications systems written by William Hazlitt.

"The Letter-Bell," composed in the last months of Hazlitt's life and published in 1831, shortly after his death, is an odd, digressive meditation on the charms of memory and on fidelity in the face of historical changes of the most wrenching sort—technological, to begin with, but also political. At the beginning of the essay, Hazlitt is at his desk composing sentences about the brevity of human life when suddenly his train of thought is interrupted by the sound of a bell outside in the street, a "loud-tinkling, interrupted sound," which in those days announced the passing of the mail carrier.[11] The sound throws him into a reverie, taking him back to the precious days of his youth. Notice the emphasis on the somatic qualities of the sound—striking the ear, vibrating on his brain—and on the active power of these vibrations to pierce and wake the subject:

> As I write this, the *Letter-Bell* passes: it has a lively, pleasant sound with it, and not only fills the street with its importunate clamour, but rings clear through the length of many half-forgotten years. It strikes upon the ear, it vibrates to the brain, it wakes me from the dream of time, it flings me back upon my first entrance into life, the period of my first coming up to town, when all around was strange, uncertain, adverse—a hubbub of confused noises. (LB, 377)

The postal service, then as now, was a communications network, although it possessed comparatively few technologies to aid in the distribution of messages. Of the few it had—a road system, highly variable in quality; a routing grid; and an audible signal to indicate the availability of a gateway to the network, for the pillar-box on the street corner would not be introduced for twenty-one years by Anthony Trollope (postal worker and novelist)—of these technologies of communication, it is the signal bell that seizes Hazlitt's imagination. About a decade later the same signal would be grafted onto the telegraph to announce an incoming message; late in the nineteenth century the same signal would become a feature of the telephone; and, today, the same signal chimes in one's computer terminal at the arrival of a message, if that feature is enabled in one's e-mail program. The sound of these signal bells is the voice of the communications network itself, a sound produced by the interactions of a vast information system, stretching around the globe even in Hazlitt's day. The bell is the network's very own sound, a voice conveying the network's (not the user's) message.

In a happy phrase, Hazlitt calls these bells "*conductors* to the imagination" (LB, 380, italics in original). They not only spark the imagination but function as relay switches as well. Hearing their "importunate clamour" breaks the circuit of attention that connects him to the present and shunts his mind into memories of "half-forgotten years." These memories are precious to him not merely because of their personal associations but also because, for many trying years, they have been the only place where the spirit of the French Revolution has continued to survive. This bitter reflection prompts Hazlitt into one of his characteristic diatribes against Wordsworth and Coleridge for betraying their former faith in liberty.

Cowards and recreants—these are the kindest words Hazlitt can find now for his former compatriots. "What would not these persons give for the unbroken integrity of their early opinions?" Hazlitt asks, and then, as if the thought of unbroken connections brings him up short, he returns to his topic of the letter bell. The transition seems as abrupt as it is hyperbolic:

This is the reason I can write an article on the *Letter-Bell*, and other such subjects; I have never given the lie to my own soul. If I have felt any impression once, I feel it more strongly a second time; and I have no wish to revile or discard my best thoughts. . . . I do not recollect having ever repented giving a letter to the postman, or wishing to retrieve it after he had once deposited it in his bag. What I have once set my hand to, I take the consequences of. . . . I am not like the person who, having sent off a letter to his mistress, who resided a hundred and twenty miles in the country, and disapproving, on second thoughts, of some expressions contained in it, took a post-chaise and four to follow and intercept it the next morning. (LB, 378–79)

As he writes these lines in 1830, Hazlitt's constancy is being vindicated, for the July Revolution in France connects the closing days of the author's career to its beginnings in the glorious days of the first French Revolution. But the odd movement from one topic to another in this passage seems to undercut the very unity of the subject about which he boasts (perhaps overmuch). In the space of a few sentences Hazlitt moves from assertions of political fidelity, to reflections on the changing mail system, to anxious comments about taking the consequences of his actions, to a ludicrous portrait of sexual vacillation. What connects these topics? More important, where does this anxiety about punishment come from, and why does the sound of a postman's bell lead him to insist on his sexual integrity?

These questions prompt one to take seriously Hazlitt's claims that his very identity is intertwined with the communications system of his youth and that changes in this system require adjustments in the way he conceptualizes himself. The overinsistence on constancy—political, sexual, and somatic—arises from the odd position in which the ringing of the letter bell puts him. For the essay charts a strange inversion in his response to the "loud-tinkling" bell. In the present, the sound "flings" him into reveries. When it "strikes upon the ear," it turns his thoughts inward. In the past, though, the bell used to wake him from his dreams. Years ago, Hazlitt confesses, "the Letter-Bell was the only sound that drew my thoughts to the world without" (LB, 379). The signal that today assures the subject of its "unbroken integrity" yesterday served to admonish its waywardness. The same sound "vibrates to the brain" with strangely opposed effects.

This is how Hazlitt is constant to himself—by growing into the opposite of what he once was. This is how he manages to feel the same impression more strongly a second time—by inverting it. I do not mean to say that Hazlitt's political convictions ever changed; far from it. But something had to change to make sure those convictions remained the same. The letter bell becomes the mark of this inversion in the subject. What makes it an appropriate sign of inversion, in this context, is the odd relation of sound devices to other modern technologies, a deviance just becoming apparent in Hazlitt's time.

The last sentence of Hazlitt's essay turns from memories of old letter-delivery systems to what seems like an anachronistic reference to the telegraph since the author died seven years before the date associated with its invention. Here is the essay's conclusion: "The telegraphs that lately communicated the intelligence of the new revolution to all France within a few hours, are a wonderful contrivance; but they are less striking and appalling than the beacon-fires (mentioned by Aeschylus), which, lighted from hill-top to hill-top, announced the taking of Troy, and the return of Agamemnon" (*LB*, 382). There is no anachronism involved, however. The telegraph to which Hazlitt refers was an optical semaphore network established by Claude Chappe in Paris in 1794.[12] This telegraph system is virtually forgotten today, but it provided continuous communication service among twenty-nine cities in France until 1855. At its height the network had 556 telegraph stations, covering some 3,000 miles, and messages sent from Paris could begin arriving at Calais in just four minutes. The stations customarily consisted of a squat tower, on the top of which was mounted a metal pole equipped with two wooden beams that could be manipulated like semaphore flags to convey the letters of the alphabet. The French were so enamored of this optical system that they lagged behind Britain and the United States in the introduction of the electric telegraph, a communications gap that plagued their country well into the twentieth century. Even after the change to the electric telegraph, France delayed adopting the international Morse code, preferring instead to operate the electric system with an optical code based on Chappe's semaphore.

The conflict between optical and aural systems that surfaces in Hazlitt's essay and that played itself out over twenty years of French policy debate was a topic of contention among U.S. and British inventors too. Although Morse patented a sound-reading system, the Morse Telegraph Company at first vigorously fought the sound system, even issuing regulations forbidding its use. In less than a decade, however, the Morse Company rule had been reversed and operators were required to receive by sound. Recording telegraphs required two employees—an operator who translated aloud the dots and dashes marked on the receiving paper and a copyist who took dictation. Operators soon found that, while listening to the clacking of the instrument, they could take down messages with fewer mistakes and that sound-reading freed their eyes and hands for writing. Sound-reading spread more rapidly in the United States than in Britain, perhaps because the rhythmic drumming action of striking downward on a key reinforced the somatic link between sound and signal. The British Needle Telegraph, invented by William Fothergill Cooke and Sir Charles Wheatstone—and later their "ABC" instruments—were operated by twisting levers to the side with a flick of the wrist. The Needle Telegraph, which was a recorder, was the dominant apparatus in Britain into the 1860s and was still employed on most private lines as late as 1888, when it began to be replaced by the telephone. Operators of these British instruments eventually learned to read the clicks of the needle by ear too, and the practice became dominant.

The role of sound in telegraphic communications was regarded by contemporary observers as one of the most startling features of this new technology. One early sound-reader is described as having "visions of sound."[13] An anonymous British poem begins, "Hark! The warning needles click," and taunts the gods of yore in its refrain: "Sing who will of Orphean lyre / Ours the wonder-working wire!"[14] Every nineteenth-century book on the telegraph contains sections on the wonders of reading by sound. One typical chapter claims: "Of all the mysterious agencies of the electric telegraph, there is nothing else so marvelous as the receiving intelligence by sound."[15]

Thomas Hardy draws on this nineteenth-century debate over the comparative advantages of sound- and sight-reading as a structural principle in his novel, *A Laodicean*. The novel's heroine, Paula Power, is a young heiress who has had a telegraph installed in her home, a castle of ancient date. A sound-reader, she "applied her ear to the instrument" to take down messages, even though the receiver would most likely have been

one of Wheatstone's "ABC" instruments.[16] Like Hazlitt, Hardy personifies the bell as the voice of the machine itself: "The telegraph had almost
the attributes of a human being at Stancy Castle. When its bell rang
people rushed to the old tapestried chamber allotted to it, and waited
its pleasure" (AL, 52). Even the wires, "the musical threads which the
post-office authorities had erected all over the country," are notable for
their sound effects when the wind makes them "hum as of a night-bee,"
something Hardy repeatedly mentions: "The wire sang on overhead
with dying falls and melodious rises . . . while above the wire rode the
stars in their courses, the low nocturn of the former seeming to be the
voices of those stars" (AL, 21). Whereas Hardy systematically links the
heroine and her female friend to the telegraph's music, he connects all
of the men in the novel—and especially the villain—with the production of images. Somerset, the hero, is an architect and the son of a famous
artist; Captain De Stancy, his unworthy rival in love, employs trumped-
up knowledge of the castle's paintings to gain access to the heroine; and
Dare, the melodramatically drawn villain of the piece, is a photographer
who doctors a photo so that the hero falsely appears drunk.

A Laodicean is one of Hardy's least-read novels, perhaps because it
is among his oddest. Uncertain of tone, it is part novel of ideas, part
gothic, part comedy of modern manners, and part love story, yet there
are fascinating touches in this work of a sort one seldom finds elsewhere
in the author's canon. Most of them occur early in the novel, in passages that connect the ambiguous sexuality of the heroine to Hardy's
theme of the "clash between ancient and modern" (AL, 34). "Laodicean"
means someone uncertain about her convictions, and the title overtly
refers both to Paula's wavering religious beliefs and to her divided loy-
alties to antiquity and to the "ultra-modern" (AL, 17). Paula, however,
wavers in her sexuality too. The few critics who have written on this
novel complain of her inability to make up her mind about which man
she will marry. As J. M. Barrie wittily puts it, "She engages to get engaged
to an architect who must not kiss her. Then she engages to get engaged
to a soldier."[17] An anonymous writer in the Saturday Review is more exas-
perated: "In A Laodicean the author showed us very queer people doing
very queer things, which seemed the odder because the background
against which the characters stood out was that of life in a country
house, and the characters themselves were of such a kind that it was

imprudent to assign to them precisely the oddities which the author did assign."[18] None of these critics ever noticed, however, that the novel's vacillating plot, with its confusions of genre and tone, corresponds to Paula's queerness and that the heroine's reluctance to kiss, much less marry, either man is based on something more than fickleness.

The reverend who compares Paula to the biblical city of Laodicea denounces her as "neither cold nor hot" (*AL*, 18), but the warmth of her feelings for another woman, Charlotte, is never in doubt. A neighbor gives the clue early on: "Now that's a curious thing again, these two girls being so fond of one another," and adds, "they are more like lovers than girl and girl" (*AL*, 50). Later, Paula herself shows some of her feelings in a comment on a statue of a recumbent woman: "'She is like Charlotte,' Paula said. And what was much like another sigh escaped her lips," then she "drew her forefingers across the marble face of the effigy, and at length took out her handkerchief, and began wiping the dust from the hollows of the features" (*AL*, 111). Charlotte is equally revealing. As she speaks of Paula, "a blush slowly rose to her cheek, as if the person spoken of had been a lover rather than a friend" (*AL*, 35).

Paula's same-sex bond destabilizes a number of elements in the novel, including the ostensible love plot, which revolves around Somerset's rivalry with Captain De Stancy. It destabilizes, as well, some of the usual markers of gender. One minor character, another woman, describes Paula's beauty as "middling," except at that time of the day when she engages in her favorite pastime, working out in a private gymnasium that she has had built on her property. Then "she looks more bewitching than at any" other time "because when she is there she wears such a pretty boy's costume, and is so charming in her movements, that you think she is a lovely youth and not a girl at all" (*AL*, 169). Somerset responds to something different but equally disturbing to his assumptions about gender. Although Paula seems "becomingly girlish and modest" to him, her "composure"—what one might read as her immunity to *his* attractions—has a queer effect not only on her looks but also on himself: "Somehow Miss Power seemed not only more woman than [Charlotte], but more woman than Somerset was man" (*AL*, 68). Far from repelling him, however, Paula's power to *un*man him seems to stimulate his desire. At one point he watches Paula caress Charlotte—"she clasped fingers behind Charlotte's neck, and smiled tenderly in her

face"—and his response is to reflect: "It seemed to be quite uncon-
sciously done, and Somerset thought it a very beautiful action," an action
that "so excited the emotional side of his nature that he could not concentrate on feet and inches" (*AL*, 84–85). Only a few lines later he is
resigning himself "to be the victim of an unrequited passion" (*AL*, 85).

By far the most striking scene in the book occurs when the malev-
olent Dare succeeds in arousing Captain De Stancy's desire for Paula
by taking him to spy on her exercises through a chink in the wall of
her private gymnasium. The dynamics of voyeurism in this act are
complex. As De Stancy watches Paula, Dare and a third man watch
him. The men, all of whom are plotting against Paula's well-being in different ways, clarify their places in the conspiracy through their different
voyeuristic positions:

> "Is she within there?" [the third man asks].
>
> Dare nodded, and whispered, "You need not have asked, if you had examined his
> face."
>
> "That's true."
>
> "A fermentation is beginning in him," said Dare, half-pitifully; "a purely chemical
> process; and when it is complete he will probably be clear, and fiery, and sparkling,
> and quite another man than the good, weak, easy fellow that he was."
>
> To precisely describe Captain De Stancy's look was impossible. A sun rising in his
> face, such was somewhat the effect. By watching him they could almost see the
> aspect of her within the wall. (AL, 174)

The conspiracy links heterosexual desire not only with the spoils of
marriage but also with a set of fraudulent architectural drawings for
plans to restore the castle to its feudal glory. Here, as elsewhere, the text
links visuality itself—whether in the scopic aggression of voyeurism
or in the deceptiveness of drawings and photographs—with an homoso-
cial bond that underwrites the heterosexual competition for the body
and estate of a woman. "What was the captain seeing?" the narrator
asks, and to emphasize the visual character of the forces that symbol-
ize Paula's violation, answers: "A sort of optical poem" (*AL*, 172).

The association of optics with male sexual aggression, in this text,
is balanced by the symmetrical counterassociation of the telegraph—
and acoustics—with a queer space, within which Paula's resistance to

violence is disguised as "feminine" indecision and delay. As the only principal characters who can read the telegraph's sounds, Paula and Charlotte hold intimate converse with one another across great distances, more than once about Somerset while he is standing in the room where the message is being received, feeling excluded by his inability to understand the instrument's clicks: "There was something curious in watching this utterance about himself, under his very nose, in language unintelligible to him" (*AL*, 42). Somerset's word "curious" understates the oddity, the queer effect, that the telegraph symbolizes in Hardy's novel. Although the contrived and melodramatic action in the second half of the novel brings the heterosexual love plot to a conclusion, with Paula's marriage to Somerset and Charlotte's retreat to a nunnery, no less, the final pages of the book are given over to ambivalence. Remembering the reverend's denunciation of her as neither cold nor hot, Paula whispers these less-than-reassuring words in her new husband's ear: "What I really am, as far as I know, is one of that body to whom lukewarmth is not an accident but a provisional necessity" (*AL*, 428).

Hardy's choice of the telegraph to represent the queer effects of Paula's desires may present difficulties of comprehension to contemporary readers, who associate advanced communications technology with disembodiment. Baudrillard has famously argued that in the "era of hyperreality," when all functions are "abolished in . . . the ecstasy of communication," the "body, landscape, time all progressively disappear."[19] Mark Dery describes well the "wraithlike nature of electronic communication—the flesh become word, the sender reincarnated as letters floating on a terminal screen."[20] Such was not how the first electric communications network was experienced. Nineteenth-century observers were fascinated by the fact that telegraphic signals could be read by any of the senses, a claim that shows up in book after book. For example, one writer tells of repairmen who commonly read the wires with their tongue "by placing one wire above and the other wire below it"; another author explains how operators would hold ends of wire in each hand and read the signal "by means of the passage of shocks" through the body.[21] John Hollingshead, writing in Dickens's *All the Year Round*, recounts how the coming of telegraphs to local pubs enabled an enterprising innkeeper to provide a "glass of ale and an elec-tric shock for four-pence."[22]

One cause of this perceived difference between the two commu-nications technologies is the differing somatic itineraries of sight and sound under modernity. As Guy Debord, among others, has maintained, sight is "the most abstract of the senses" and hence, most "adaptable to present-day society's generalized abstraction."[23] Debord emphasizes that in the society of the spectacle sight has been separated from the other senses and elevated to "the special place once occupied by touch."[24] By contrast, the conditions of modernization have made sound appear to retain a closer connection with the sense of touch, in part because the body's role in producing sound waves has not been eliminated in daily life by technology. The subject experiences this activity of production in a strained vocal cord, a gasp for breath, a hoarse throat or dry mouth after prolonged speech, the sibilance of the lips in a whisper, the thrust of the solar plexus in a grunt. Similarly, the manual operation of the telegraph worked against the abstraction of sound from the tactile realm. Even today computer manufacturers design keyboards to produce a clicking noise in an effort to link, through the agency of sound, the fingers' actions to the letters materializing on the screen.

I do not mean to romanticize the job of working in a telegraph office. From the middle of the nineteenth century onward the central stations in large cities like London and New York achieved a degree of regimentation depressing to behold, and the rationalization of this workplace particularly capitalized on the increasing gendering of the labor force.[25] Indeed, more than one cultural critic has suggested that nineteenth-century communications technologies such as the type-writer, telephone, and telegraph played a decisive role in moving women into the office.[26] Thus Trollope, in his story "The Telegraph Girl," describes his heroine at her labors with "eight hundred female com-panions, all congregated together in one vast room."[27] Sound technologies did not escape the process of modernization and, in fact, played their own part in the regimentation of the work environment (witness the role of steam whistles in factories).

What I do claim, however, is that our understanding of sound has been historically constructed so as to make it appear less abstract than vision, and thus, less integral to the development of modernity. Debord is right when he claims sight is more adaptable than sound to modernity's demand for abstraction, if one recognizes that the subject's experience of sight *and* sound is historically conditioned. Nineteenth-century acoustic technology reinforced rather than severed the connection among the senses, particularly sound and touch. Unlike nineteenth-century optical technology, which transformed particular objects into abstract images the better to circulate as commodities, the voice in the machine operated to connect one somatic experience with another. By consolidating the sensory effects of the signal, sound technology appears to intensify rather than abstract. Hence the remarkable power of sound to provoke memories—in Hazlitt's words, to "ring clear through the length of many half-forgotten years." This aural effect lies behind one of the hyperbolic claims in Hazlitt's essay: "If I have felt any impression once, I feel it more strongly a second time."

One can clarify this difference by comparing an optical technology like the stereoscope, which Crary calls the "most significant form of visual imagery in the nineteenth century, with the exception of photographs,"[28] with sound-producing technologies from the same period. As it happens, Sir Charles Wheatstone, who was knighted for his role in inventing the telegraph, also invented the stereoscope. This apparent coincidence is not as surprising as it may at first seem. The link between his optical and electrical researches was wave-theory. Wheatstone, son of a musical instrument dealer, began his research career by investigating the properties of acoustical waves. At the age of nineteen, he created a sensation in London by exhibiting a musical instrument called the "Enchanted Lyre," in which a replica of an ancient lyre was hung from the ceiling by a thin cord and was made to play musical pieces for hours on end without any apparent human intervention. This exhibition turned out to be a serious scientific demonstration of the ability of sound waves to travel more rapidly through solids than air. The lyre was connected to the sounding board of a piano in a room above, and the sound was propagated down through the wire. Wheatstone's publication of his results was the first of many contributions to acoustical wave-theory that are still regarded as seminal. His contributions to optical research are even more highly regarded: he and Sir David Brewster are credited with being the first people to uncover the principles behind binocular vision.

Wheatstone's stereoscope illustrated the way in which binocular vision functioned by radically separating the images seen by each eye. Since the viewer could see the two different images positioned on opposite sides of the instrument, the illusion of three-dimensional synthesis created by the stereoscope made clear that the visual field was itself fragmented. By breaking down the principles behind binocular vision, the stereoscope, in Crary's words, "discloses a fundamentally disunified and aggregate field of disjunct elements,"[29] a disclosure that signals a break with classical principles of perspective around which the observing subject had been organized for centuries. Thus Wheatstone's stereoscope was "based on a radical abstraction and reconstruction of optical experience."[30]

Wheatstone's Enchanted Lyre and his later Kaleidophone did not have the effect of disclosing the radical abstraction of sensory experience. In fact, his acoustical experiments and devices consistently underscored the relationship between physical contact and the propagation of sound. His instruments demonstrated for audiences "the augmentation of sound which results from the connexion of a vibrating body with other bodies capable of entering into simultaneous vibration with it."[31] In one demonstration he showed that a wire held in the air next to a flute could not transmit the sound, but if the wire touched the side of the instrument, the music could be heard at a distant sounding board. In another, he proved that "the sounds of an entire orchestra may be transmitted," although dimly, because of the air intervening between the sounding board and the music. All the same, Wheatstone wrote, "The effect of an experiment of this kind is very pleasing."[32]

The telegraph, in similar fashion, was perceived as connecting people to one another, and the experience of communicating by wires was one of amazing immediacy, even though the signal was terribly slow by today's standards. The phrase "annihilating distance" turns up over and over again in publications about the telegraph, but as the word itself indicates, the technology actually made distance internal to the signal. The word "telegraph," which preexisted the electrical apparatus now associated with the term (witness Chappe's semaphore system), means "writing at a distance"—and that is exactly what it did. The signal produced by a machine at one location was produced again by a machine at a distance. Hence there is no intrinsic reason why the experience should not have been one of thrilling dislocation, like the disembodied sense of "thereness" felt by many in cyberspace. The way in which sound seemed to consolidate and intensify sensory experiences, however, militated against this interpretation of the technology. Listening could have the effect of splitting the subject—between present and past, say, as in Hazlitt's essay—but the impression was one not of diminishment but of superabundance.

All of these somatic effects—intensification and immediacy, combined with a sense that distance has been internalized, brought inside the subject, resulting in a split but oddly augmented identity—are on view in what is perhaps the most successful treatment of the telegraph in English literature, Henry James's "In the Cage." This fascinating story revolves around an unnamed lady telegraphist who regards herself as the "contact" through which an entire communications network flows.[33] She works in a small station in a grocery, separated off by a wood and wire cage, with an appropriately named instrument at its center—the "sounder" (*ITC*, 174). As Jennifer Wicke has pointed out, women such as the telegraphist "mediate exchange. Communication flows through them, telegraphically or otherwise enhanced."[34] Although Wicke has no occasion to mention it, this enhancement is explicitly described in electrical terms: "The great thing was the flashes" that come from her "contact with the human herd" (*ITC*, 178), flashes that fire each of her senses in turn:

> As the weeks went on there she lived more and more into the world of whiffs and glimpses, she found her divinations work faster and stretch further. It was a prodigious view as the pressure heightened, a panorama fed with facts and figures, flushed with a torrent of colour and accompanied with wondrous world-music. (*ITC*, 186)

The telegraphist is an early version of Donna Haraway's cyborg, a woman wired into the information network, the interface between a vast technological network and a human system of customers and exchange.[35]

James fully registers the oddity of the telegraphist's position, what he calls "the queer extension of her experience, the double life that, in the cage, she grew at last to lead" (*ITC*, 186). "Queer" is apt, given the sexual ambiguities opened up by this story. Eve Kosofsky Sedgwick, in an English Institute essay now a decade old, first drew attention to James's use of this word in another late story, "The Beast in the Jungle."[36] Since then, Eric Savoy has traced the historical context for "In the Cage" back to the homosexual scandals of the 1890s, particularly the Cleveland Street Affair of 1889–90, which centered on the incriminating testimony of telegraph boys and "the Post Office's anxiety about the operations of its 'particularly sensitive telegraph branch'."[37] If "queer" is apt, "extension" is equally apropos, given the way in which the telegraph seems to bring distance inside the subject, allowing it to incorporate two positions without contradiction. For the telegraphist, the sense of a "double life" does not invalidate convictions the way the photographic double-exposure in Hardy's novel did. Rather it has the odd effect, so common in James, of both multiplying and intensifying experiences: hence "there were more impressions to be gathered and really—for it came to that—more life to be led" (ITC, 178).

Since "In the Cage" has lately begun to attract the attention that it deserves,[38] I concentrate on the neglected somatic dimension of the telegraph network—and on a related sexual motif. The dangers of the telegraphist's sexuality have sometimes been referred to the suggestion—toyed with at several points in the story—of prostitution and blackmail. Savoy nicely illustrates how these topics represent "James's displacement of fin-de-siècle homosexual panic into the narrative economies of heterosexual transgression."[39] What has not been noticed is that the displacement, in one crucial instance, moves in the other direction—from the heterosexual to the homosexual register. Much of the plot concerns the telegraphist's knowledge of an adulterous intrigue between an upper-class gentleman, Captain Everard, and a married woman, Lady Bradeen. Although the telegraphist, in the course of her work, meets Captain Everard often enough to fall obsessively in love with him, she is alone with the recipient of his secret telegrams only once. Lady Bradeen, who has come into the station to send a wire, makes a mistake in the private code that she and her lover have devised, a slip that could potentially expose their affair. The telegraphist catches this slip and, to the amazement of the sender, supplies the missing word. This act, of course, transgresses all the rules of the telegraph service, for the woman behind the counter is supposed to be a neutral, expressionless, transparent interface. James treats it as one of the climaxes of the story: "It was as if [the telegraphist] had bodily leaped—cleared the top of the cage and alighted on her interlocutress" (*ITC*, 213). Even before this transgressive act, however, the scene has had a queer dimension.

When she first sees Lady Bradeen, the telegraphist finds that her feelings for Captain Everard make his lover an intensely interesting object: "The girl looked straight through the cage at the eyes and lips that must so often have been so near his own—looked at them with a strange passion" (*ITC*, 211). The homoerotics of this kind of transference are familiar, although fiction more often chronicles two men triangulating their love for one another through a mutually desired woman. "She was with the absent through her ladyship," James remarks, and then he adds a further twist, "and with her ladyship through the absent" (*ITC*, 211). So intense is this "strange passion" that, in a bewildering reversal, her desire for the man appears as if it had been stimulated by her response to the woman rather than vice versa: "But, gracious, how handsome *was* her ladyship, and what an added price it gave him that the air of intimacy he threw out should have flowed originally from such a source!" (*ITC*, 211).

The encounter indeed represents a "queer extension of her experience," one that reproduces the oddness of the telegraph in its very structure. To be with the sender and receiver at the same instant, to feel physically present at two ends of a communications circuit, such was the way many nineteenth-century subjects experienced the "sounder." This somatic effect, discussed now in a number of different contexts, does not fit neatly with other, more "modern" aspects of James's London, such as the commodification of language in the telegraph office. If the transformation of words into commodities is the most modern feature of James's story, as several critics have maintained,[40] then the telegraphist's queer relation to this process vexes the story's own relation to modernity. James undoubtedly means to capture the modern tendency toward abstraction when he describes the telegraphist counting and reckoning the cost of the words in the messages she transmits. But this process of commodification fails to encompass every aspect of the woman's situation. Mr. Mudge, the telegraphist's stolid fiancé, makes the point. He wants her to view her relationship with customers in more rather than less commercial terms. He does not like "to see anything *but* money made out of his betters" (*ITC*, 203). This wish, James wryly comments, is the "straight" view of her position. "Yet [Mr. Mudge] was troubled by the suspicion of subtleties on his companion's part that spoiled the straight view. He couldn't understand people's hating what they liked or liking what they hated" (*ITC*, 203), which is exactly the "perverse" way in which the telegraphist experiences her situation.

The queerness of her position corresponds to the odd, still unassimilated position of the telegraph network in the regime of modernity. Marvin claims that, "in a historical sense, the computer is no more than an instantaneous telegraph with a prodigious memory, and all the communications inventions in between have simply been elaborations on the telegraph's original work."[41] I hope to have shown that this early acoustical instrument has a more complicated place than that. The telegraph, that forgotten technology in histories of modernity, offers an alternative site for thinking about language machines. It has an odd relation to other communications networks, and an odd relation to the dominant story of modernity.

Let me conclude by suggesting that the best way to understand these odd relations is not by shifting the putative origin of modernism thirty, forty, or even fifty years earlier. Such adjustments merely relocate the boundaries of the period and leave intact the larger assumptions about its unity and comprehensiveness. If modernity both inhabits and is deployed in response to a dominant scopic regime, then attending to the subject's experience of acoustic technology may help make audible queer modes of social experience not assimilable to the grand narratives of modernity.[42]

NOTES

1. I learned about *Orten v. Welch* from Carolyn Marvin, *When Old Technologies Were New: Thinking about Electric Communication in the Late Nineteenth Century* (New York: Oxford University Press, 1988), pp. 93–94. Similar stories can be found in many nineteenth-century publications about the growth of the telegraph system. By the last decades of the century, tales of telegraph romance and telegraph fraud had become staples of journalism and popular fiction.

2. Daniel R. Headrick, *The Invisible Weapon: Telecommunications and International Politics 1851–1945* (New York: Oxford University Press, 1991), p. 9, notes that the origins of broadcast media have received far more attention than those of point-to-point communication, which is the mode of technology that underlies the internet. In addition

to Headrick's own work and that of the "notable exceptions" he cites (Ithiel de Sola Pool, *The Social Impact of the Telephone* [Cambridge, MA: Harvard University Press, 1976] and *Technologies of Freedom* [Cambridge, MA: Harvard University Press, 1983]; Marvin, *When Old Technologies Were New*, and Stephen Kern, *The Culture of Time and Space, 1880–1918* [Cambridge, MA: Harvard University Press, 1983]), I have located only a few other significant examples of this sort of study. They are Marshall McLuhan's chapter on the telegraph in *Understanding Media: The Extensions of Man* (New York: New American Library, 1964), pp. 246–57; James W. Carey, "Technology and Ideology: The Case of the Telegraph," in *Communication as Culture: Essays on Media and Society* (Boston: Unwin Hyman, 1989), pp. 201–30; Friedrich A. Kittler, *Discourse Networks 1800/1900*, trans. Michael Metteer, with Chris Cullens (Stanford, CA: Stanford University Press, 1990); and Scott Bukatman, "Gibson's Typewriter," in *Flame Wars: The Discourse of Cyberculture*, ed. Mark Dery (Durham, NC: Duke University Press, 1994), pp. 71–90.

3. Marvin, *When Old Technologies Were New*, p. 3.

4. Jonathan Crary, *Techniques of the Observer: On Vision and Modernity in the Nineteenth Century* (Cambridge, MA: MIT Press, 1990), p. 7.

5. See Raymond Williams, *Marxism and Literature* (New York: Oxford University Press, 1977), pp. 120–27.

6. For an account of Sherlock Holmes's engagement with the telegraph, see Robert N. Brodie, "'Take a Wire, Like a Good Fellow': The Telegraph in the Canon" in *The Baker Street Journal* 41 (September 1991), pp. 148–52.

7. Alfred Vail, *The American Electro Magnetic Telegraph: With the Reports of Congress, and a Description of All Telegraphs Known, Employing Electricity or Galvanism* (1845; reprinted in *Eyewitness to Early American Telegraphy* [New York: Arno Press, 1974]), pp. 77–78.

8. This poem, "The Telegraph," is quoted in its entirety in George B. Prescott, *History, Theory, and Practice of the Electric Telegraph* (Boston: Ticknor and Fields, 1860), pp. 371–72.

9. Prescott, *History, Theory, and Practice of the Electric Telegraph*, p. 214.

10. J. C. Parkinson, *The Ocean Telegraph to India: A Narrative and a Diary* (Edinburgh: William Blackwood, 1870), pp. 269–71.

11. William A. Hazlitt, "The Letter–Bell" in *Uncollected Essays*, vol. 17 of *The Complete Works of William Hazlitt*, ed. P. P. Howe (New York: AMS Press, 1967). Subsequent references to this essay will be included in the text as LB.

12. The fascinating history of Chappe's telegraph is told in Gerard J. Holzmann and Björn Pehrson, *The Early History of Data Networks* (Los Alamitos, CA: IEEE Computer Society Press, 1995), from which most of the details in my account are drawn.

13. See John Wilson Townsend, *The Life of James Francis Leonard, The First Practical Sound-Reader of the Morse Alphabet*, vol. 24 of the Filson Club Publications (Louisville, KY: John P. Morton, 1909), p. 18. Townsend goes on to invoke the Moses comparison: "What a wonderful time, labor, and money saver the sound system has proved to be,

and how grateful the world should be that the keen ear and rapid penmanship of James F. Leonard enabled him to become the Moses of the situation!" (20).

14. Quoted in Prescott, *History, Theory, and Practice of the Electric Telegraph*, pp. 232–33.

15. Taliaferro P. Shaffner, *The Telegraph Manual: A Complete History and Description of the Semaphoric, Electric and Magnetic Telegraphs of Europe, Asia, Africa, and America, Ancient and Modern* (New York: Pudney and Russell, 1859), pp. 456–57.

16. Thomas Hardy, *A Laodicean; or, The Castle of the De Stancys. A Story of To-Day*, ed. Jane Gatewood (1881; Oxford: Oxford University Press, 1991), p. 42. Subsequent references to this novel will be included in the text as AL.

17. J. M. Barrie, "Thomas Hardy: The Historian of Wessex," *Contemporary Review* (1889); reprinted in *Thomas Hardy: The Critical Heritage*, ed. R. G. Cox (New York: Barnes & Noble, 1970), p. 165.

18. [Unsigned review], *Saturday Review* 54 (18. November 1882), pp. 674–75; reprinted in *Thomas Hardy: The Critical Heritage*, p. 97.

19. Jean Baudrillard, "The Ecstasy of Communication" in *The Anti-Aesthetic: Essays on Postmodern Culture*, ed. Hal Foster (Port Townsend, Wash.: Bay Press, 1983), pp. 128, 131, 129.

20. Mark Dery, "Flame Wars" in *Flame Wars: The Discourse of Cyberculture*, ed. Mark Dery (Durham, NC: Duke University Press, 1994), p. 1.

21. See Shaffner, *The Telegraph Manual*, p. 464; Prescott, *History, Theory, and Practice of the Electric Telegraph*, p. 341.

22. John Hollingshead, "House-Top Telegraphs" in *All the Year Round* (26. November 1859), p. 106.

23. Guy Debord, *The Society of the Spectacle*, trans. Donald Nicholson-Smith (New York: Zone Books, 1994), p. 17.

24. Ibid.

25. The most sophisticated analysis of the role of women in the telegraph industry, particularly in the United States, is Katherine Stubbs, "Operating Fantasies: Gender, Class and the Technology of the Telegraph" in *Plastic Bodies: Working-Class Women in American Literature and Culture, 1860–1940*, unpublished manuscript.

26. See Kittler, *Discourse Networks 1800/1900*, pp. 347–68; Jennifer Wicke, "Henry James's Second Wave" in *Henry James Review* 10 (1989), p. 147.

27. Anthony Trollope, "The Telegraph Girl" in *Why Frau Frohmann Raised Her Prices and Other Stories* (1877; New York: Arno Press, 1981), p. 265.

28. Crary, *Techniques of the Observer*, p. 116.

29. Ibid., p. 125.

30. Ibid., p. 9.

31. Charles Wheatstone, "On the Transmission of Musical Sounds through Solid Linear Conductors, and on their subsequent Reciprocation" in *The Scientific Papers of Sir Charles Wheatstone* (London: The Physical Society of London, 1879), p. 50.

32. Ibid., p. 59.

33. Henry James, "In the Cage" in *In the Cage and Other Tales*, ed. Morton Dauwen Zabel (New York: Norton, 1969), p. 178. Subsequent references to this work will be included in the text as ITC; all italics in quotations are James's own.

34. "Henry James's Second Wave," p. 148. Stubbs also notes the telegraph operator's position as a "mediating agent" in the communications network and comments on her attempts "to change her status from industrial toiler to brain worker, to move from the working-class subjection of manual labor to the bourgeois respectability of the information specialist" ("Operating Fantasies," pp. 8, 36).

35. See Donna Haraway, "A Cyborg Manifesto: Science, Technology and Socialist-Feminism in the Late Twentieth Century" in *Simians, Cyborgs, and Women: The Reinvention of Nature* (New York: Routledge, 1991), pp. 149–81. For a discussion of some of the hidden affiliations between Haraway's cyborg and aspects of nineteenth-century culture, see Jay Clayton, "Concealed Circuits: Frankenstein's Monster, the Medusa, and the Cyborg" in *Raritan* 15 (1996), pp. 53–69.

36. Eve Kosofsky Sedgwick, "The Beast in the Closet: James and the Writing of Homosexual Panic" in *Sex, Politics, and Science in the Nineteenth-Century Novel*, ed. Ruth Bernard Yeazell (Baltimore: Johns Hopkins University Press, 1986), p. 172.

37. Eric Savoy, "'In the Cage' and the Queer Effects of Gay History" in *Novel* 28 (1995), p. 290; quoting Colin Simpson, Lewis Chester, and David Leitch, *The Cleveland Street Affair* (Boston: Little, Brown, 1976), p. 18.

38. In addition to Wicke, Savoy, and Stubbs cited above, valuable recent treatments of James's story include Dale M. Bauer and Andrew Lakritz, "Language, Class, and Sexuality in Henry James's 'In the Cage'" in *New Orleans Review* 14:3.(1987), pp. 61–69; Naomi Schor, *Reading In Detail: Aesthetics And The Feminine* (New York: Methuen, 1987), pp. 123–24; Priscilla L. Walton, *The Disruption of the Feminine in Henry James* (Toronto: University of Toronto Press, 1992), pp. 91–100; and John Carlos Rowe, "Spectral Mechanics: Technology, Gender, and Work in 'In the Cage'," Henry James Sesquicentennial Conference, New York University, June 1993.

39. Savoy, "The Queer Effects of Gay History," p. 287.

40. See, e.g., Wicke, "Henry James's Second Wave," p. 151.

41. Marvin, *When Old Technologies Were New*, p. 3.

42. I owe a large debt to Mark Schoenfield, who hand delivered to me a very old message, Hazlitt's "The Letter-Bell." Later he read an early version of this essay at a critical juncture in the writing process. I also want to thank Valerie Traub and Mark Wolleager for insightful comments.

PERFORMING TALKING CURES

ARTAUD'S

VOICE

To CONTEMPLATE a curative voice in the despairing silence of contemporary progressive politics in the United States is to recognize some immediate and crucial limits to what we might call a politics of voice. Having a name or the ability to name is not the same thing as "having" a voice or the ability to voice objection or assent. One of the lessons learned in the swift collapse of affirmative action legislation in the 1990s is the naiveté of the hope that the ability to name an identity, to consolidate a community around race or gender, is sufficient to give such groups a strong voice, a powerful political platform from which to defend such identities. While many would point out that the Left, in focusing so exclusively on naming and selling identity categories, lost sight of the more difficult tasks of creating political voice, such an accusation would overlook again the inherent political and philosophical problem of placing faith in voice at all. Part of this may be due to the inherent formlessness of voice itself, a formlessness that is at once the beckoning lure of voice as a crucial aspect of avant-garde art, and a formlessness that is the source of its amorphous malleability and political fickleness.

Voice has been at the center of a radical twentieth century performance theory and practice that stretches from Antonin Artaud to Diamanda Galas. Both artists give specific weight to a phenomenological ideal that views theatre as curative. Crucial to both Artaud and Galas is the performance of the scream, a projection of voice that at once shatters and sutures the distance between the performer and the auditor. While it would be worth exploring whether or not this avant-garde theory and practice, despite its limitations and faultlines, has anything of value to say about the political problem raised by the voicelessness of the Left, I will concentrate here on the difficulties and possibilities of Artaud's conception of voice and body. While Artaud's idea of a body without organs has had an important impact on contemporary theory, much of that discussion has elided the particular force of presence that animates the idea for Artaud.[1] This is largely because contemporary theory has tended to think that most claims about presence are naive, reactionary, or otherwise misguided. Of course some are. But Artaud's conception of the body without organs suggests a different way to think about both the present tense and theatre's faith in presence, in the tense present of our present plague.

Such a rethinking returns us to the most sustained attack on the metaphysics of presence—the extraordinary work of Jacques Derrida. Theatre turns up in Derrida's project often, but perhaps the most salient instances are in his essays on John Longshaw Austin and Artaud. I will begin with Austin because he will help us hear why presence matters for more than voice (what Derrida usually calls speech). While there has been much discussion of the distinctions and similarities between linguistic performatives and theatrical performances, thus far critical commentary has neglected the important interrelationship between Austin, Derrida, and Artaud that informs those distinctions and similarities.[2]

It is worth repeating that in *How to Do Things with Words* Austin condenses and disavows the epistemology of theatre in order to create an epistemology for the speech act, especially the performative speech act. Austin's consolidation and disavowal of theatre has in turn prompted the dramatic dueling encounter between Derrida and John Searle, and has led to the strange but telling misreadings of Judith Butler's use of drag as a response to the normative coercions of gender performances.[3] In other words, Austin's disavowal of the theatrical prompts his readers to make sure theatre returns to the discussion.

In Lecture 2, section 2 of *How to Do Things with Words*, Austin carefully delineates what he will exclude from his theory of the performative speech act: "a performative utterance will, for example, *be in a peculiar way hollow or void* if said by an actor on the stage, or if introduced in a poem, or spoken in soliloquy. This applies in a similar manner to any and every utterance—a sea-change in special circumstances. Language in such circumstances is in special ways—intelligibly—used not seriously, but in ways *parasitic* upon its normal use—ways that fall under the doctrine of *etoilations* of language. All of this we are *excluding* from consideration. Our performative utterances, felicitous or not, are to be understood as issued in ordinary circumstances."[4] In other words, Austin's theory of the performative leaves out performance as such.

Derrida's gloss on this paragraph of Austin's is itself a remarkable piece of theatre, enacting at the level of the sign the consequences of repressing theatre. In Derrida's "Signature, Event, Context," his emphatic citings of the words he wants to infect the ear of his reader, are exuberantly "parasitic" or metacitic. His citations are like nervous tics; they pass through the punctured skin of Austin's textual body and infuse his own. Derrida absorbs Austin's repression of theatre and acts out that prohibition by re-citing Austin's argument. He is like an actor reading a script from someone else's play, more particularly the script written by Artaud for a theatre of cruelty, a theatre dedicated to curing the collective body from the parasites hatched by language. Derrida asks, "Is it that in excluding the general theory of this parasitism, Austin, who nonetheless pretends to describe the facts and events of ordinary language, makes us accept as ordinary a teleological and ethical determination?" Derrida's chief complaint against Austin's theory is that it is inadequate to an understanding of citation, of "a general iterability without which there would not even be a successful performative." [5] In other words, what gives language its locutionary force is its iterability, its general citationality. The "success" of a performative speech act for Derrida is derived from the fact that it repeats an iterable statement, that it is a citation. Austin's desire to isolate performative speech acts from the world of theatrical performance is repelled by Derrida's infiltrating performance as a reader. Derrida becomes a parasitologist in order to trace the infection swimming in performances' sea change. Derrida learned to study parasites while reading Artaud (and looking at his paintings).[6]

Derrida argues that the iterability of the sign makes it impossible for language ever to be fully present to itself. Since a sign can only begin by repeating itself, its meaning is independent of both its addressee and its "user." But theatre and performance both require an addressee that is fully present to itself (hence Herbert Blau's point that a "universal of performance" is the acknowledgment that one is present to it—as maker or observer or both).[9] The quest for presence at the heart of western theatre's aesthetic ideal at least since Stanislavski makes it oddly resistant to the force of deconstruction which takes on faith the full force of presence's impossibility.

It could be said, perhaps overly simply but nonetheless truly, that whereas deconstruction insists on "the implacable necessity" of difference and *différance*, twentieth century western theatre continually dreams of presence without difference. This dream is at the foundation of theatre's conservative allure (its "entertainment" value) and its radical, even perverse genius. From Meyerhold's biomechanics to Eugenio Barba's "theatre anthropology," western theatre of this century has pursued with a literally maddening passion a universal body-speech.[10] Part of the problem of evaluating this pursuit is that such an evaluation must be carried out through writing, video, and film; the dissemination of what theatre and performance learn is undone by the "implacable necessity" of conveying that learning in other representational forms, in forms that invariably make theatre "other."

Silent film had begun to forge a somatic system of gesture, affect, and expressive meaning that would make films "universal." Assuming that a technical apparatus that could come ever closer to "real" life was to be preferred to an apparatus that could not reproduce sound, silent film abandoned its aspiration to create a universal body-speech; psychoanalysis and theatre took it up. Psychoanalysis developed theories of the symptom that led to notions of somatic conversions, while theatre became obsessed with the technical training of voice, gesture, and expression.[11] This training, as Artaud was quick to point out, has a lot in common with toilet training. What leaves the body, Lacan's *objet petit à*, is almost always subject to the fetishistic logic of conversion.

III.

Artaud, a gifted silent film actor, was not a happy man when film began to speak. Dedicated to unifying the body and voice, Artaud could not abide the mechanical, clumsy suturing of voice to actor that early sound films employed.[12] Decrying dubbing, the mechanical and false joining of different voices to screen bodies, Artaud invested his ideal theatre with a voice that could not be divided from flesh. For Artaud, such unity was not metaphorical. The technology of cinematic sound represented for Artaud the terror he felt in relation to the body's vulnerability to contagion, to parasites, to organisms that did not belong in the body. Cinematic sound contributed to the breakdown of the body's unity and Artaud fiercely resisted it.

In his two essays on Artaud written in the sixties, "La parole soufflée" and "The Theatre of Cruelty and the Closure of Representation," essays that in every way haunt his reading of Austin, Derrida tries to follow the spirit of Artaud's thinking as far as he can.[13] He recognizes that Artaud's thought cannot be sustained within the limits of logocentrism; it would indeed bring about the closure of representation, the end of philosophy. The iterability of the sign, so central to Derrida's project that it becomes, by default, celebrated, was for Artaud the source of incredible anguish. Artaud would emphatically reject Derrida's project. "Let us leave textual criticism to graduate students," Artaud writes in *The Theatre and Its Double*, "and recognize that what has been said is not still to be said; that an expression does not have the same value twice, does not live two lives; that all words, once spoken, are dead and function only at the moment they are uttered, that a form, once it has served, cannot be used again and asks only to be replaced by another, and that the theatre is the only place in the world where a gesture, once made, can never be made the same way twice."[14] The iterability of the (speech) act that Derrida argues is the performative force of the signifier is plucked out of Artaud's cruel theatre, like Gloucester's eye. For Artaud, the iterability of the (speech) act divides and infects the body, making it vulnerable to parasites and in desperate need of a cure.

An expanded political conception of voice needs Artaud's theatre to liberate it from its incarceration in the mouth. For what we must come to hear is that by severing the body and assigning body parts exclusive functions, we lose the soundscape of the entire body and render sounds that issue from sources other than the mouth unworthy of audition. Similarly, by listening exclusively for articulations from incredibly narrow sources in the collective social body, we create partial social subjects and render others voiceless. Just as we divide body parts and subject them to hierarchies that in turn become vulnerable to parasites and prohibit a curative cultural becoming, so too do we parcel and degrade the full amplification of bodily sound by insisting voice comes exclusively from the mouth and enters only "the *ear* of the other." The particular force of this theatrical insight for progressive politics is that it recalls us to the demands of active audition. Artaud himself did not trust voices that could only enter ears; he wanted to amplify sounds capable of shattering bones.

Insofar as writing aligns itself with the conveyance of "things" (what Derrida calls language's "communicative function") it works to destroy the contagion of the "truth" that Artaud's theatre wanted to expose. "I don't give a damn if my sentences sound French or Papuan, but if I drive in a violent word, I want it to suppurate in the sentence like a hundred-holed eccymosis."[15] This is a more radically embodied idea of a performative speech act than Austin's, and a more violently literal notion of deconstructing the signifier than Derrida's. The terrific challenge of writing about Artaud is to take on faith, as he did, the value of thinking that resisted thought's imperative to take a form, to exist *as* form.

Artaud argued that poetry should be read once and burned; yet he sought to have his poetry published. He wanted to wean theatre from literary drama, and yet he staged canonical plays himself. In speaking of Artaud's project it is necessary to emphasize how thoroughly self-divided it was, if only to take note of what drove his passion for a curative art. Artaud wanted to find a curative magic for the parasites eating body parts, parasites that enter the body at the moment logo-centrism insists that bodies take parts. He imagined a curative theatre in which sound was continuous with body, in which the distinction between word and flesh, between sound and sight, would be dissolved. He wanted to create a theatre in which bodily senses, fully released from partiality, would be released into a present, a presence that was formless—in the beyond of speech, voice, or thought itself. In order to reach such a radical formlessness, theatre had to create and endure the violent limit of a perpetually incomplete act of becoming, in an endless present tense. Artaud's theatre of cruelty imagined a drama of completely saturating presence in a present that had already consumed all end points, including the one promised by death. The "cure" that Artaud's theatre promises is one that insists that transformation is the most potent purpose of the speech act and the theatrical event. The transformation of the present at the heart of Artaud's aspiration (for his theatre and for himself) required a body without organs, a body thoroughly theatrical, a body that had cast off its recognizable form and moved instead in a circular present where sound was continuously projected and consumed, and breath itself was not a matter of in and out, but rather a matter of simple air, always there.

Artaud's conception of theatre is fundamentally, shockingly, curative: "There is plague / cholera / smallpox / only because dance / and consequently theatre / have not yet begun to exist" (quoted in Derrida, *Writing and Difference*, 184). The plague, like the theatre, insists that bodies are continuous and connected. The abscess carried by the theatre and the plague can carry either a killing parasite or a collective cure. Theatre is above all a physical collective act; lumbering toward existence, theatre stands as the beckoning lure of a new cultural body. Artaud imagines theatre as a promise, and as a promise his theatre carries the locutionary force of a performative speech act. Theatre cannot be comprised of deeds done; it cannot risk the deadening iterative force of the past tense. For Artaud, theatre is the tension of presence or it is nothing.

Artaud's theatre insists on the truths of bodily senses as well as the truths of reason and the truths of reason's parasites; what theatre "knows" comes from the delirium and contagion of a precisely imagined unreality. "[T]he images of poetry in the theatre are a spiritual force that begins its trajectory in the senses and does without reality altogether" (*Theatre and Its Double*, 25); "[T]he theatre, like the plague, is a delirium and is communicative" (*Theatre and Its Double*, 27). The phantasms released by theatre, according to Artaud, can be collectively curative because they are constructions of will, of the desire that constitutes the event of collective spectatorship. Life itself can be reproduced by a belief in the contagious phantasm of what is not (yet) here: "We must believe in a sense of life renewed by the theatre, a sense of life in which man fearlessly makes himself master of what does not yet exist, and brings it into being. And everything that has been born can still be brought to life if we are not satisfied to remain mere recording organisms" (*Theatre and Its Double*, 13).

Artaud viewed theatre as a stage upon which a public talking cure could be enacted. Borrowing the thesis of Breuer's and Freud's early theory of the talking cure, a theory borne out by a clinical practice in which somatic speech, the symptom, could be "removed" after it was "acted out" for the listening spectator/doctor, Artaud based his idea of the theatrical talking cure on a similar acting out and mimicry. "I propose to bring back into theatre this elementary magical idea, taken up by modern psychoanalysts, which consists in effecting the patient's cure by making him assume the apparent and exterior attitudes of the desired condition" (*Theatre and Its Double*, 80). Whereas Freud's deepest aspiration was to cure the collective soul by treating individual patients, Artaud's plan was to cure the collective soul through public theatre. Precisely because theatre is public and collective, and psychoanalysis private and individual, Artaud thought theatre had a greater curative potential. In a 1933 letter to Natalie Clifford Barney, Artaud wrote, "[The theatre] must abandon individual psychology, enter into mass passions, into the conditions of the collective spirit, grasp the collective wavelengths, in short, change the subject" (quoted in Weiss, 279). Concluding "The Theatre and The Plague," Artaud writes, "It appears that by means of the plague, a gigantic abscess, as much moral as social, has been collectively drained; and that like the plague, the theatre has been created to drain abscesses collectively.[. . .] The theatre like the plague is a crisis which is resolved by death or cure" (*Theatre and Its Double*, 31).

Artaud's search for a collective cure can be seen as (in part) a response (however indirect) to the cruelty of his horrendous political moment. The politics of division upon which the Nazis based their ascension was the logical termination point of a system of thought dedicated to division and separation. Such thinking reproduced a resistant response that was itself also self-divided and separatist. Perhaps a few could summon a voice to defend the Jews, and perhaps a few more could find a voice to defend the queers. But it seemed impossible to find a voice capable of defending everyone. Artaud allows us to see that this failure is in keeping with the way in which voice itself is separated from the body (by technology, but also more fundamentally by logocentrism's divisive logic). For example, voice could be turned into an aesthetic ideal if it was harnessed to music and if it originated from the mouth, but who would defend and develop the voice of the anus? Unable even to insist on the value of the body's own connected soundscape, how could one argue for humanity's? "Cutting out the vermin,"

one of the violently iterative phrases of the Nazi regime, was itself supported by a rhetoric of the human body that insisted on higher and
lower organs. Artaud's literalism, his dogged insistence that thought and
body could not be divided, allows us to see the structure of logic that
connects divisions in the physical body with divisions in the social body
and vice versa. Artaud wanted his theatre to espouse a "magical" rather
than rational language because logocentrism itself must collapse, he
argued, if we are to be cured.

In a fascinating and much-quoted epistolary exchange with Jacques
Rivière, the editor of *La Nouvelle Revue Française*, who had rejected
Artaud's first poems submitted for publication in 1923, Artaud attempted
to defend his poems, which Rivière had found less than coherent, formally or intellectually: "The dispersiveness of my poems, their formal
defects, the constant sagging of my thinking are to be attributed to
[. . .] a central collapse of the mind, to a kind of erosion, both essential and fleeting, of my thinking . . . There is thus something that is
destroying my thinking, a something which does not prevent me from
being what I might be, but which leaves me, if I may say so, in abeyance"
(quoted in Derrida, *Writing and Difference*, 177). The strange seeping
away from thinking, an action both essential and fleeting, encourages
a becoming that encompasses the abeyance and loss that is vital to voice
itself. Artaud refused the consolations of form, in part because he sus-
pected that form always falls short of what it wants most to secure.
Artaud felt the terror of form and formlessness with a theatrical, heightened, always-present intensity. When he attempt to find a new form,
a new conception for the body, he felt the violence of his failure. To
borrow and distort the words of Judith Butler, Artaud knew that "there
is no reference to a pure body which is not at the same time a further
[de]formation of that body" (*Bodies*, 10). Artaud's "pure body" was
always already a theatrical body, a body that played in what Lacan
believed was tragic theatre's true home, the "space between two deaths."[16]

Artaud's intelligence comprised the theatre that held him—in the
sense of both propping him up and of arresting him—making it impossible for him to abandon it. In this sense, his intelligence was
theatrical—all of his work, the paintings, the self-portraits, the poetry,
the manifestos, the radio program, the public lectures, the letters, are
best understood as attempts to create that theatre. Artaud needed the-

atre so he might become himself. Theatre becomes itself through its disappearance and Artaud's many contradictions and self-dramatizations are exemplary literalizations of Artaud's own aspiration to be theatrical, to live up to the ideal of theatre through self-dramatizations. In such a script it is hard to keep hold of "the line" between reality and illusion, between authenticity and performance, between madness and reason. Drawing the line is an instance of partiality; it creates a separation where one does not exist.

Artaud argued for a body without organs because the body itself had not come into being, and already it was being divided, taken apart, given specialties. "Reality has not yet been constructed because the true organs of the human body have not yet been assembled and put in place. / The theatre of cruelty has been created to complete this putting into place and to undertake, through a new dance of the body of man, the disruption of this world of microbes which is but coagulated nothingness. / The theatre of cruelty wants to make eyelids dance cheek to cheek with elbows, patellas, femurs and toes, and have this dance be seen" (quoted in Derrida, *Writing and Difference*, 187). The theatre of cruelty rivals God: it seeks to create a new body, but unlike God, it longs to be seen.

Artaud's cruel theatre would make manifest the performative promise of embodied redemption, but with a perverse twist : "The body is the body, / it is alone / and has no need of organs, / the body is never an organism, / organisms are the enemies of bodies, / everything one does transpires by itself without the aid of any organ, / every organ is a parasite, / it overlaps with a parasitic function / destined to bring into existence a being which should not be there" (quoted in Derrida, *Writing and Difference*, 186). Whereas the locutionary coherence of language reveals itself as iteration, citation, copy—thereby making language users to some degree dead letters—the force of Artaud's theatre requires a body that will be manifest once only. The body that "should" be reproduced in Artaud's theatre is a body of pure surface, a body with no secrets or secretions. A body without organs eliminates the surface/depth binary so integral to logocentrism (upon which the distinction between absence and presence is based); more radically, it eliminates the distinction between living and dying, because in eliminating parasites, Artaud also eliminates death.[17] Or more accurately, the drama Artaud most wanted to stage was the battle that takes place on the other side of death, an encounter that could only take place in a phantasmal space (which is to say a theatrical space) that is simultaneously real and not-real. (Artaud suffered enough mental anguish to know that an imagined event has no less force than an empirical one.) It is here that Artaud's most brilliant insights can be seen. For if in his theatre, "all words, once spoken, are dead," so too is the body that speaks them.

For Artaud, having conceived the phantasm of the theatre of cruelty (as) himself, theatre could contribute to a reconception of the temporality of death. If theatre's force was a promise, perhaps its most compelling promise was that death was an act, one among many, and like other acts, could be survived. "[M]ost certainly I am long dead, I am already suicided. That is to say, I have already been suicided. But what would you think of an anterior suicide, of a suicide that would make us retrace our steps, but from the other side of existence, and not from the side of death?" (quoted in Weiss, 295). Like Christ after the Resurrection, Artaud has survived his own death. The question that arises in both cases is: what kind of body is it that lives after death? For Christian theologians, Christ's resurrected body was incorruptible because all of his blood was used in salvation and the body that returned to verify the Resurrection was a body without blood.[18] Artaud's solution is similar: the body that lives after death is a body without organs.[19] Thus, for this body, death is something that has happened in the past tense: its business in and for theatre is to regain the endlessness of the present tense that the ideology of death-in-the-future forecloses. "[S]uicide will be for me only a means of violently regaining myself, of brutally bursting into my own being, of forestalling the uncertain advances of God[. . .] I can neither live nor die, neither not wish to die nor to live. And all men are like me" (quoted in Weiss, 285–86). Suspended in an impossible temporality and bound by contradictory desire, Artaud demanded a cure from the uncertain advances and disappointments of God, a typically inattentive spectator of Artaud's theatre. Eventually Artaud recorded his demand in a radio program, aptly named, "To Have Done with the Judgment of God."[20]

The ferocity of Artaud's insistence on the ideal of a body without organs, a concept that is "mad" in the sense that such a body cannot live, has distracted critics and theatre historians from Artaud's startling point—a point that Artaud himself could only approach at an angle, most frequently through the metaphor of plague. Let us, for a moment anyway, take Artaud at his word; let's not try to turn him into a coherent aesthetician. Artaud wants to make a body without organs the animate center of a living theatre; yet such a body cannot live. The death of the body is the drama of the theatre of cruelty, and for Artaud, the only drama worth making occurs on the other side of that death, in the "afterwards" that sustains the interpretive force of psychoanalytic trauma and amplifies the body's most profound expressivity.

In the echo of theatrical voice, the aftersound that stays in the air after the "life" of sound has ended, one can hear a different body—one that remains after death has come and gone. Such a sound vibrates between death and cure—between the cure by death and a cure for death. It is the still present tension of that oscillation that makes Artaud's theatre taut enough to echo across our bodies, caught now in the theatre of cruelty of our present plague. This theatre requires both a different conception of presentness and a different conception of presence, than "the metaphysics of presence" critiqued by Derrida. This is the present that Blanchot understood: "It is the abyss of the present, the time without present with which I have no relation, toward which I am unable to project myself. For in it, I do not die. I forfeit the power of dying. In this abyss they die—they never cease to die, and they never succeed in dying" (quoted in Deleuze, 152).

The centrality of incoherence in Artaud's thought, a formlessness that he valued as highly as any of the other features of his thinking, helps us understand one of the most powerful features of voice. Sophisticated concepts of voice note that sound becomes incorporeal at the moment it exits the body. But such notions implicitly participate in severing the body into parts and blessing the mouth as the source of bodily utterance. Artaud encourages us to hear a more dramatic body-voice, to listen to the sounds that emanate from the entire body, a flesh-speech that hears the voice that emanates from the mouth as just one source for somatic utterance. Artaud's ideal body hurls sound out of the body so as to consume it, to take it in, to hear it in an audition that occurs across the whole body. If there is not one source for voice, neither is there one end, one death, for the body.

Artaud's ideal body comes to its becoming through its encounter with an audience. The strange dispersiveness of the word across the body (as against "in the ear") of the other is the drama of sound's life to which Artaud dedicated himself. Artaud helps us remember that we cannot concentrate on developing a politics of voice independent from developing a politics of audition. Listening with the full body is radically demanding, even cruel. For it necessitates temporarily abandoning one's body in order to let it be the stage for the other's body. There is something of this in the psychoanalytic idea that the free associations of the analysand must be met by the analyst's freely associative listening. Such a listening requires at once a completely evacuated self *and* a completely inhabited self; evacuated in the sense that the auditor listens only to the sounds of the other, and in that hearing the listener is most fully recalled to him or herself.

Such sounds are loudest perhaps when the body is in pain or enraptured. Artaud tried to convey the interior and exterior sounds of a dream recorded by Saint Remys, the viceroy of Sardinia, in 1720. Artaud rehearses the Viceroy's dream that he is infected by the plague that he sees ravaging the whole of his state. A language of a dream recited two centuries after it happened, Artaud knew, would provoke a phantasm of its own. From the gathering force of his hallucinatory incantation, Artaud seeks to express the agony of a body besieged by plague. Its gruesomeness rivals the famous opening paragraphs of Foucault's *Discipline and Punish*, in which torture is rendered in the language of an eighteenth-century eye witness.[21] Artaud's description of physical torture is even more horrifying, because its specificity is the product of a fevered *affective and affected* imagination, rather than the product of a chillingly precise factual document. "Then he is seized by a terrible fatigue, the fatigue of a centralized magnetic seduction, of his molecules divided and drawn toward their annihilation. His crazed body fluids, unsettled and commingled, seem to be flooding through his flesh. His gorge rises, the inside of his stomach seems as if it were trying to gush out between his teeth. . . . his eyes, first inflamed, then glazed; his swelling gasping tongue, first white, then red, then black, as if charred and split—everything proclaims an unprecedented organic upheaval. Soon the body fluids, furrowed like the earth struck by lightning, like lava kneaded by subterranean forces, search for an outlet . . ." (*Theatre and Its Double*, 19). Such descriptions are made even more delirious and therefore more communicable when performed by an actor with the physical skills of Artaud. Anaïs Nin describes the scene when Artaud read this text at the Sorbonne in 1933:

"His face was contorted with anguish, one could see perspiration dampening his hair. His eyes dilated, his muscles became cramped, his fingers struggled to retain their flexibility. He made one feel the parched and burning throat, the pains, the fever, the fire in the guts. He was in agony. He was screaming. He was delirious. He was enacting his own death, his own crucifixion."[22] Nin's description of Artaud's performance mimics his description of "the typical plague victim." His flesh-speech, utterance that involves much more than the mouth, passes into the body of her writing like a parasite.[23]

What was Artaud after with this noisy performance? This screeching symphony of body fluids plummeting through his prose? I think he wanted to find a way to hear himself and he could not do so until his speech left and returned to him. The scream is that utterance which attempts to sound, at once, internally and externally, across the body with force sufficient enough to still the division of time. In Artaud's phantasmatic theatre, the one he projected so as not to be the sole auditor of his own screams, he would teach us how to hear the "shrieks of splitting stones, noises of branches, noises of the cutting and rolling of wood, [which] compose a sort of animated material murmur in the air, in space, a visual as well as an audible whispering. And after an instant the magic identification is made: WE KNOW IT IS WE WHO WERE SPEAKING" (*Theatre and Its Double*, 67, emphasis in original). As Artaud slides across the tenses of his sentences, his internal scream fills the theatre between us, and as we listen to its echo, distorted and vulnerable to time's static, we might sense an identification that is at once beyond history and beyond speech. We know it was him; the him in us that snares something more than our ears; the him that is here with us, hearing this, the hymn of historical, hallucinatory, hysterical citation, a citation that I hope acts with something other than the parasitic tic that Derrida declared the signifier's main event.

What Artaud's theatre of cruelty is striving for is the reproduction of a new body, a body that cannot encompass the possessive form upon which our imaginations of bodies so often flounder—politically, erotically, socially, and philosophically. "A true man," Artaud argued, "has no sex," by which he meant to emphasize the limitations of the possessive "has" for encompassing such a radical formlessness as sex. Extrapolating from Artaud's formula, I would like to suggest that "a true person has no voice," for in the very gesture of "having" it, voice is strangled. What I am calling here flesh-speech, an ecstatic murmuring of body fluids that is simultaneously projected and devoured, is the philosophical ideal of a political voice precisely because it cannot be severed, had, ignored, or stolen by its auditor. Such a voice also has a philosophical appeal precisely because it does not submit to the divide between life and death.

Just as cinema has taught us about the optics and psychic resonance of the afterimage, so can radio and audiotape teach us about the aural echo and psychic amplification of the aftersound. Gregory Whitehead has written provocatively about the voices of the dead that provide the electrical zing of radio air waves.[24] Whitehead likens this dead air to the aftersound of the body that literally shakes a newborn corpse, a death rattle in the literal meaning of that term. Artaud was subject to extensive electrical shock (he had over fifty-one treatments) and wrote, "Electricity is a body, a weight, the pestling of a face"[25] In his portraits and self-portraits, in his screams and in his radio text, "To Have Done with the Judgment of God," Artaud attempted to amplify the sound of that chipping, whirring erosion.

"For man is not only *dispersed* in his body, he is also dispersed on the outside of things, like a corpse who forgot his own body and because his body forgot itself; and the man who does not live through all of himself at each instant commits the error of believing himself to be this self, mind, idea, conception, notion, which floats upon a point of the body, instead of being at every instant his entire body" (quoted in Weiss, 292). Similarly, a voice must not be content to carry words, it must rather strain to hear and thereby convey the soundscape in which the entire body lives and dies, at every instant; and this is true for both the physical and social body.[26] The physical body doubles the social body: when we specify and feel the agony of an organ, it has infected the collective body, the "us" which Artaud believed theatre could cure.

Artaud understood that theatre, precisely because it exists and comes into being for the spectator, creates a body that is fundamentally social. The body created by theatre is a body that can never be possessed or owned. More radically, such a body cannot carry the interiority presupposed by organs. The theatrical body is created only in and for the present tense, and only in relation to the spectator. It comes into being for the other who observes it, for the other who calls it into its becoming. The spectator, by being present to this body in the unfolding of its appearance, and as it sounds itself out of the abyss of the simultaneously real and phantasmatic space that is theatre's only home, both conjures and cures the theatrical body by honoring it as manifestation, as presence whose depth is social, rather than private and individual. Such an honoring also rehearses and inspires the spectator to contemplate the sociality, rather than the interiority, of his or her own body.

Theatre, for Artaud, is that place where voices and sounds become attached to bodies. Whereas the talkie launched a technology in which voice became separate from the body, theatre for Artaud is the technology that gives body to voices that would otherwise remain unheard. For a man haunted by voices as Artaud was, theatre was curative because it allowed those voices to be heard—sounds that could be recognized only after they left his body. In insisting so emphatically on both a theatre of voice and the theatricality of voice, Artaud made manifest the collectivity of our aural world. Awash in sounds that lie beneath and beyond the articulations of our various languages, we dangle from a lattice of noise that exists both prior to and after our ability to hear it. While Derrida wants to recall us to the force of the signifier's iterability, Artaud wants theatre to amplify the soundscape that is the precondition of signification itself.

Too often scholars say that Artaud failed to realize his theatre of cruelty; they insist that his achievement was theoretical and not "actual." But this division is exactly what Artaud threw his body against. He lived the theatre of cruelty, and somehow, through the flames of electric shock, voices, and an infected, cancer-ridden body, Artaud wrote and drew that theatre's psychic and linguistic *mise en scène*. Artaud's life was dedicated to making that theatrical body live. Caustic, bold, poetic, mad, passionate, Artaud imagined a theatrical body of spectacular utterance, one capable of staging the formlessness of the despair and anguish that fuels our desire to be cured.

NOTES

1. See Gilles Deleuze, *The Logic of Sense*, trans. Mark Lester with Charles Strivale, ed. Constantin V. Boundas (New York: Columbia University Press, 1990) and Gilles Deleuze and Felix Guattari, *Anti-Oedipus: Capitalism and Schizophrenia*, trans. Robert Hurley, Mark Seem, and Helen R. Lane (Minneapolis: University of Minnesota Press,

1983) for some of the most interesting commentary on the ramifications of the body without organs. Herbert Blau's "Universals of Performance; or, Amoritizing play" in *By Means of Performance: Intercultural Studies of Theatre and Ritual*, eds. Richard Schechner and Willa Appel, (Cambridge: University of Cambridge Press, 1990), pp. 250–272 has an excellent discussion of Artaud's belief in presence that is informed by contemporary theory's critique of the metaphysics of presence.

2. See Eve Sedgwick and Andrew Parker, eds., *Performance and Performativity* (New York: Routledge, 1995) for a comprehensive discussion of the distinction between performatives and performance; see also Peggy Phelan, "Reciting the Citation of Others, or, A Second Introduction" in *Acting Out: Feminist Performances*, eds. Lynda Hart and Peggy Phelan (Ann Arbor: University of Michigan Press, 1993) for a discussion weighted more to theatrical events than to linguistic ones.

3. Much of the next section of this argument is indebted to conversations I've had with Jon McKenzie. His excellent *Performance Studies and the Lecture Machine* (dissertation, Tisch School of the Arts, New York University, 1995) covers much of the same material at far greater length and with more nuance.

4. J.L. Austin, *How To Do Things With Words*, 2nd ed., eds. J. O. Urmson and Marina Sbisa (Cambridge: Harvard University Press), p. 22, emphasis in the original.

5. Jacques Derrida, "Signature, Event, Context" in *A Derrida Reader*, trans. and ed. Peggy Kamuf (New York: Columbia University Press, 1991), p. 103.

6. Artaud's extraordinary paintings and drawings include many self-portraits. See Antonin Artaud, *Dessins et Portraits*, eds. Paule Thevenin and Jacques Derrida (Paris: Gallimard, 1986), in which Derrida's essay "Forcener le Subjectile" appears.

7. See McKenzie as well as Judith Butler, *Gender Trouble: Feminism and the Subversion of Identity* (New York: Routledge, 1990).

8. Judith Butler, *Bodies That Matter* (New York: Routledge, 1993).

9. Many people would object to Blau's argument and in certain ways I myself take some issue with it. But I employ it here because it helps us see a bit more clearly why the erosion between performance and performatives at the heart of much contemporary critical theory is a problem. "Queer acts," for example, are both more than and less than theatrical events and/or speech acts.

10. There is still much work to be done on early cinema and classical psychoanalysis. Many of the theoreticians and practitioners associated with the magazine *Close Up*, for example, believed that silent film could make Freud's emerging theory of a universal psychic subject manifest in the universal language that silent film was developing.

    For an excellent discussion of theatre's pursuit of this somatic language and a lucid discussion of the philosophy, science, and pseudoscience that supported it, see Joseph R. Roach, *The Player's Passion: Studies in the Science of Acting* (Newark: University of Delaware Press, 1985).

11. I am painfully aware of the crude consolidation of history I am writing here; in many ways what I assert here is so brief it appears to be ridiculous. But I am doing so anyway, aware of accusations that this is pure fantasy, because I want to sketch,

however broadly, the intertwining of film, psychoanalysis, *and* theatre in the quest for a somatic language. The consolidation I undertake here is itself a symptomatic conversion of history. Forgive me, even though I do know what terrible deeds I do.

12. See Mikhail Yamplosky, "Voice Devoured; Artaud and Borges on Dubbing" in *October* 63 (1993), pp. 57–75 for an excellent discussion of why Artaud hated dubbing.

13. Jacques Derrida, "La parole soufflée" and "The Theater of Cruelty and the Closure of Representation" in *Writing and Difference*, trans. Alan Bass (Chicago: University of Chicago Press, 1978).

14. Antonin Artaud, *The Theatre and Its Double*, trans. Mary Caroline Richards (New York: Grove Press, 1958), p. 75.

15. Quoted in Allen Weiss, "Radio, Death, and the Devil: Artaud's *Pour En Finir Avec Le Jugement de Dieu*," in *Wireless Imagination: Sound, Radio, and the Avant-Garde*, eds. Gregory Whitehead and Douglas Kahn (Cambridge, MA: MIT Press, 1992), p. 289.

16. Jacques Lacan, "The Essence of Tragedy: A commentary on Sophocles' *Antigone*" in *The Seminars of Jacques Lacan, Book VII: The Ethics of Psychoanalysis*, ed. Jacques-Allain Miller, trans. Dennis Porter (New York: Norton, 1992) pp. 243–90

17. This is partially why Artaud often referred to himself as already suicided. This aspect of Artaud's thought and practice stands (mutely) behind Lacan's proposition that suicide is the only successful act and that theatre is a place of play between two deaths. See Lacan, pp. 243–90.

18. See Phelan, "Bodies at the Vanishing Point" in *Mourning Sex* (New York: Routledge, 1997) for a fuller discussion.

19. It is tempting to suggest that the death of Artaud's sister, whose intestines were crushed, and Artaud's own response to electroshock—internal hemorrhaging—were instrumental in shaping his belief in the redemptive powers of a body without organs. But I think this temptation should be resisted because it has the consequence of repathologizing Artaud's thought. What is astonishing about Artaud is the passionate lucidity of much of his writing and his painting (especially the portraits and self-portraits).

20. The best treatment of Artaud's radio work is in Weiss, pp. 269–308. An English transcript of Artaud's radio play, translated by Clayton Eshelmann, follows Weiss' article.

21. Michel Foucault, *Discipline and Punish: The Birth of the Prison*, trans. Alan Sheridan (New York: Vintage Books, Random House, 1979), pp. 3–6.

22. Anaïs Nin, *The Diary, 1931–34* (New York: The Swallow Press and Harcourt Brace & World, 1966), pp. 191–92.

23. The same mimicry informs the accounts of Artaud's final public appearance in 1947. See Ruby Cohn, *From Desire to Godot: Pocket Theatre of Postwar Paris* (Berkeley: University of California Press, 1987), pp. 51–63 and James Miller *The Passion of Michel Foucault* (New York: Simon and Schuster, 1993), pp. 94–96. Miller's book is pretty alarming, but it makes a few very important observations about Artaud's influence on Foucault, and Miller is the first to try to do more than observe the ways in which

Deleuze and Guattari have transformed Artaud's body without organs in their own work. Allen Weiss is writing a full account of Artaud, Deleuze, and Guattari. It is worth noting here that Deleuze's *The Logic of Sense*, especially in the discussion of surface and depth, also owes a lot to Artaud's theatrical body.

24. Gregory Whitehead and Douglas Kahn, eds., *Wireless Imagination: Sound, Radio, and the Avant-Garde* (Cambridge: MIT Press, 1992).

25. Artaud, "Interjections," in *Watchfiends and Rack Screams: Works from the Final Period by Antonin Artaud*, ed. and trans. Clayton E. Shleman and Bernard Bador (Boston: Exact Change, 1995), p. 258.

26. After he was submerged in a soundproof isolation chamber, John Cage, one of Artaud's true heirs, was stunned to hear the symphony of noise that permeated his body. His musical compositions consolidated in performance the inescapable noise from which voice, music, and speech emerge as recognizable sound.

10

GREGORY L. ULMER

PART ONE
XANADU: A REMAKE
I

KUBLA
HONKY TONK

VOICE

IN

CYBER-PIDGIN

The main justification for honky-tonk elements in architectural order is their very existence. They are what we have.

—Robert Venturi

MY AMBITION is to compose a remake of "Kubla Khan." The success of the remake in other registers of arts and letters (from James Joyce to Hollywood) makes it worth trying in the field of criticism and theory. Commentators explain that a film is remade when its themes resonate once again with the social or historical circumstances existing in our culture. The tradition of dialogue has its own rationale for reviving a work from the past. In this tradition composers do not simply repeat the previous work, but ask themselves the same question the original addressed in its own time. Drawing upon the various uses of the remake is more than a convenience if one is exploring the method of choragraphy (or chorography), as I have noted elsewhere,[1] since this method has no standard form of its own, but calls for the sampling of an existing practice immanent within the object of study. Meaning arises choragraphically through evocation, in any case, and lacks a direct conceptual equivalent.

No one needs to be reminded that "Kubla Khan" is subtitled, "Or, a Vision in a Dream: A Fragment." Nor that it is the product of a legendary scene of writing, an account of which often accompanies the poem in publication. Samuel Taylor Coleridge had retired to a lonely farmhouse in part to recover his health. Having taken a prescribed "anodyne" (some extract of opium, the historians say), the poet fell asleep while reading a book about the palace of Kubla Khan. While asleep Coleridge dreamed that he wrote a poem, which, upon awaking, he still remembered. He immediately began to transcribe the dream poem, but soon was distracted by a visitor who kept him away from his writing for over an hour. When the poet returned to his page, the memory was gone. That this story is most likely apocryphal has not prevented it from being revisited in any number of studies of the creative process.

I invoke this scene once again to pose to it a question about the scene of writing appropriate to the era of the computer, the Internet, interactive multimedia, hypertext, digital electronic storage, and retrieval of information. The potential relevance of Coleridge to the question of online creativity has been established by Ted Nelson, originator of the term "hypertext," who named his vision of globally connected information "Project Xanadu" after Coleridge's poem. This name acknowledged the romantic quality of the vision, long before it was technically possible, of the "hackers' dream"—total information instantly available to everyone everywhere.

Nelson also suggested that the greatest software designer was Orson Welles; or rather Welles would have been the greatest software designer if he had lived in the age of computers. This assertion makes sense in the context of Nelson's view that making a movie is a better interface metaphor for what it is like to write in hypermedia than are the book or desktop metaphors that still tend to dominate our conception of byteracy (computeracy, electracy). This association of Welles with software adds to my determination to remake "Kubla Khan," or at least its scene of writing, since the estate that Welles named "Xanadu" in *Citizen Kane* is located in Florida. My remake continues this series, from Coleridge to Welles to Nelson to me.

My hope is that a sampling of this series will offer some guidance for the problem confronting me: how to conduct the practice of humanities education online? Specifically, the remake may help me rethink the place of the exotic in our cultural codes. Is the Internet still colonialism by other means? How might we design the forms and practices of byteracy to take into account the postcolonial context of the new apparatus? At the least, I want this experiment to demonstrate a heuretic (as distinct from hermeneutic) way to work with the traditional objects of study in my discipline. At the most, I hope to discover a principle of design for Internet authoring.

2

> As if this earth in fast thick pants were breathing,
> A mighty fountain momently was forced:
> Amid whose swift half-intermitted burst
> Huge fragments vaulted like rebounding hail,
> Or chaffy grain beneath the thresher's flail.

Coleridge's reference to the thresher's flail evokes for me one of the key images of *chora* in Plato's *Timaeus*, which is to say that one purpose of my remake is to continue my inquiry into the nature of choragraphy. *Chora* is a theoretical invention. The Greeks recognized at least two kinds of space or place—*topos* and *chora*. To simplify the matter for now, *topos* names the abstract quality of place as a container, and *chora* names the sacred nature of specific places. The Greek sense of place included both dimensions together, but with the development of literacy the two notions became separated. Aristotle, in his codification of rhetoric, that is, dropped *chora*, which still had been important in Plato, and retained *topos* as his metaphor for the places of memory (*inventio*). The project of choragraphy, developed out of the Derrida-Eisenman collaboration on a design for Villette Park, is the application to electronic design of a rhetoric in which chora figures the places of invention.

In the *Timaeus*, Plato addressed one of the profound metaphysical questions of his day—the problem of how being and becoming were related—by proposing a third term, selected from the vernacular and elevated to philosophical status—*chora*—to name a space of mediation. He characterized this place with a variety of metaphors in order to suggest the effect of this mediation, which was to bring order out of chaos. Metaphors were essential because *chora* could not be treated directly; it was that which made appearance possible but itself did not appear. "As, when grain is shaken and winnowed by fans and other instruments used in the threshing of corn, the close and heavy particles are borne away and settle in one direction, and the loose and light particles in another. In this manner, the four kinds of elements were then shaken by the receiving vessel, which, moving like a winnowing machine, scattered far away from one another the elements most unlike, and forced the most similar elements into close contact."[2]

The association of *chora* with the four elements (earth, air, fire, and water) directs the choragrapher to the tradition of the music of the spheres. Another image for bringing the four elements into order is musical: the tuning of a lute. In his history of the term *Stimmung*, Leo Spitzer notes the importance of *Timaeus* in figuring the world soul as musical: the importance of music in classical education through the Middle Ages was based on the idea of morality as a tuning of the individual soul to this world harmony.[3] Heidegger returned to this tradition as part of his return to the Greeks, designating *Stimmung* as one of the existentials grounding one's being in the world. It names the ground of feeling that lets us know where we are "at," how we are doing, how things are with us. Translated as "atmosphere," "ambiance," "mood," the attunement of modern man is "dread," according to Heidegger. A modern mood of anxiety has replaced the Greek attunement of wonder.[4] A root term of *Stimmung* is *Stimme*, meaning "voice."

3

In *Heuretics* I began an exploration of the usefulness of attunement as a principle of writing. Everything I discovered there—summed up as the "square"—showed me the fourfold pattern of this attunement. My remake of "Kubla Khan" indicates, however, that I had not gone far enough. Coleridge's Xanadu, that is, has more to teach me about the nature of *chora* as place. The lesson begins with the question: where is Xanadu, exactly? The answer, available in both scholarly and popular versions,[5] is that Xanadu is a composite diegesis (just like most Hollywood movies)— "diegesis" referring to the imaginary space and time of the world created in the poem. "Xanadu" is a hybrid image made of elements drawn from four locations. These four locations, none of which Coleridge had visited but about which he had read, were four of the most exotic sites of otherness, of "elsewhere," of anyplace out of this world, available to a romantic imagination. This use of the exotic as the emblem of curiosity and imagination is one of the features that has to be revisited in my remake, directed as it is toward

Internet circumstances in which, in principle, the exotic is interactive.

An inventory of the sites alluded to in the poem should begin with the namesake of "Xanadu" itself, Shangdu, which "lay in what is now the Zhenglan Banner of the Autonomous Region of Inner Mongolia, in northeast China" (Alexander, xv). It was the capital city of Kubla Khan. The remake takes into account our current relations with China, as distinct from those of Coleridge's day, including the human rights violations exemplified by the diplomatic crisis associated with the imprisonment of Harry Wu. The name "Wu," moreover, puns on the acronym for the latest development in MUDs or multiuser domains— the convergence of MUDs with object-oriented programming (MOO) with World Wide Web hypertext display (WWW). The acronym for this merged MUD-WWW configuration is WOO.

The second exotic location alluded to in "Xanadu" is the holy caves of ice in Kashmir. The caves in question are near Pahalgam, "at approximately seven thousand feet at the northern end of the Lidder valley, between the junction of the Aru and the Sheshnag, two branches of the majestic Lidder River, which flow through defiles at the valley head" (105). A headline in *The New York Times* on August 21, 1995, helps me update these sacred caves for my remake: "Terror in Paradise Keeps Tourists from Kashmir." Kashmir, the Himalayan State that was once India's greatest tourist attraction after the Taj Mahal, now is on the index of the State Department. Muslim separatists took several European hostages. To show their seriousness, they executed a Norwegian tourist by the name of Hans Christian Ostro, on whose abdomen they carved the signature of their organization.

The third sacred location (*chora*) referenced in "Xanadu" is Mount Abora, the place about which the Abyssinian maid sang. Located in east central Africa, the holy site in question is Gishen Mariam in the Ambasel range, forty miles north of Dessie (166). Although much of the news about Ethiopia in the early 1990s dealt with the coups and skirmishes that led to the independence of Eritrea from Ethiopia, the region is still associated in our culture with images of famine.

And the fourth exotic, sacred locale of the poem, site of the mighty fountain itself and the underground river? It is Alachua County, Gainesville, Florida—my place of residence since 1972 and hometown of the University of Florida. The experience of realizing that I lived in one of the four most exotic places in the world, according to the romantic imagination, can only be described as "uncanny," to express the encounter of the familiar in the foreign in this discovery. As part of her project to visit the four sites composing the diegesis of "Xanadu," Caroline Alexander came to Gainesville, and she describes it in the same travel journalism prose used to describe how she negotiated access to the other far-flung outposts on the map. Fortunately she does not mention that more tourists have been murdered in Florida than in Kashmir, nor had *Money* magazine yet ranked Gainesville as the best city in which to live in the entire United States (1995), making it a fit counterpart in my remake for Kubla Khan's "stately pleasure-dome."

Coleridge's source was Bartram's *Travels*, one of the most popular books of the later eighteenth century which gave an account of the karst topography of northern Florida. Indeed, Bartram's description of the underground rivers, sinkholes, springs, poljes, and the other features of limestone geology shaped by a semitropical climate is one of the major sources of the language of the poem. In my remake the "Ancestral voices prophesying war" might note that the name "karst" applied to limestone topography originates in the region of Bosnia-Herzegovinia, whose landscape is the prototype for these features.

4

I live in Xanadu. I did not know I was moving to Xanadu when I came to Gainesville in 1972. The Chamber of Commerce makes no fuss about it. To learn that Xanadu is Gainesville (at least in part) has the status in chorography of the insight that the morning star and the evening star are one and the same—a touchstone of epistemology in certain branches of philosophy. I had known of the association of Bartram with Gainesville since the mid-1980s, when Mel New, a specialist in the eighteenth century in my department, included quotations from Bartram in the brochure we published to promote our graduate program. Ted Nelson's interest in *Kubla Khan* got me to read John Livingston Lowes, which completed the link at the level of information (Bartram as source for Coleridge), but the relevance of this fact had not yet registered as an insight.

In the fall of 1994 I began teaching courses in the new computer lab, established at Florida with the help of a million-dollar grant for equipment from IBM. Equipped with its own MOO and all the other tools of online computing (email, the internet), the lab gave me a chance to organize a course entirely around the hyper-rhetoric of choragraphy, whose method I had defined theoretically in *Heuretics*. The lab offered the students the possibility of composing a home page for the World Wide Web using HTML (hypertext markup language) for Internet publication. When I started thinking about this interface metaphor for screen design—the "home page"—I finally realized the relevance of Xanadu as a relay for teaching and research. Xanadu supplied a relay for home page design. Every home page is Xanadu. The home page, that is, as a support and guide for online learning, may be structured as a composite diegesis of four distinct places "sacred" to the individual user.

This context triggered a recollection of Walter Benjamin's four-part psychogeography, as described by Susan Buck-Morss. Benjamin's "home," we might say, was located at the null point of the intersection of two axes: to the west was Paris, origin of bourgeois society in the political sense; to the east was Moscow and the end of bourgeois society; to the south was Naples and the origins of Western civilization in Mediterranean culture; to the north was Berlin, Benjamin's childhood home.[6] Benjamin's *inventio* was grounded in a mood or atmosphere informed by this composite location: Paris-Moscow-Naples-Berlin—the cities that formatted his imagination. A salient feature of this foursome in my context was the fact that one of the four was Benjamin's "hometown."

5

Xanadu as a composite diegesis of sacred sites supplied a useful relay for mapping the poetics of "mystory" onto a rhetoric of the home page. This new context allowed me to continue the refinement of mystoriography begun in *Teletheory*, in which the genre is defined and then tested in an experiment entitled "Derrida at the Little Bighorn."[7] In *Heuretics* the mystory is generalized into choragraphy. Choragraphy, that is, makes explicit the structuration of mystory. The key is the notion of the "popcycle"—the four discourses of the ideological apparatuses most responsible for subject formation in modernity: the Family, Entertainment, School, and Discipline (specialized knowledge of one's work). Choragraphy showed that individuals could compose a figure of their cognitive style, could write the conditions capable of evoking their founding mood, by locating their material position within each one of the discourses. The popcycle is constituted by the codes and practices of each of the four principal institutions of interpellation (so to speak); the mystory is one individual's specific passage through these institutions.

The power of choragraphy to guide learning comes only with the experience of making a mystory. The effect of juxtaposing the details of one's position in each discourse of the popcycle may be characterized as "uncanny"—it is the pedagogical equivalent of the "encounter" explored by the surrealists and others, in the unexpected convergence of individual with collective phenomena, of the present with the past, of the sort Breton expresses in *Nadja*.[8] I finally understood in the context of the tradition of *Stimmung* (the principle of cosmological harmony) the relationship of the mystory to the four levels of medieval allegory. I recognized that mystory gives a heuretic turn to medieval allegory, which is to say that in mystory secularized individuals generate an allegory out of the chance interferences of their historical circumstances.

The literal level in the medieval schema is the Old Testament story of the nation of Israel. In the popcycle this level is occupied by the institution of schooling, K–12, with the required teaching of state history as the metonym for ideological functioning of school. Mystorians replace the literal level of Israel with a specific event in the histories of their home state or nation. The allegorical level in the medieval schema is provided by the life of Christ. In the popcycle the story of Christ in particular and religion as an institution in general are replaced with the institution of Entertainment: the mystorians select as the data for this level a media star or celebrity with which they identify. The moral level of the medieval schema is occupied by the individual believer. In the popcycle this level consists of the institution of the Family, as expressed in the details of the mystorians' personal experience. The world historical record of anagogy in the medieval schema is replaced in the popcycle with the theory of the mystorians' particular career field.

In *Teletheory* these levels (excluding Entertainment) were simply juxtaposed in order to find the pattern of repetitions that appeared by chance, but that, once noticed, became motivated figures of one's personal signature. In *Heuretics* I learned that it was possible to "tune" the four levels—to use the pattern of the mystory to produce a mediated, indirect expression of the "premises" or subject positioning of the author in collective historical culture. Now the application of Xanadu to the problematic of the home page as an interface metaphor for screen design has shown me how to use the mystory as a guide for disciplinary research. Again, Walter Benjamin supplied a confirmation of the potential usefulness of a mystorical schema.

> Suddenly and with compelling force, I was struck by the idea of drawing a diagram of my life, and knew at the same moment exactly how it was to be done. With a very simple question I interrogated my past life, and the answers were inscribed, as if of their own accord, on a sheet of paper that I had with me. A year or two later, when I lost this sheet, I was inconsolable. Now reconstructing its outline in thought without directly reproducing it, I should speak of a labyrinth. I am not concerned here with what is installed in the chamber at its enigmatic center, ego or fate, but all the more with the many entrances leading into the interior. These entrances I call primal acquaintances; each of them is a graphic symbol of my acquaintance with a person whom I met, not through other people, but through neighborhood, family relationships, school comradeship, mistaken identity, companionship on travels, or other such situations. So many primal relationships, so many entrances to the maze. . . . "If a man has character," says Nietzsche, "he will have the same experience over and over again." Whether or not this is true on a large scale, on a small one there are perhaps paths that lead us again and again to people who have one and the same function for us: PASSAGEWAYS that always, in the most diverse periods of life, guide us to the friend, the betrayer, the beloved, the pupil, or the master. This is what the sketch of my life revealed to me as it took shape before me on that Paris afternoon. Against the background of the city, the people who had surrounded me closed together to form a figure.[9]

The length of the citation is justified by the importance of Benjamin's observation to chorography, and to the lesson of Xanadu for home page design. The frustrating aspect for admirers of Benjamin has been that he never revealed the *inventio* he used to produce his "figure." The Xanadu principle offers one way to turn Benjamin's figure into a design method. The method is to "tune" the four discourses of the popcycle into a composite scene, by finding a thread of whatever sort at whatever level of detail that runs through and crosses the boundaries of these different dimensions of experience. The difference between this mystorical "allegory" and the medieval version is that while the latter is held together by totalizing isotopies or absolute homologies attaching the believer's personal existence as a sinner to the salvation of the world by Christ, the former is a turbulent disorder brought into a figure or constellated by the evocative repetition of a few details. The goal of the tuning exercise is to identify the figures—the historical persons transformed into concepts, or conceptual personae,[10] whose actantial position in the diegesis of Home is that of "donor"—the character(s) who help the protagonist solve the problem of the narrative world.

PART TWO
KAWLIGA KHAN
THE PHANTOM TRAILER

The year is 1953. The decade that set the design of the ideograms of cyber-pidgin. My father, mother, sister, and I are in a trailer, a mobile home, parked on concrete blocks on some land down by the Yellowstone River that was part of my father's business, the Miles City Sand and Gravel Company. We are together at the dinner table. It is not so much a table as a counter in the dining area of the trailer. One end of the counter is attached to the wall. A shelf space is recessed into the wall, and on one of the shelves our radio is playing, tuned to the local radio station, KATL. This radio was turned on every waking moment. The playlist was programmed for a week, and it never seemed to change; a certain number of times a week, in a nearly predictable rhythm of repetition, you could hear the Sons of the Pioneers singing "Cool Cool Water." After I got my driver's license and started cruising the drag with all the other teenagers, I could listen at night to KOMA in Oklahoma, which played the new rock music. I used my allowance to buy at the Melody Shop 45rpm singles of the songs I heard on KOMA. I never bought a copy of anything I heard on KATL.

The odd thing about this memory is that we never lived in a trailer. We moved from a rented house to our own home—a three bedroom house with a free-standing garage—when I was in the seventh grade. The mortgage on this house was a financial burden, and the one thing my folks argued about was this expense. The argument consisted in essence of a choice between this mortgaged house and a trailer at the Sand and Gravel, the latter being in a sense "free." In memory these two places have begun to merge—the house and the trailer. I realize now that these dwellings were metonyms for something else, for what distinguished them was not only square footage and building materials. The tracks of the Northern Pacific Railroad make a diagonal slash through the town. Our house was on the right side of the tracks, and the trailer was on the wrong side, the left (out) side, the working-class side. If my father had moved into the trailer as he claimed he wanted to do, he would have moved in without his wife and children: that was my mother's position.

The map of Home for me, then, has these two material axes: KATL–KOMA; house-trailer. I want to locate on this map a particular scene of writing that involved the naming of our cat. Like almost every cat I have ever roomed with, this one—an orange and white tom—showed up as a stray and moved in. So it was 1953 and we were seated at the kitchen counter in the trailer/house. The cat jumped up onto the counter and began persuading us to adopt it. This was a very persuasive cat. Among its accomplishments was that my mother cooked it scrambled eggs for breakfast every morning of its life, or at least its life with us. How did this happen? She did not cook eggs for the rest of the family every morning. These were not leftovers, an extra egg while she was at it. We ate cereal and toast. The cat had its own schedule, which did not coincide with ours. I never understood how this ritual started. There was a huge scene between my mother and my grandmother when the latter came to stay with the kids while my folks went on a trip. My grandmother disliked cats, and she was not pleased to learn that part of her duties included scrambling eggs for our cat.

The scene of writing in this Home voice has to do with how we named the cat. The radio was tuned to KATL, a station that played the songs of Hank Williams Sr. on a regular basis. It was 1953, a year when *Billboard* chart number one for many weeks was *Kaw-liga*, and number two was *Your Cheatin' Heart*. A song about a wooden Indian. "Poor ol' Kaw-li-ga, he never got a kiss. Poor ol' Kaw-li-ga, he don't know what he missed. Is it any wonder that his face is red. Kaw-li-ga that poor ol' wooden head." While the song was playing the cat rubbed up against

the radio and started to purr. By whatever process, the family agreed
at that moment that the cat could stay, and that it was named Kawliga.

THE BABY BLUE CADILLAC

Hank Williams Sr. is my Voice of Entertainment. It is the same mystery
as Kawliga's scrambled eggs. I do not know how or when exactly Hank
acquired this status. When I was growing up I hated country and loved
rock. I hated the piles of gravel at the Sand and Gravel plant, but I liked
the music on KOMA that we could hear in Montana at night coming
all the way from Oklahoma. Hank's "voice" in this structure consists of
two elements. The first element is his yodel, the way he flipped his
singing in and out of falsetto. "If you're tired of breaking other hearts,
you can come back again and break mine." On "breaking" the voice
flips into falsetto, breaking the word into two parts. The second element is the electric pedal steel guitar. Commentators agree that the
signature sound of Hank's music, which included his backup group,
the Drifting Cowboys, was the sustained wailing glissando that is distinctive to the steel guitar. The opening bars of *Your Cheatin' Heart* are
exemplary of this quality. I had forgotten that, as part of Hank's crossover
success, *Kaw-liga* was mixed with an orchestral string background. I
remember only the yodel and the slide glissando.

"Kawliga Khan" (my remake) borrows from two unknown songs
that Hank never finished. Hank was a country romantic in that his songs
exemplify "authenticity." He was a natural, they say. Although he attended
school until he was nineteen, he had only made it to the ninth grade.
He learned his music in the streets, hanging out with a Black street
musician named Rufus "Tee Tot" Payne. Hank was twelve when he
started the drinking that made him an alcoholic. His drug use is ascribed
to his need for relief from the pains associated with the symptoms of
spina bifida oculta, from which he suffered. His songs reflect the hard
life he actually lived growing up in south Alabama.[11]

The scene of writing for my Entertainment Voice is a hybrid of
these two unknown songs, both interrupted during the early stages of
composition. One is the last song Hank ever wrote. On New Year's Eve,
1952, Hank got into the back seat of his baby blue Cadillac convert-
ible. Heavy snows had grounded his flight to Canton, Ohio, where he
was to play in a concert on New Year's Day. There is more to the story,

having to do with the drugs prescribed by his quack doctor, his drinking problem, his poor health. The short of it is that when the driver stopped in the dawn hours somewhere in West Virginia to check on his passenger, Hank was dead. He was 29 years old. Clutched in his hand, the story goes, was a new song he had been working on. That Hank was at the peak of his songwriting skills was evident from the two songs completed in his last recording session—*Kaw-liga* and *Your Cheatin' Heart*. This new song was, like most country songs, about a problem: we lived, we loved, you left.

Not much is known about this legendary final song. To fill in the gaps I merge it with a further scene that has fascinated me for some time. Hank Williams and the Drifting Cowboys were engaged in 1951 as the featured act of a touring show intended to promote the popular patent medicine, Hadacol. The active ingredients in this medicine were alcohol (12 percent) and laxative. The product sold well in the mostly dry South, but the inventor, Dudley LeBlanc, wanted a national distribution. To gain legitimacy, LeBlanc engaged some of the biggest stars of the day—Jack Benny, Cesar Romero, Milton Berle, and Bob Hope, to name only a few. The stars were to join the main act—Hank and his band—just for a few days each. One of the stars with whom Hank was supposed to perform was Carmen Miranda (Koon, 36).

Carmen Miranda, whose presence in cinema in the 1940s was a manifestation of the Good Neighbor Policy pursued during the war years, had introduced the samba into American popular culture.[12] Before coming to the United States, Carmen had a successful career as a samba singer in Brazil. I have not been able to find any information about the meeting of Hank Williams and Carmen Miranda on the Hadacol Caravan. The Caravan was cut short after thirty-four shows when the company folded due to problems over taxes and false advertising (Koon, 38). Could there have been a phantom song, a syncretic invention crossing country with samba? Elvis did not make his country-blues hybrid until 1954, around the same time that Carmen collapsed and died after a performance on Jimmy Durante's television show. The phantom song that haunts the history of rock, or the song this history forgot, is the one Hank and Carmen might have coauthored. The scene of this collaboration between country and samba may or may not have taken place in 1951, and it is an opportunity whose future remains open. The original Carnaval music of Brazil, before samba, was called "choro" (literally, "sobbing, crying").[13]

STRING THEORY

I am following a thread rather than a story or an argument. A string. The first mystory I composed, "Derrida at the Little Bighorn," turned up the word *ficelle* in the voice of history (School). I found it on the battlefield of Custer's Last Stand, or rather on the map of the battlefield published in the visitor's guide. The five companies that died with Custer were named, following military conventions, with a letter of the alphabet. The historian who designed the map placed the letters of the five companies on the map to designate the defensive position the units assumed in their last hour of life. C-E-F-I-L. The letters may be read as an anagram of the French word *ficelle* (allowing for the extra letters that mark gender in French spelling). *Ficelle* was the term Jacques Lacan used to refer to the loops of string that he tied into knots to demonstrate to his seminars the topologies of the unconscious.

The word already had a history as a theoretical term, having been used by Henry James, in his preface to *The Ambassadors*, to name those secondary characters included in a novel to meet the needs of the form. Lacan featured a painting by Holbein entitled "The Ambassadors"— famous for the death's head smeared across its foreground in anamorphic perspective— in one of his seminars. What were these two ambassadors sent to tell me? "Ficelle" means (among other things) "the thread of a plot," a meaning to which James may have been alluding with his choice of terms. Further development of the mystory into choragraphy has helped me understand how I should read the figure in my own carpet, my own diagrammed labyrinth. The figures that recur in the diagram show me my superego. The four voices I found speaking through my popcycle were my father (Family), Custer (School), Gary Cooper (Entertainment), and Jacques Derrida (Discipline). A heuristic device for negotiating with this figure is to look for the ficelle, the supporting character, for each one of these *imagoes*. A preliminary incomplete list of my countersuperego, then, is Mom, Chief Gall, and Marlene Dietrich.

A further question now is how to extend this device into a method of research. The lesson of choragraphy is that of the choral word—to work with all the meanings of a term. These *ficelles* are the strings on the world lute that I need to tune to compose electronically. The music of the spheres, *Stimmung*, voice, mood, atmosphere. In this discourse of theory, in which it is possible to speculate about cosmology, "voice" names a category of grammar. To write in the active voice is to designate agency, making clear the party responsible for an action. The passive voice is condemned in most handbooks because it may erase this assignment of responsibility. These guidelines or heuristic rules of thumb made sense within literacy, whose apparatus includes "selfhood" as its principle of subjectivation. The clear borders separating self from other, inside from outside, that were drawn within literacy are dissolving in the emergent apparatus of byteracy. "Kawliga Khan" is composed in the middle voice, to explore and perhaps redraw the borders of my identity.

In choragraphy the string I am following is literally part of a guitar. A heuristic rule of heuretics (the logic of invention) is to examine a scene in terms of an invention that might be found in it. One of the inventions prominently displayed in my voices of Family and Entertainment is that of the slide guitar. The provisional contested border of the subject's inside/outside is traced between experience and history, memory and research. What is the status of the slide guitar? In my experience the slide guitar originated in country music. Whatever my tastes were or are, the sound of the pedal steel guitar in the opening bars of *Your Cheatin' Heart* evoke the essence of Home for me. The juxtaposition of this experience with some research produces a shock, an "encounter" (Cohen).

The shock is that the steel guitar was invented in Hawaii. I should have known this fact, since steel guitar is often identified in the credits as "Hawaiian steel." The steel guitar developed from the slack key tunings introduced by Hawaiian musicians, so called because the tuning of the strings was slackened to achieve an open chord (Broughton, 650). Strumming the strings of a guitar tuned DBGDGD produces a G chord. Placing a finger (barring) or steel bar across the strings at the fifth and seventh frets gives the other two chords used for any three-chord song. "The steel guitar developed from the slack key and is played horizontally with the strings facing upward. The steel rod is pressed on the strings with the left hand to produce a harmonious sliding sound.

The first electric guitar, a Richenbacher nicknamed the 'frying pan', was actually a Hawaiian lap steel guitar made in 1931" (650).

The different voices of the popcycle are given an open tuning. Slack-key tuning and the resulting style of playing, including the barred chords, give instructions for how to write in choragraphy. The sound that marks Home for me is threaded through Hank Williams and *Stimmung*. Where else does it go? A little more history shows me the larger scene within which my listening to *Kaw-liga* is inscribed. A worldwide craze for Hawaiian guitar music was launched in 1915 at the San Francisco Panama-Pacific Expo which celebrated the opening of the Panama Canal. The music was featured in the pavilion sponsored by the new territory of Hawaii. The music, and more particularly the style of the steel guitar, became popular worldwide, spread by tours and by the sale of recordings. The records of Jimmy Rogers, who adapted steel style to country, were popular in Africa in the 1930s.

This research, in other words, led me into the area of world music, and finally to the juju music of King Sunny Ade. Reading a description of the juju sound was like finding the place at which the other end of the rainbow touches ground: "I was fascinated by the melding of 'deep'Yoruba praise singing and drumming, guitar techniques from soul music, Latin American dance rhythms, church hymns and country-and-western melodies, pedal steel guitar licks and Indian film music themes, and by the fact that this modernist bricolage could so effectively evoke traditional values."[14] The best word to describe the effect of listening to a CD of juju music is "uncanny"—the discovery of the familiar in the unfamiliar—when I heard come floating in over the top of the multiple complex drumming rhythms that predominate in African modes the glissando of the electric pedal steel guitar. I now pronounce the name of the famous drink invented at the University of Florida like the last name of the juju king (Gator Ah-day).

APPARATUS CATASTROPHE

What does it mean when King Sunny Ade shows up in "Kawliga Khan"? The inference path that produced him follows neither the forms of narrative nor of argument. The narrative and arguments that are involved are organized in turn by pattern, by repetition of material details. The logic is conductive rather than inductive, deductive, or abductive (the inference path moves from material thing to another thing, without recourse to the abstractions of rules and cases). While it is too early to be able to say very much about the nature of the emerging electronic apparatus, grammatology suggests where we might look for symptoms of what to expect. What are the symptoms that evoke the qualities of technology, social institution, and psychology of identity of byteracy?

The technology of the Internet is the clue that establishes the pattern. The Internet originated as a military idea, as a feature of our strategy of defense against a nuclear strike. To deprive the enemy (the Soviet Union) of a target, our national communications infrastructure would have no center. Instead packet switching was invented: messages are addressed and routed by whatever links are available. The material signal is broken into pieces independent of one another, routed by whatever lines are open, and reassembled at the destination. This defense practice of packet switching resonates in the psychological register of the apparatus with the defenses of the ego involved with repression. The dream work that allows communication between the different registers of the psyche, between the unconscious and conscious mind, may be understood as a kind of packet switching: condensation, displacement, secondary elaboration, symbolization. The impulse of signification is routed and reassembled in the understanding by means of these operations.

I had been aware of this analogy between the destroyed network of the military still able to function after suffering a first nuclear strike and the ruined messages of dream work, scrambled into nonsense yet received and understood in a way by the dreamer. I had not thought of a match for this pattern at the level of social institutions until the composition of "Kawliga Khan." The equivalent at this social historical level is the Black Atlantic—the continuation of African culture through the catastrophe of the Middle Passage, the diaspora of slavery disseminating individuals throughout the Americas, and the practices of syncretism that enabled the members to reassemble their culture in new forms fashioned out of the materials ready to hand in the colonizing culture. Syncretism—the formation of cross-cultural hybrids in religion, music, crafts, arts, and letters—is the dream work, the packet switching, of Black Atlantic culture. The defensive powers of fetish charms are still invoked in the American South, for example, even if the flash of the spirit is now materialized by a hubcap.[15]

The computer connected to the Internet is a choral device, mediating, supplying a place to sort the different materials of the chaos of world cultures into a signifying order. To read the pattern that appears in the tuning of the discourses of the popcycle into a mystory, the designer must understand the destroyed, ruined quality of the network producing the scene and its image. The description of this network as "ruined," however, reflects a literate bias. Choral logic lacks the pure, clean lines of an abstract inference pattern. Instead, it traces its paths through the surface details of material existence. Since the packet is never "sent," but is only assembled at the point of reception, the speed of the post is that of the incalculable flash of a profane illumination.

CYBER-PIDGIN

My remake as research produced this image: the slack key tunings associated with the steel guitar. It is a question not only of the tunings, but their dissemination. "Common Hawaiian slack-key tunings in C, G, and F—for example, 'taro patch' (5-1-5-1-3-5, ascending)—are identical to tunings used by Lagosian guitarists. The international distribution of such tuning systems along trade routes has yet to be adequately investigated" (Waterman, 47). Such images are the basic units of the reasoning suited for the apparatus of byteracy with its catastropic figures made of syncretic dream packets. The catastrope or interface metaphor for electronic design practice is that of world music. The "trade route" of these tunings figures the inference paths of the mystory, and follows the materializations of the inventions that pass through the different registers of the popcycle.

World music includes a more basic version of the metaphor—pidgin language. The three terms are interrelated and mutually illuminating—syncretism, world music, and pidgin. First used in anthropology to describe the symbolic fusion of West African deities with Catholic saints, syncretism was defined as "the tendency to identify those elements in a new culture with similar elements in the old one, enabling the persons experiencing the contact to move from one to the other and back again, with psychological ease" (Waterman, 9). Waterman makes the analogy explicit: "guitar patterns and songs learned from gramophone records were adapted by palmwine performers for use in informal social gatherings. This process involved a schematization of patterns, much in the manner of a pidgin language" (47).

The purpose of the interface metaphor—a postcolonialized version of a pidgin language—is to figure the global dimension of Internet interactivity. The metaphor applies to both the inside and outside registers of the design method: to the exchanges across the levels of the mystory within the composers' design and to the exchanges among all the composers online. Pidgins arose in the special spaces that formed when European traders and colonizers encountered non-Western peoples. Pidgins have no native speakers and are reduced in function, with the grammatical structure usually derived from the language of the dominant culture in the encounter, with many additions from the subordinate culture. Eventually the pidgin may evolve into a creole—a full-featured language—among the children of pidgin speakers. What does this phenomenon suggest about the future of a global society in an electronic apparatus? The nature of such a society may be intuited in the syncretic scene of juju invention. "It should be noted that the metaphoric forging of correspondences between musical and social order is not limited to structural analogies. . . . The experiential impact of the metaphor 'good music is the ideal society writ small' depends upon the generation of sensuous textures. An effective performance of juju predicates not only the structure of the ideal society, but also its 'feel': intense, vibrant, loud, buzzing, and fluid" (Waterman, 220).

Waterman's central point about the moral, political, social lesson of juju has to do with a new attitude toward hybrid formations, to creolization. A postcolonial internet pidgin must abandon the colonialist denigration of the "creole," and the ideological atmosphere in which colonizer and colonized alike favored modernist "purity" and despised the mixed (75). This exploration of hybrids across cultures and categories sets the program of choragraphic research for the immediate future. A fundamental component of this institutional dimension of the electronic apparatus is the practice of byteracy—the choragraphic home page, with its four voices articulated simultaneously using the inventive methods of slack-key tuning.

NOTES

1. Gregory L. Ulmer, *Heuretics: The Logic of Invention* (Baltimore: Johns Hopkins University Press, 1994).

2. Plato, *Timaeus* in *The Collected Dialogues*, eds. Edith Hamilton and Huntington Cairns, (Princeton: Princeton, 1963), pp. 52d–53a.

3. Leo Spitzer, *Classical and Christian Ideas of World Harmony: Prolegomena to an Interpretation of the Word "Stimmung"* (Baltimore: Johns Hopkins University Press, 1963), p. 34.

4. Michel Haar, *The Song of the Earth: Heidegger and the Grounds of the History of Being*, trans. Reginald Lilly (Bloomington: Indiana University Press, 1993).

5. John Livingston Lowes, *The Road to Xanadu: A Study in the Ways of the Imagination* (Boston: Houghton Mifflin, 1955), provides a scholarly version; Caroline Alexander, *The Way to Xanadu: Journeys to a Legendary Realm* (New York: Knopf, 1994), gives a popular one.

6. Susan Buck-Morss, *The Dialectics of Seeing: Walter Benjamin and the Arcades Project* (Cambridge: MIT Press, 1989), p. 25.

7. Gregory L. Ulmer, *Teletheory: Grammatology in the Age of Video* (New York: Routledge, 1989).

8. Margaret Cohen, *Profane Illumination: Walter Benjamin and the Paris of Surrealist Revolution* (Berkeley: California University Press, 1993).

9. Walter Benjamin, *Reflections: Essays, Aphorisms, Autobiographical Writings*, trans. Edmund Jephcott (New York: Harcourt, 1978), pp. 30–31.

10. Gilles Deleuze and Felix Guattari, *What Is Philosophy?*, trans. Hugh Tomlinson and Graham Burchell (New York: Columbia, 1994).

11. George William Koon, *Hank Williams: A Bio-Bibliography* (Westport, CT: Greenwood, 1983).

12. Gregory L. Ulmer, "The Miranda Warnings: An Experiment in Hyperrhetoric" in *Hyper/Text/Theory*, ed. George P. Landow (Baltimore: Johns Hopkins University Press, 1994).

13. Simon Broughton, et al., eds., *World Music: The Rough Guide* (London: Rough Guides, 1994), p. 558.

14. Christopher Alan Waterman, *Jùjú: A Social History and Ethnography of an African Popular Music* (Chicago: Chicago University Press, 1990), p. 2.

15. Robert Farris Thompson, *Flash of the Spirit: African and Afro-American Art and Philosophy* (New York: Vintage, 1984), pp. 146–158.

JAY CLAYTON is Professor of English at Vanderbilt University. He is the author of *Romantic Vision and the Novel* and *The Pleasures of Babel: Contemporary American Literature and Theory*. His current essay is part of a book titled *Charles Dickens in Cyberspace, Or, History in an Age of Cultural Studies*.

VINAY DHARWADKER is Associate Professor of English at the University of Oklahoma. He is the author of *Sunday at the Lodi Gardens*, a book of poems. He has co-edited *The Oxford Anthology of Modern Indian Poetry*, *The Collected Poems of A. K. Ramanujan*, and *Contemporary Literature of Asia*. His work on Indian and postcolonial literatures and in literary theory has appeared in various journals and edited collections.

MARY ANN DOANE is Harrison S. Kravis University Professor and Professor of Modern Culture and Media at Brown University. She is the author of *The Desire to Desire: The Woman's Film of the 1940s* and *Femmes Fatales: Feminism, Film Theory, Psychoanalysis*. She is currently writing a book on technologies of temporality in modernity.

JONATHAN GOLDBERG is Sir William Osler Professor of English at The Johns Hopkins University and also holds an appointment at Duke University. He is the author of *Writing Matter: From the Hands of the English Renaissance* and several other books on early modern literature and culture. The essay in this volume is part of a forthcoming book on women writers in the English Renaissance.

N. KATHERINE HAYLES is Professor of English at the University of California at Los Angeles. She teaches and writes on the relations between literature and science in the twentieth century. Her most recent book project, *Virtual Bodies: How We Became Posthuman*, explores the cultural and historical construction of the cyborg.

MARSHA KINDER is Professor of Critical Studies in the School of Cinema-Television at the University of Southern California. Her most recent books are *Playing with Power in Movies, Television and Video Games* and *Blood Cinema: The Reconstruction of National Identity in Spain*, and the forthcoming *Refiguring Spain: Cinema/Media/Representation* and *Kids' Culture*. She is also the general editor of a bilingual CD-ROM series on national media.

JEFFREY MASTEN is Gardner Cowles Associate Professor in the Humanities at Harvard University. He has written *Textual Intercourse: Collaboration, Authorship, and Sexualities in Renaissance Drama*, as well as essays on textual materiality published in *ELH*, *Textual Practice*, *Queering the Renaissance*, *Field Work*, *Reading Mary Wroth*, and *A New History of Early English Drama*.

MEREDITH L. MCGILL teaches in the English Department at Rutgers University. She has published articles on Edgar Allan Poe and literary nationalism, on nineteenth-century American copyright law, and on Robert Lowell and Wallace Stevens. She is currently completing a book on antebellum American literature and reprint culture.

PEGGY PHELAN is Chair of the Department of Performance Studies, Tisch School of the Arts, New York University. She is the author of *Unmarked: the Politics of Performance* and *Mourning Sex: Performing Public Memories*. With Lynda Hart, she is the co-editor of *Acting Out: Feminist Performances*.

PETER STALLYBRASS is Professor of English at the University of Pennsylvania. He is co-author with Allon White of *The Politics and Poetics of Transgression*, co-editor with David Scott Kastan of *Staging the Renaissance*, and co-editor with Maureen Quilligan and Margreta de Grazia of *Subject and Object in Renaissance Culture*. He is at present completing a book with Ann Rosalind Jones entitled *Worn Worlds: Clothes and Identity in Renaissance England*.

GREGORY L. ULMER is Professor of English and Media Studies at the University of Florida in Gainesville. He is the author of *Heuretics: The Logic of Invention.* He is also the moderator of Electronic Learning Forum, an online practice devoted to distance learning.

NANCY VICKERS is Professor of French and Italian and of Comparative Literature at the University of Southern California. She is co-editor with Margaret Ferguson and Maureen Quilligan of *Rewriting the Renaissance: The Discourses of Sexual Difference in Early Modern Europe.* She is now working on a study of lyric as it is reshaped by the technologies of electronic reproduction—recorded sound, music video, and interactive media.

ILLUSTRATION CREDITS

CHAPTER 2

Figure 2.1   page 43

Payson, Dunton, and Scribner, *Manual of Penmanship* (New York, 1873), p. 25. Courtesy of the American Antiquarian Society.

Figure 2.2   page 46

Benjamin Franklin Foster, *Practical Penmanship* (Albany, 1832), Plate 3, Fig. 5. Courtesy of the American Antiquarian Society.

Figure 2.3   page 52

Spencerian Key to Practical Penmanship (New York, 1866), p. 29. Courtesy of the American Antiquarian Society.

Figure 2.4   page 53

Spencerian Key to Practical Penmanship (New York, 1866), frontispiece. Courtesy of the American Antiquarian Society.

Figure 2.5   page 54

Reply of Payson, Dunton & Scribner to the Absurd Claims of the Spencerian Authors to Originality (Boston, 1871), Plate III. Courtesy of the American Antiquarian Society.

Figure 2.6   page 55

Reply of Payson, Dunton & Scribner to the Absurd Claims of the Spencerian Authors to Originality (Boston, 1871), last page. Courtesy of the American Antiquarian Society.

Figure 2.7   page 65

Facsimile reprint, *Some Letters of Edgar Allan Poe to E. H. N. Patterson of Oquawka, Illinois*, ed. Eugene Field (Chicago, 1898). Courtesy of the American Antiquarian Society.

CHAPTER 6

Figure 6.1   page 161

"How to choose composition," in *Jinjo Shogaku Shintei Gaten Dai Roku Gaku Nen Dan Sei Yo* (Elementary Grade Drawing Manual for Sixth Grade Boys). Tokyo, Board of Education, 1910.

Figure 6.2   page 169

The "trinity of beasts," image from *A TV Dante*, by Tom Phillips and Peter Greenaway.

Figure 6.3   page 171

The head of Tom Phillips, image from *A TV Dante*, by Tom Phillips and Peter Greenaway.

Figure 6.4   page 175

Image from *Where on Earth Is Carmen Sandiego*, Fox Children's Network, 1994.

CHAPTER 7

Figure 7.1   page 193

Roman Verostko, *Illuminated Universal Turing Machine*, 1995. By permission of the artist.

Figure 7.2   page 194

Andy Kopra, *The Ornament of Grammar*, displayed at the SIGGRAPH Art Exhibit, August 1995, Los Angeles, California. By permission of the artist.

Figure 7.3   page 195

Bibliophile browsing *The Ornament of Grammar*, by Andy Kopra. By permission of the artist.